W9-CFN-509

Triumph of Hope

NORTH SEA
BALTIC SEA
LITH.
DANZIG
EAST PRUSSIA
Niemen R.
Hamburg/Freihafen
Ravensbrück
Berlin
Weser R.
Wista R.
NETHERLANDS
Oder R.
Elbe R.
Rhein R.
GREATER
GERMANY
Taucha
Pönitz
Leipzig
POLAND
N
BELGIUM
Theresienstadt
Auschwitz
LUXEMBOURG
Main R.
0
100
MILES
Prague
Opava
Ostrava
Bielsko
Protectorate of
Bohemia and Moravia
WEST BESKIDS
EAST BESKIDS
Prerov
Trinec
TATRA MTS
Ceske
Budejovice
Brno
Vyskov
Pozorice
SUDETENLAND
FRANCE
SLOVAKIA
Danube R.
Tisza R.
HUNGARY
ROMANIA
SWITZERLAND
LIECHTENSTEIN

Triumph of Hope

From Theresienstadt and Auschwitz to Israel

~

Ruth Elias

Translated from the German by
Margot Bettauer Dembo

Published in association with the United States Holocaust Memorial Museum

John Wiley & Sons, Inc.
New York • Chichester • Weinheim • Brisbane • Singapore • Toronto

Published by John Wiley & Sons, Inc.

German edition published in 1988 as *Die Hoffnung erhielt mich am Leben.* New German edition published 1990.

This text is printed on acid-free paper. ♾

Library of Congress Cataloging-in-Publication Data

Elias, Ruth
[Die Hoffnung erhielt mich am Leben. English]
Triumph of hope: from Theresienstadt and Auschwitz to Israel/
Ruth Elias; translated from the German by Margot Bettauer Dembo.
p. cm.
Includes index.
ISBN 0-471-16365-1 (cloth: alk. paper)
1. Elias, Ruth, 1922– . 2. Jews—Czech Republic—Ostrava—Biography. 3. Holocaust, Jewish (1939–1945)—Personal narratives. 4. Theresienstadt (Concentration camp). 5. Auschwitz (Concentration camp). 6. Holocaust survivors—Israel—Biography. 7. Immigrants—Israel—Biography. 8. Ostrava (Czech Republic)—Biography.
I. Title.
DS135.C97E45313 1998
940.53′18′092—dc21
[B] 97-37418

Printed in the United States of America

10 9 8 7 6 5 4 3 2 1

This book is dedicated to my beloved and wonderful little family.

Contents

Time is passing quickly for me these days. I tend to look ahead, for the years have taught me not to look back. But from time to time I do—and then the immediate and pervasive sensation I have is of the concentration camp. It haunts me and has left deep scars. I cannot rid myself of it, even though I have tried all my life to push it aside. It keeps coming back, so I am condemned to live with it. I can't describe the sensation to anyone who has not gone through this kind of hell; after all, nobody can comprehend the incomprehensible. In a way, my persecutors have succeeded: Memories of their deeds continue to pursue me. To escape this feeling, at least in part, I keep running. Ever since my time in the camps I have been hurrying onward, moving forward without much thought or reflection. Running, always running. I am convinced that I have lost out on much that is beautiful because I could never stop long enough to get deeply involved in some of the things I would have liked to do. Will I ever be rid of this restlessness? The only time I seem able to relax is with my grandchildren. When I look at them I want to cry. Sometimes I think I have been allowed this happiness only in a dream, to experience something I once thought I would never have. My grandchildren are my triumph over my persecutors, and I rejoice that I have been able to start a new family whose roots are in our homeland. In Israel.

My dear grandchildren . . .

This book is dedicated to you. Your fathers grew up without a family. When they were still little boys, my heart would ache each time they asked me, "Why don't we have a grandpa and a grandma? Why don't we have any uncles and aunts? Why do all our friends get presents from relatives and we don't? Why do we celebrate the holidays without a family?" Their words hurt me deeply. How could I possibly explain to them, while they were still children, why they were denied these things? Your grandfather and I made a big mistake in bringing up our sons: We didn't want to burden them with our past, so we never told them about it. We wanted them to grow up as free citizens in a free Israel, without any involvement in what had happened to their parents. Consequently, a certain distance developed between them and us, a lack of understanding that is beginning to fade only now that they themselves are parents.

Years from now you will understand what I have written. When you are older you will learn about it in school, you will read books and see films about it, but it probably will sound only like a chapter from a history book. Whenever you hear or read about the "persecution of the Jews during the Nazi period," think of your grandfather Kurt and grandmother Ruth, who endured this hell and who, in spite of the Nazis, managed to survive and pass along to future generations the truth about the horrors through which they lived. Soon my generation will be gone—that is Nature's law—and then only this account will testify to what happened to us.

I'm glad I could write this book for you, glad that you have grandparents, uncles, aunts, and cousins. Please treasure the bonds of family. Don't ever let anyone destroy these ties, even though sometimes there may be disagreements among you. It was such a bond that gave me the strength to survive. Yes, I survived, but then came the day when I realized that I was alone. All alone.

1

Growing Up in Ostrava

IT WAS A SMALL HOUSE. A little shop in front, at the back a large yard with a huge chestnut tree, a stall for our horse and a shed for the carriage—all enclosed by a wooden fence. On weekdays we gathered for meals in the roomy kitchen that was presided over by our cook, Herminka, who invariably became upset when I refused to eat the good food she had prepared. We sat at a long kitchen table covered with a blue-and-white checkered oilcloth: my father; my mother; my sister, Edith, who had inherited my mother's good looks—a beauty so striking that people would turn around to stare at her on the street—and I, a plain little girl who always stayed in the background, embarrassed because I was not as pretty. Quite an average family, the Hupperts, living in Přívoz, a suburb of Ostrava, in that portion of Czechoslovakia known as Moravia.

Fanny Ringer, my grandmother on my mother's side, lived nearby. Once a week my sister and I got dressed up and went to visit her. On our best behavior, we would spend one or two hours there,

The house in which I was born (top) and one of our family's shops. Photographed in 1965.

consuming enormous amounts of sweets, but always glad to return to our own backyard.

Our paternal grandmother, Emilie Huppert—we called her Oma, the German word for "grandma"—lived in Marianské Hory (Marienberg), which, like Přívoz, was a suburb of Ostrava. We had to take the streetcar to get there, and because it was far and the trip took a long time we didn't visit her very often. But whenever we did, it was always with great enthusiasm. She lived in a large one-story house with many small rooms. Facing the street was a store where one could buy just about anything—food, spices, candy, liquor, soap, shoelaces, and lots of other things. The smell in that place was wonderful.

The image of my grandmother is deeply engraved in my memory. A stately, vigorous woman, she presided over the store and managed everything by herself. Nothing escaped her. Although she was strict, she had a kind and loving heart. As soon as we arrived, she would give each of us a small colored candy stick that, when licked, would turn our mouths red, blue, or orange. The more we licked, the smaller and pointier the stick became. Then Edith and I would run into the big courtyard, where a huge lilac bush grew. In spring I couldn't get enough of this bush, with its glorious fragrance and lush white panicles of blossoms. Nearby stood a linden tree, its trunk encircled by a narrow bench. In bloom it gave off a marvelous aroma. During linden blossom time we visited Oma quite frequently because the flowers had to be collected and dried to make linden-blossom tea, which replaced the regular tea Oma drank. She had to be frugal because she was rather poor.

Not far from the house was a small field that provided fodder for the horse. Some of this was dried as hay and stored in the barn for the winter. Chickens ran around the yard, and Oma knew exactly where to find their eggs. There were geese and ducks too, and Oma "stuffed" the geese. I always felt sorry for one of these creatures when she forced her homemade *Schlischken* into its throat, massaging the thin neck until the mixture had gone down. The poor goose grew so fat that after a while she couldn't move anymore, so she just sat there in a large shallow basket lined with straw. What was she waiting for? Oma deftly continued with the stuffing, testing the goose's weight every time she lifted her. Sometimes two or three geese were stuffed at the same time. On our next visit, if the geese were gone I knew they had been slaughtered, and this always made me sad. But then I would get a piece of homemade bread sliced from a huge loaf and spread with goose fat, goose liver, and onions. How wonderful that tasted! The goose fat would dribble down my chin, and the poor slaughtered goose was forgotten.

The kitchen was the largest room in Oma's house. In the center was a big table made of rough wood, which was scrubbed down with a stiff brush after the main meal every day. A large tiled stove contained a huge oven for baking bread. The stovetop was made of slate, I think. It had two round cutouts with covers that could be lifted to stir up the fire inside. This cooktop, which was big enough to hold four or five large pots, had a metal rim that was polished daily with emery paper until it sparkled. The gleaming rim was a housewife's pride and joy, and proof of her industriousness. The fire in the stove was fanned through two side doors that had decorative handles. It took a good deal of expertise to get a fire going. First we put in some crumpled paper, and on top of that went chips of wood that had been prepared the night before. After the fire had been lit, we had to wait until it was blazing before we could add thicker pieces of wood and finally the coal. There was never a shortage of coal because Ostrava was a coal-mining town, and coal was delivered, cheap, to the house. When there wasn't enough money to buy regular coal we would have to make do with coal dust, which was even cheaper, but then the chimney sweep had to come more often.

Ah yes, the chimney sweep. I used to wonder: Did he dress in black to begin with, or did his clothes turn black from his work? As an honored guest in Oma's house he was always served wurst with bread and beer. The chimneys were a very important part of the house. Every room had a tiled stove, a *Kachelofen,* that gave off wonderful warmth in the winter, and the chimney from each stove had to be kept clean of soot. The chimney sweep arrived carrying a black ladder; slung over his shoulder was a rope, at the end of which was a round black brush and a rock. All the chimney sweeps I ever met were very slim because, it was said, they sometimes had to climb down the chimney to remove stubborn clumps of soot. Our chimney sweep's black clothes were tight-fitting and he wore a small black beret. Early in the morning his face was clean, but the rims of his eyes were always black, a mark of his trade. He could never get them clean because soap would have stung his eyes. By the time he had cleaned the first chimney, his entire face was black, except for the whites of his eyes. There's an old superstition that says touching a chimney sweep with your index finger brings you good luck. So naturally chimney sweeps were very popular. Ours would begin his work by climbing up onto the roof and lowering the rope with the round brush and the rock down the chimney until clouds of soot burgeoned out through the kitchen and the other rooms. After he left, we always had to do a thorough housecleaning.

I remember all these details of Oma's house in Marianské Hory especially well because when I was almost six years old my father and mother were divorced, and for a time Edith and I lived with Oma. We could not understand or grasp what divorce meant, but we were happy to be in Oma's care because we liked living in her house.

There was no running water in the house, but in the courtyard there was a wonderful well from which we hauled up water in a pail tied to a rope. The pail was lowered into the well with a hand crank. In the winter this was hard work. I still don't know how Oma got water when there was a heavy frost. Melted snow or rainwater collected in barrels was used for the laundry. The house had no bathroom. We were bathed only once a week in a big washtub set up on two wooden trestles in the kitchen. The tub had an opening at the bottom that could be closed with a wooden stopper. Giant potfuls of water were heated on the stove and then poured into the tub. Edith and I took turns bathing in the same water, and as it cooled off more hot water had to be added. Oma scrubbed us with a brush and dried us off with a large linen towel. Then the stopper was pulled out and the water ran into pails placed under the tub.

At the end of the big courtyard there was a horse stall, a barn, and a little house for the maid and the coachman. In those days we never saw our grandfather, Opa Heinrich Huppert. Much later I found out that he had gone to Bielsko, Poland, leaving Oma with twelve children. She had to take care of all those children, feed them and clothe them, which wasn't easy considering her meager income from the grocery store. Actually, making sure the children had clothes to wear wasn't that hard because only the oldest boy and the oldest girl would get new clothes and these would then be handed down to the younger ones.

The only way Oma could feed and care for her children was to send the boys, once they had reached the age of fourteen, into apprenticeships. Each had to learn a trade, because there was no money to send them to school. My father, Fritz, was apprenticed to a master locksmith in Vienna. He slept in the workshop. A corner of it was boarded off, and there they set up a bed for him. The master was also responsible for feeding his apprentice, but the food was so meager that Father often went hungry. Nor was the little bit of pocket money he received every week enough to buy food or clothes, and he began to look around for a way to improve his lot.

He had heard that opera singers regularly hired claques to applaud long and vigorously after every aria they sang; they did this because a singer's performance was judged by how loud and how prolonged the applause was. That's how Father earned extra money. Among the singers for whom he worked were Enrico Caruso and Maria Jeritza. In addition to getting paid, he had a chance to sit in the splendid Vienna Opera House, surrounded by distinguished and elegantly dressed people. It was his first encounter with culture, especially with music. This job marked the beginning of his great love for music, and although in his impoverished circumstances he could not afford lessons, music continued to enrich his life.

After Father finished his apprenticeship, he began to work on his own as a locksmith in Vienna. Later he moved back to Ostrava to be near his family. Since he wasn't earning much as a locksmith, he decided to go into another business. He bought a little house in Přívoz, borrowing heavily to set up a butcher shop there.

Father would get up at four in the morning to be ready when the railway workers passed the store on their way to work at five o'clock. They would stop to buy some wurst or meat, so the little store was very busy at that early hour. It stayed open until late at night, with Father working hard to pay off his heavy burden of debt. Once he was halfway there, he began to think of marriage.

My mother, Malvine—née Ringer—was a striking beauty. She was only sixteen years old when she married Father. After the wedding she immediately took over managing the household. Soon she was pregnant with her first child, and a year after the wedding my sister, Edith, was born.

In those days women didn't go to the hospital to have children. Instead, a midwife came to the house. The same midwife returned two years later to assist at my birth. She was a small, delicate woman who came often to see how "her" children were getting along. My mother always gave her presents of wurst and meat, which made these visits quite rewarding for her.

Our occasional trips to Oma's house became more frequent, and each time we would stay longer. Then came the day we were told that our mother had left home and from now on we would be living with Oma. I wasn't quite six years old. I wanted my mother to stay with us and couldn't understand why she didn't want me anymore. Father told us that Mother would never come back. I always held it against him that he had sent her away. Why did other children have their mothers at home, and why didn't we? But our days with Oma were so exciting and eventful that soon I stopped thinking about Přívoz and my mother. Unfortunately, the happy life at

Oma's house didn't last long; she became ill and died shortly after we went to stay with her.

Edith and I were then taken in by Father's brother Hugo and his wife, Irma, who had no children of their own. Losing two people whom I dearly loved had an effect on me psychologically. I became sullen and disobedient and was often punished. I would have to stand in a corner with my face to the wall, and sometimes I was even sent to bed without supper. Uncle Hugo usually came to my defense and spoiled me inordinately even though Aunt Irma, who was trying to be a mother to us, didn't approve.

I was grateful to Uncle Hugo for his love, which took the place of the maternal love I had been deprived of at such an early age. And, in turn, I loved him with all my heart—more than I loved my father, I believe. I respected Father, perhaps I was even afraid of him, but I can scarcely remember getting any affectionate fatherly caresses. By contrast, Uncle Hugo opened his arms wide whenever he saw me, and I could always run over and cuddle up to him. I felt secure and safe with him, a feeling I had lost when my parents' home broke up.

Aunt Irma now took a firm hand in our education and upbringing. She hired nannies for us. These women came and went frequently, probably because I was so obstreperous. None of them understood that I longed to have my mother back, that my misbehavior had deeper roots than mere willfulness. Aunt Irma kept saying nasty things about my mother, things I didn't at first want to hear or believe. Again and again she would tell me that my mother didn't want me, otherwise she would have come to get me, and that I must not show affection for her if I ever ran into her. With constant repetition, Aunt Irma's words began to take hold.

I don't know where my mother was living at that time. But one day, while I was walking home from school, a woman grabbed me and held me close. I can still feel her kisses on my face and hear her voice choked with tears: "My Rutinko, my Rutinko!" ("My little Ruthie, my little Ruthie!") I was seven or eight years old, and when

I realized who she was, I tried desperately to free myself from her embrace. "Go away," I screamed. "You're not my mother anymore! Go away! Let me go." I arrived home sobbing hysterically. Naturally, I couldn't tell anyone about this encounter. I was ashamed; perhaps I was afraid of my father's or Aunt Irma's reaction. I just don't know.

My mother had given me a present. She must have found out that I was taking piano lessons, and as she held me close she pressed a book of waltz music for the piano into my hands. I was still clutching the book when I got home. In panic I hid it. When someone found it and I was asked where it came from, I lied. In later years I often played the waltzes from that book as a reminder of my mother. I never saw or heard from her again. It was rumored that she had emigrated to Palestine, married a Greek there, and moved with him to Salonika.

We lived with Uncle Hugo and Aunt Irma for several years. Meanwhile, Father sold his little house, intending to join Uncle Hugo in enlarging and expanding his meat and sausage business. There was already one store in Uncle Hugo's house, and Father bought another one.

Uncle Hugo's house was large. In the backyard a one-story building for the staff had been constructed, and it wasn't long before the business grew to employ thirty-five people. Herminka and two helpers prepared meals for the family, as well as for the workers. A maid did the housecleaning, while the whole family worked in the business. A young girl from Aunt Irma's hometown, Skoczow, near Bielsko, was hired as a salesgirl in one of the stores. Her name was Ženka Frischler; she lived with us and was just like a member of the family.

Two horse-drawn carriages stood in the rear courtyard, and a horse was kept in the stable. One of the carriages was used for the business, and the other one, painted a bright yellow, was ours to use for pleasure. A coachman took care of the horse and the carriages. Later the carriages were replaced by a car, and Lada, a chauffeur who always wore a chauffeur's cap, was hired.

It was extraordinary that we should have had a car in the days of horse-drawn carriages and wagons. Not only that: This vehicle was truly unique. During the week it was a truck. The truck body was attached to the driver's compartment with four large bolts. On weekends these bolts were unscrewed and the truck body was put on blocks. Then four men with two long rods lifted a passenger-car body off another set of blocks and bolted it to the driver's compartment. A built-in bench in the passenger compartment could seat three grown-ups or four children. In front of this bench was a collapsible seat that had room for three people. Up front, next to the chauffeur, there was room for three more. So the car, which we called the family bus, could accommodate nine or ten people. At the back of the driver's compartment was a sliding window that usually stayed open during family outings so that we could talk to one another. All the windows in the passenger compartment were equipped with pull-down shades. The headlights were individually mounted on the fenders and the horn was attached outside. To blow the horn, you squeezed a rubber ball and the sound would come out through a golden funnel. Lada was always polishing the bus and kept it gleaming. For family excursions he proudly wore special gloves with large cuffs, which lent him an imposing air.

One entered the back courtyard of Uncle Hugo's house through a large iron gate. Near that gate was the kennel of our black-and-white Great Dane, Bella. She and I were very fond of each other. She was bigger and stronger than I, and whenever I went to see her she would jump up, putting her front paws on my shoulders and knocking me over. I paid no attention to constant admonishments not to go near her because she would dirty my clothes. I needed the dog's affection, so I gladly put up with being scolded.

On one side of the house, under the kitchen window, there was a narrow garden with a green bench and a large pear tree. When the pears were ripe I would climb into the tree to pick them. There were also wonderful currant and gooseberry bushes. The kitchen window was so low that I could sit on the sill, swing my legs over, and find myself in the garden. I remember digging around in that garden, trying to grow my first green vegetables and flowers, but my efforts never seemed to come to anything.

The building behind the house, where the wurst and meats were made and cured, was continually being upgraded and expanded. Pretty soon it became a small sausage factory, with new machines for cutting, mixing, and stuffing; everything ran on electricity. A three-room refrigeration plant was built to keep the meat fresh. The smokehouse was nearby, managed by Adolf. An expert in woods, he knew exactly what type of wood was best for smoking each kind of meat or wurst to give it just the right flavor. Two giant smoking ovens were big enough to accommodate innumerable rods holding strung-up hams, rolled hams, bacon, hot dogs, kielbasas, salamis, and many other wursts. This was Adolf's domain: Only he was allowed to enter here; I don't remember ever having seen anyone else inside. We were always happy when Adolf gave us a piece of hot wurst straight from the smoker. Nothing could possibly taste more delicious. Summer or winter, Adolf worked shirtless, his body gleaming with sweat. Wherever he went he exuded the aroma of smoked meat.

When Father joined Uncle Hugo, he brought with him Alfred Klatt, an assistant from his small shop. Because Klatt was loyal and devoted, he was entrusted with all the secret recipes for making the wurst products. We called him *Mr.* Klatt out of respect for his expertise, and he became the foreman of the wurst-making operation. When Mr. Klatt got married, Father and Uncle Hugo helped him find an apartment. They looked after his family and were always willing to give them advice.

And then there was Mr. Müller, our bookkeeper, who worked next to the shop in a small room that contained a big iron safe, a desk, and shelves. The safe was opened by turning an iron ring. I didn't know what else was kept in there, but I often saw the day's receipts being counted and then locked up until the money could be taken to the bank the next day. Mr. Müller, a tall, thin man who wore a pince-nez, dressed impeccably, and carried an umbrella even when the sun was shining, arrived at work punctually every morning. He would begin his morning ritual by taking off his coat and hat and hanging them up beside his umbrella. Then he would slip black sleeve protectors over his jacket sleeves or, in the summer, over his shirt sleeves. Mr. Müller was married but had no children, and he became fond of Edith and me. We found his pedantic bookkeeper's mannerisms peculiar, and behind his back we often giggled at him and his sleeve protectors.

In the main store there was a section for kosher meat, located off to one side so that the meat would not come into contact with the nonkosher products. The kosher section, which was open only two or three hours a day, was supervised by Cantor Schimkowitz, who also arrived punctually every day. Since there were not many customers for the kosher meat, the cantor, sitting on a white bench, always had time to get into deep conversations about Jewish philosophy with Father or Uncle Hugo. Our house and the business were located directly behind the Přívoz/Oderfurt church and rectory, and whenever the priest, a good friend of my father's, had the time he would come over and join in these conversations. This developed into a Christian-Jewish friendship in which other members of the family participated. From time to time, Edith and I were invited to visit the rectory. The priest would then tell us about the Christian religion, and sometimes he took us by the hand and led us through his church. We learned a lot about our own religion from Cantor Schimkowitz, who taught us many precepts to follow in life. I did not understand the meaning of some of these principles until many years later.

The business continued to grow, and soon Father and Uncle Hugo purchased a short-order restaurant—a one-dish fast-food buffet, actually—on the main street of Ostrava. This meant more employees and more work, for the little business in the back courtyard had turned into a thriving wurst factory. Every day several trucks came to pick up the wurst and meat products to transport them to stores, restaurants, and inns. And every day around one o'clock, after school let out, Edith and I went to the buffet to help out with the lunchtime customers. This was no hardship for me; I loved working among the little round tables, each surrounded by gaily colored stools—red, yellow, green, and blue. The goulash-like soup we served—delicious and filling—had made the buffet so popular that it was always packed at that hour. Workers from all the shops and offices in the vicinity streamed in to have a bowl, served with two kaiser rolls. Large chunks of meat and cubed potatoes floated in the thick reddish-brown soup, and beads of fat swam on the surface; the aroma spread into the surrounding streets and drew in even more customers. One could scarcely find a seat at lunchtime. The whole meal cost 1.20 koruny, which was very little.

But because the buffet led to a lot of additional work and worry, Father and Uncle Hugo decided that it was more than they could handle, and they sold it to their sister Hanča. She renamed it Buffet Anka and substituted fish and delicatessen for the soup. The wonderful fragrance of goulash soup disappeared, to be replaced by the smell of fish. On my way home from school I often thought of the beautiful hours I had spent in the buffet.

Father, Edith, and I lived in two rooms in Uncle Hugo's house. During the week we hardly saw Father, who left the responsibility for our education entirely in Aunt Irma's hands. She knew how to influence and guide us. In addition, there was always a nanny, who saw to it that our room and our clothes were neat and that we were kept busy. Our days followed a precise schedule. In the morning we would get dressed in our good clothes and go for a walk. If we met Father, Uncle Hugo, or Aunt Irma, we had to curtsy and give them a kiss. Before we went out, Aunt Irma would check to see that we were dressed properly; somehow she always found something to complain about. The family was very concerned that the Huppert girls should always look immaculate and behave perfectly, so no one would have cause for gossip. After our parents' divorce there was plenty of that, since divorce was very unusual in those days.

Once we started going to school, the walks with the nanny were switched to the afternoon. Carrying a pail and shovel, a ball, or some other toy, we would go to one of the nearby parks, sometimes even to a cemetery. The nanny would sit on a bench and read a romance novel, leaving us to our games. After exactly one hour, she took us home again. We would have supper and then go to bed. If by chance one of the grown-ups was there, we would get a good-night kiss. But this rarely happened, because the family stores were still open at that hour.

I was happiest when I was sick in bed, because then everyone worried about me and I got to see Father, Uncle Hugo, or Aunt Irma at least twice a day. Dr. Gessler, the family doctor, would come to the house carrying a brown leather bag in which there were all sorts of little bottles, tongue depressors, and other mysterious things. Dr. Gessler was familiar with not only our bodies, he also seemed to know our minds and souls. He was goodness personified and always treated me with love and understanding. I don't think he ever used a stethoscope. Rather, he would first put his ear against my chest and listen. Then he would lay his hand flat on my chest or back and tap on it with the knuckle of his index finger. Everyone had to be absolutely quiet to permit him to hear the sound the tapping made. Amazingly, his diagnoses were invariably correct. After the examination, provided I had been a good girl and had not cried, I got a candy. Of course, that's what I had been waiting for and why I never cried. Dr. Gessler then pulled out his prescription pad, and the nanny would be sent to the pharmacy to pick up the medicine, which was specially prepared and brewed by the pharmacist. I swallowed these gruesome preparations only out of love for Dr. Gessler.

When I came down with a high fever, Dr. Gessler never prescribed medicines; instead, he ordered a cold body compress. I was terrified of this procedure. Two heavy wool blankets were put on my bed, and a sheet dipped in cold water was placed on top of them. Sometimes two people were needed to get me, kicking and screaming, to put my feverishly hot body on the cold wet sheet. It seemed like sadistic torture. Then, with my hands immobilized inside, the icy sheet and the blankets were wrapped around me. On top of all this they put a down quilt. I would begin to perspire profusely. This lasted for at least half an hour, sometimes longer. What a relief when they finally unwrapped me! Once the blankets were off, lo and behold, the fever was gone.

I'll never forget my first day at school. I wore a dark-blue sailor dress with a square collar trimmed with three stripes of white braid, brown cotton stockings, black laced boots (supposedly to make my ankles slender, but it didn't work), and a navy-blue coat with a velvet collar. On my back I carried the traditional school bag, from which dangled a slate, a slate pencil, and a sponge. There were no paper notebooks in the first grade; everything was written on the slate with that special pencil. Once the slate was full and there was no more room to write, you wiped it all off with the damp sponge. The slate even had fine red lines running across it to teach us to write neatly. The upward strokes were very thin lines; for the downward ones, you had to press hard. This gave the script a sculpted look.

On that first day of school, I climbed into our carriage and the coachman drove me ceremonially to the Jewish grammar school on Kostelní Street. The nanny came with me. But when we walked into the classroom my joy vanished. I saw that all the other children were accompanied by their mothers, and I began to cry bitterly and ran out of the room. The school janitor spotted me and forcefully brought me back, and so I received my first punishment. The grown-ups said I had *Schulangst*—that I was afraid of school—and for quite some time I was taken to school against my will. But gradually I came to like it there because my teacher, Grete Gross, understood my problem and showed her affection for me in front of the whole class. In those days Miss Gross became a substitute mother for me, and I felt drawn to her during the four years that I attended the school.

When I left the house in the mornings I stopped off at the shop, giving a kiss and a curtsy to each member of the family. They would look me over to make sure that I was properly dressed before handing me a midmorning snack—a roll with a lot of delicious wurst and an apple or orange. It wasn't long before I became the most popular girl in class because of this breakfast package. I was bored with wurst and wanted nothing but a piece of plain bread and butter, whereas my classmates all longed for the wurst. We set up a barter deal, and suddenly everybody wanted to be my friend so they could exchange their buttered sandwiches for my wurst.

School was about two and a half miles from our house, and I walked there and back every day. Only when it rained or on very cold days was I taken by horse and carriage, and later by car. Many of the children envied or admired me for that. If we passed one of my classmates, I would ask the coachman or the driver to pick him or her up. These little courtesies helped me cope with my feeling of inferiority at not having a mother around. But on other occasions there were problems. For instance, I was never invited to birthday parties or to visit a girlfriend. It wasn't until much later that I realized the reason for this exclusion: I was the child of divorced parents, and divorce was socially unacceptable. Because of the wurst, I was popular in class but not outside school. There, the influence the other children's parents had on them made me a pariah.

When she discovered that I had a good ear and a love for music, Miss Gross recommended that I take piano lessons. Father bought a piano, and I started lessons with Aranka Wasserberger. This drastically changed my daily routine: In the mornings there was school; after lunch, homework; twice a week, piano lessons; and every day, practice. No one had to force me to practice. On the contrary, I had to be dragged away from the piano; it had become my best friend. I was able to forget everything when I was playing, and I spent many hours at the keyboard—some happy, some sad. Miss Wasserberger nurtured this musical talent, and I always did well at her recitals. Year after year, I would get a prize for being her best pupil. After a time, she decided that I should prepare to take the entrance examinations for the Prague Conservatory. Anxious to make it, I practiced harder than ever.

Father and Uncle Hugo were descended from the Jewish priestly lineage—they were Cohanim. Since they were both well-to-do members of the congregation, they had seats in the first row of the synagogue. On the High Holy Days—Rosh Hashanah, the New Year; and Yom Kippur, the Day of Atonement—our shops were closed. Wearing new clothes, everyone in the family went to the synagogue. Cantor Schimkowitz led the services, and as a special honor Father was called up to the lectern to bless the Torah. Then the Torah was carried up and down the aisles of the synagogue and the children could touch it, a great privilege indeed. That was the only time Edith and I were allowed downstairs. The rest of the time we had to sit in the balcony with the women, separated from the men.

Years later, we sang in the synagogue choir on Shabbat and holidays. I was the youngest choir member. The organ was played by a non-Jew, since there was a religious restriction against doing any kind of work on Shabbat and on many major holidays. Cantor Schimkowitz taught us the music. But I didn't stay in the choir very long; I was simply not willing to spend my evenings in the company of grown-ups.

We were home from school on the Jewish as well as the Christian holidays, and this provided a welcome change from the usual routine. In synagogue my sister and I didn't have the patience to stay up in the women's balcony for very long. Wearing our new dresses, we would run out to the courtyard to play hide-and-seek with the other children. Our games often got quite noisy, and the *shammes* (synagogue sexton) would come out and ask us to behave. Sometimes, to back him up, he would bring Father, who would warn us to be quiet. But the silence didn't last long. When we went home in the evening, our new dresses soiled, we would be scolded and reproached for being "a disgrace to the family."

The day before Yom Kippur, Edith and I had an important assignment. We were given several pounds of nice-looking apples and told to stick cloves into them. These apples were then doled out to the fasting women in the balcony, who were only allowed to sniff them. The smell supposedly would drive away their hunger pangs for a while.

Since we lived near the synagogue, many friends and acquaintances came to our house after the Yom Kippur service to break their twenty-four-hour fast. First everyone had a small glass of kümmel, a caraway-flavored liqueur; that was followed by salt herring. Wonderfully aromatic coffee would be poured from large pots, and Herminka would bring in her specialty: yeast-cake rolls filled with poppy seeds and raisins. Our guests showered her with compliments. They would then walk home, refreshed, and Father would tell us that feeding the hungry was a mitzvah—a good deed—that every good Jew must perform. Father's words have stayed with me, and I have followed his teaching whenever I could. Every day a different needy family would come to eat lunch with us. Or if they were too proud to stay, they were given food to take home.

Father was a member of the Zionist movement, and he insisted that Edith and I also learn about Zionism. Conspicuously displayed at home, in our shops, and in the restaurant were blue collection boxes for the Jewish National Fund, each marked with the Star of David. Many customers would drop in generous donations, and Edith and I regularly contributed some of our pocket money. There was a lot of discussion at our house about the founding of a Jewish state. My sister and I became members of Maccabi Hatzair, a movement that combined sports with Zionism. We participated enthusiastically in these sports activities and attended all the lectures because this was a way to meet other young Jewish people. We were never allowed to attend any of the meetings that were held outside Ostrava, however, or to go on camping trips. Unfortunately, this kept us somewhat apart from the other children. Aunt Irma insisted that we were always to be closely supervised and home by 8 P.M. In the beginning the nanny, and later our governess, would pick us up from the meetings. How embarrassing for Edith and me! But Aunt Irma kept saying she had to protect our reputation.

Ostrava is located in the foothills of the Beskids, north of the High Tatra mountain range. In good weather we took the "family bus" into the countryside to go hiking. On these excursions I got to know and love nature. Father would come along, spending all his time with us. In the summer, when it got hot, we would drive to one of the nearby rivers, and there Father taught me to swim. First he took a long stick and fastened a rope to one end. Wrapping a towel around my chest, he tied it into a tight knot at the back. Then he attached the rope to the towel. Next he told me to float, facing downstream, while he ran along the shore holding on to me with the stick and the rope. The current carried me along. It was marvelous, and I hardly noticed when Father lowered the stick and I was swimming on my own. This game was repeated two or three times until I realized that I was really swimming without any help. Father would then come into the water and we would swim far downstream side by side, just the two of us. Of course, we had to walk all the way back, but what a happy time these precious hours with my father were for me! I wished they would never end.

When winter came we went skating, but I didn't enjoy merely going round and round the rink. I missed the open country and nature. One day—I wasn't much more than eight years old—Father bought some short children's skis for Edith and me and took us on our first ski trip to the lowest of the Beskids, Mount Ondřejnik. In those days there were no ski lifts. Father tied the skis and one of the poles together and showed me how to carry this bundle on my shoulder; in my free hand I held the other pole to help in climbing the mountain. Father led the way, and Edith and I followed in his tracks. The climb was very strenuous for me, but Father didn't relent. Just when we had made it up the last, steep stretch, and could see a ski hut nearby, I slipped back down the slope.

Father, who had already reached the edge of the forest, yelled down to me, "Get up on your feet and climb." I began to cry. I didn't want to negotiate the nearly perpendicular stretch again, but he was adamant. He did not come to help me, saying that if I wanted to I could wait there until he and Edith came back down. So I had no choice but to do it on my own. This little scene is firmly imprinted on my mind. The experience taught me never to give up but to keep trying.

A few years later, Father rented a small farm cottage on Mount Visalaja, one of the smaller mountains in the Beskids. The car trip from Ostrava to the base of the mountain took about an hour, and from there we hiked up to the cottage. This was the most wonderful time of my childhood. Weather permitting, we spent every weekend and all our vacations up there. On Saturday, as soon as the store closed, we would pile into the car and drive out of the city. Each of us had a backpack filled with food and other things that were needed at the cottage. Attached to a button on our jackets was a flashlight that lit our way as we climbed in the dark. In the summer we walked up, but in the winter we skied. Father had bought us sealskins, which were fastened to the bottom of our skis to keep us from slipping backward.

As soon as we arrived at the cottage, we lit a kerosene lamp. It had a large light-green shade with painted flowers. Then we brought wood in from the shed and started a fire in the large broad *Kachelofen.* In no time the fire was crackling in the stove, there was fragrant tea to drink, and a cozy, peaceful mood prevailed.

Father had brought along a hand-cranked phonograph with a large dark-green, funnel-shaped speaker on which there was a picture of a little white dog and the inscription "His Master's Voice." The needle had to be changed frequently, but we had plenty of extra needles. Before long, we had accumulated quite a collection of records in the cottage. Father had become fond of opera during his apprenticeship in Vienna, and we had just about every opera ever recorded. There were also lots of cabaret songs, and gradually, as a result of my music lessons, I saw to it that classical recordings found a place on the shelves. The one thing I often missed up on the mountain was my piano, especially during the long summer vacations we spent there with our governess. But it would have been impossible to transport a piano up to the cottage. I begged Father to buy an accordion for me, and he finally agreed. After that there was a lot of singing and gaiety in the cottage. Cantor Schimkowitz, who was in charge of my Jewish education, was shocked when he heard about the accordion and demanded that Father get rid of it immediately. "Mr. Huppert," he said, "the accordion just isn't a suitable instrument for a Jewish girl to play." But the accordion stayed and contributed much joy to the wonderful hours we spent up on the mountain, singing and dancing. Here Edith and I were the center of Father's attention, and he was our closest friend. In the summer we would take long hikes through the woods, and Father, who knew all about mushrooms, taught us how to identify and collect them. When we went back to the cottage, we would clean the mushrooms, slice them, and string them into long chains to be hung up to dry. Almost every day during the summer we ate mushrooms prepared in various ways: mushrooms with scrambled eggs, mushroom soup with potatoes, mushroom omelettes, or as an accompaniment to meat.

Father also taught us how to identify various other plants in the forest. We would carry large cans with us to collect blueberries, raspberries, strawberries, or blackberries, depending upon the season. When we brought back blueberries, the cook would make a yeast cake covered with berries and streusel, or we would eat them fresh, slathered with sweet cream. Our lips, teeth, and tongues would turn dark blue.

There was always something to do. We got milk and eggs from the nearest farmstead, about a fifteen-minute walk away. In the summer we collected pine-tree splinters to be used later for starting fires in the stove. Father bought logs from the woodcutters in the forest, and we sawed these into smaller pieces with a bow saw. How nice it was when Father and I used the saw together, pulling it back and forth in a regular rhythm while the sawdust collected at our feet. The cut wood was then piled up in the barn so that it could dry and be ready for winter.

Though Aunt Irma and Uncle Hugo were always there, I was closest to Father. Even when we weren't talking, I felt secure when I was near him. For me the time on Mount Visalaja was filled with love for him.

Not far from our place was a cottage that belonged to one of Father's cousins, Friedel Wurzel, a superb skier, who taught Edith and me to race. There were wide meadows on Mount Visalaja that were ideal for practicing. Friedel also taught me how to slalom, and when I won first prize in the school slalom competition everyone was very proud. After that I participated in all the slalom races and won several cups.

When I finished grammar school, it was decided that I would attend the German high school for girls on Matiční Street, a school with a good reputation and a high academic standing. I would have preferred to go to a Czech school, but Aunt Irma would not hear of it. She now replaced our nanny with a governess, who supervised my homework. I was constantly reminded that I had to prove I came from a good home.

I longed for my former teachers—Grete Gross, Mr. Panzer, and even the strict principal, Mr. Kraus. I had become very fond of them all during my early school years. At the Jewish elementary school, boys and girls attended classes together, and I was an enthusiastic participant in all the boys' games. I especially liked soccer and was always pleased when the boys asked me to play. Now I was at a girls' high school, in a new and formal environment. For example, if we met one of our teachers on the street we were not permitted to say hello but only to nod respectfully. Dr. Holz, the principal, was Jewish, but otherwise the school had no Jewish teachers. While the Christian students attended religious classes, the Jewish girls went walking in a nearby park. Jewish religious instruction was provided in the afternoon by Dr. Färber, who took great pains with us. His classes were a real learning experience, and we always looked forward to them. There were few friendships between Jewish and Christian girls in the school; even during the breaks we kept apart as though in obedience to an unwritten law. As I recall, some of the Christian girls were the children of German parents and may have been exposed to antisemitic ideas at home.

Aunt Irma and our governess were constantly urging me to get better grades and to do well, not only academically but also in sports and in piano lessons. I took part in athletic contests, swimming, and gymnastics in school and in the Maccabi Club. These activities filled my days.

Family life followed its usual course. On weekdays there was work; weekends were spent on Mount Visalaja. There were family reunions on rainy Sundays, wonderful hours with our cousins, and that kept the family connections intact. The family get-togethers on holidays would be either at our house or we would cross the border to Bielsko to visit Opa Huppert, who owned a restaurant in the Zigeunerwald near Bielsko, a very popular spot for excursions. Because he lived so far from the nearest synagogue, Opa, a pious man, had converted one of the rooms in his home into a sanctuary that housed a Torah scroll. The children were not allowed to set foot in this holy place. Opa was a gray-haired, dignified gentleman who sported a pointed beard. His sons and daughters always spoke to him with great respect. Although we played rowdy games in the Zigeunerwald, I can't remember ever having played with Opa or even having spoken to him. When we arrived he would give us a kiss, but we never formed a close relationship with him, probably because these visits were so rare.

On the other hand, we often saw Father's brothers and sisters. His oldest sister, Aunt Resi, and her husband, Uncle Julius Färber (not to be confused with Dr. Färber), lived in Svinov, a suburb of Ostrava, where they owned an inn near the train station. As soon as we arrived, Aunt Resi would offer us orangeade mixed with sparkling soda that was so delicious I still remember it. Drinks nowadays just don't seem to have the special flavor her orangeade had. I liked Aunt Resi because she looked very much like Oma and because she was always kind to Edith and me.

Aunt Messner, whose first name was Irma but whom we always called by her last name so we wouldn't get her mixed up with Uncle Hugo's wife, lived in Hrušov, another suburb of Ostrava. She sold fabrics in a dark, dimly lit basement shop where the walls were lined with shelves filled with bolts of fabric. Of all my father's sisters, it was Aunt Messner I saw most frequently; I could walk to her place in only three-quarters of an hour. Because I loved the open countryside, I often walked to Hrušov by myself, passing the coal yards on the way. The town had a swimming pool, and I liked to swim there. This pool was made entirely of wood and was surrounded by planks and a barrier so that you wouldn't accidentally fall into the water. Both men and women wore full-length bathing suits in those days, and the women's suits extended down to their knees. But it wasn't long before I was forbidden to go on these excursions, because it was considered inappropriate for a girl to walk past the coal yards by herself.

Aunt Alma Spitzer, Father's youngest sister, lived in Brno. She had two sons, Theo and Lixi, who were my age. We saw them only rarely, since Brno was quite far away. But we would see them more often later on. Aunt Alma and her family would play an important role in our lives.

Aunt Hanča, who lived in Ostrava and owned a delicatessen near the main street, was an elegant, stately lady. She circulated in what were considered the higher social circles and often went to the Palace Coffee House, a meeting place for the fashionable Jews of Ostrava. I had little contact with her sons, who were much older than I. But whenever I happened to pass by her delicatessen, I went in because it was a treat to see the platters of colorful open-face sandwiches topped with all sorts of delicious things: slices of sausage rolled into little funnels, smoked salmon, sardines, cheese, hard-boiled eggs decorated with caviar, pickles cut into fan shapes—all of it gorgeous to look at, never mind the eating. There were rows of beautifully decorated salads in bowls, including my favorite, the herring salad with mayonnaise. Aunt Hanča would give me a sandwich and something to drink, and if she was in an especially good mood, or if I had been particularly well behaved, I also got some of the herring salad. (It was she who later bought our buffet on the main street.)

Two of Father's brothers, Uncle Emil and Uncle Otto, lived in Marianské Hory, near Oma's house. I saw them infrequently. Uncle Emil had no children. Uncle Otto, the youngest brother, had a daughter named Alenka who was much younger than I, so we weren't close.

Aunt Regina Heitlinger lived in Trinec, a small town near the Polish border. We would see her when we went to visit Opa in Bielsko or when there was a family reunion. One of her two sons, Heini, was my age, so at family reunions I always had someone to play with and then, when I was older, to talk to. Aunt Regina owned a large, fashionable fabric store and was well-to-do. In addition to Father's brothers and sisters, there were countless cousins. Oma's maiden name was Wurzel, and she had many brothers and sisters. In fact, almost everybody named Wurzel in Ostrava and the surrounding area was related to Father.

We were a huge family, and although we were scattered we kept in touch with one another. During the Jewish holidays our house was always full of visiting relatives. I especially remember Passover seders, a time of great excitement and nervousness for me because for many years I was the youngest at the table and had to recite the *Mah nishtanah,* the four questions. A huge table would be set with our best Rosenthal dishes, silver cutlery, and crystal goblets. Father presided at the head of the table. While the first prayers were being said, Herminka would peek in from the kitchen, where she waited for the signal to start cooking the matzo balls, which had to be served as soon as they were done. She was proud of these *knoedel,* which were as light as a feather and tasted of nutmeg. The matzo-ball soup was followed by several marvelous dishes, most of which went only half eaten because everyone already had filled up on the soup. As part of the seder ritual, you had to drink a lot of wine. This always put us children in high spirits, and we would traipse around, play games, and laugh a lot, annoying the grown-ups no end. Father felt compelled to finish the seder shortly after dinner was over because the children just couldn't sit still until the rest of the Haggadah had been read. In spite of that, I remember these seders as something quite beautiful because they were like a big family reunion that instilled in us a feeling of togetherness.

What we children liked best was the major housecleaning that preceded Passover. All evidence of bread had to be removed; every last crumb had to be found and thrown out. Then large packages of matzo were delivered to the house and distributed to all the employees. They called it Jewish bread and considered it a delicacy. There were also several packages of egg matzo—special treats for the family. We weren't allowed to help ourselves to these because they were very expensive. I'd love to eat one of those egg matzos again, but I haven't found anything quite like them since.

For some mysterious reason, when I reached my thirteenth birthday Edith and I were sent to a girls' finishing school in Opava, a small town about an hour's drive from Ostrava. We were told that we would get a better education there to prepare us for life. We went home only for the Easter and Christmas holidays, and Father and Uncle Hugo visited us but rarely.

The high school Edith and I attended was located directly across from the finishing-school residence. I had to get used to new teachers, new surroundings, and sharing a room with two strange girls. What I missed most, though, were my piano lessons with Aranka Wasserberger. Even though Edith was with me, I felt lonely, an outsider. I hated being there and didn't see how we could be getting a better education there than at home. Once again, our days followed a prescribed routine. There were prayers before each meal. Since Edith and I were the only Jewish girls, we didn't have to fold our hands in prayer; instead, we stood silently next to the other girls. The Christian students often made fun of us. The academic part wasn't hard for me, but my grades kept slipping, though this had nothing to do with my work or my ability.

At night, after the lights were turned out and the teacher on duty had made her rounds through the dormitories, I was sometimes pulled out of bed by the other girls and ordered to do all sorts of forbidden things. For instance, I had to prove my fearlessness by climbing down and then back up a rope of sheets that had been knotted together and hung out a window. Once they forced me to smoke a cigarette. This brought on a fit of coughing, revulsion, and vomiting. The other girls laughed and jeered. Was this the superior education I was supposed to be getting here?

On Sundays we often went for walks. Opava was near the German border, and frequently we found ourselves heading in that direction—possibly because our teachers steered us there. Whenever we approached the border, a few of the students would leave the group, run across to the German side, and kiss the ground. At first I had no idea why they did this, but later I found out that they were the daughters of ethnic Germans who had been brought up to love Germany and to hate Czechoslovakia. Was this the better class of people Father wanted us to meet?

One Sunday Father suddenly appeared and took us for a walk. He told us that he was going to get married again and that we would be taken out of the Opava school. I was already fourteen, and Edith was sixteen. Now I understood why we had been exiled to Opava. From that moment on, even before I met Lore, who was to be Father's new wife, I subconsciously developed an antipathy toward her: She was taking Father away from me. If he had remarried soon after the divorce, while we were still little girls, we would have gotten used to it. But now, as teenagers, it was hard to accept. In the meantime we had developed a pleasant, comradely relationship with Father. He considered it important that we behaved well and studied hard; that made him happy. He had devoted his free time to us, imbued us with a love of music and nature, and encouraged us to participate in sports. He even had taught us how to dance. He was proud of his daughters. True, ours was not a close, loving relationship, but it had many other good qualities. Now a stranger was about to take all this away from us. When Father left that day, I cried bitterly.

After we returned to Ostrava, we moved out of Uncle Hugo and Aunt Irma's house and into a big apartment in Přívoz, which was furnished according to Lore's taste. My piano was put into the room Edith and I shared. A cook and a maid were hired. And so I was suddenly torn from a colorful and busy life and the many familiar things I had become so fond of, from Uncle Hugo and his love for me, and from the dog Bella. I blamed it all on Lore, and I began to hate her.

Father and Aunt Irma made things worse by their lack of sensitivity. I went back to the same school I had left the year before. One morning I was told that Father would be getting married at eleven o'clock that day—and I had to go to school as if it were any other day! From my seat in the classroom, I could see the town-hall clock. When the eleven o'clock class started, I began to cry. The teacher asked why, but I couldn't explain in front of the whole class that my father was getting married at that moment and that I felt like an outcast.

Father and Lore left for their honeymoon immediately after the ceremony. Edith and I remained behind with the cook and the maid in a strange new apartment. We began to scheme how to annoy Lore, and we became quite good at it. We did everything we could to make trouble for this woman, who surely wanted to be a good and loving wife to our father. There were endless arguments, and eventually things reached the point where we stopped talking to her entirely—a situation that was particularly painful at mealtimes. Edith and I kept running to Aunt Irma with our complaints, and she didn't have much sympathy for Lore. She felt that after being in charge of us and the shops for so many years, her authority had been snatched from her and she now had to share it with someone else. She ended up taking our side in every argument, and this only reinforced our dislike for Lore. On family excursions, Father and Lore often went off by themselves, and we remained with the other members of the family.

My sister, meanwhile, had grown into a beautiful young woman. When she turned seventeen, she left school to learn dressmaking

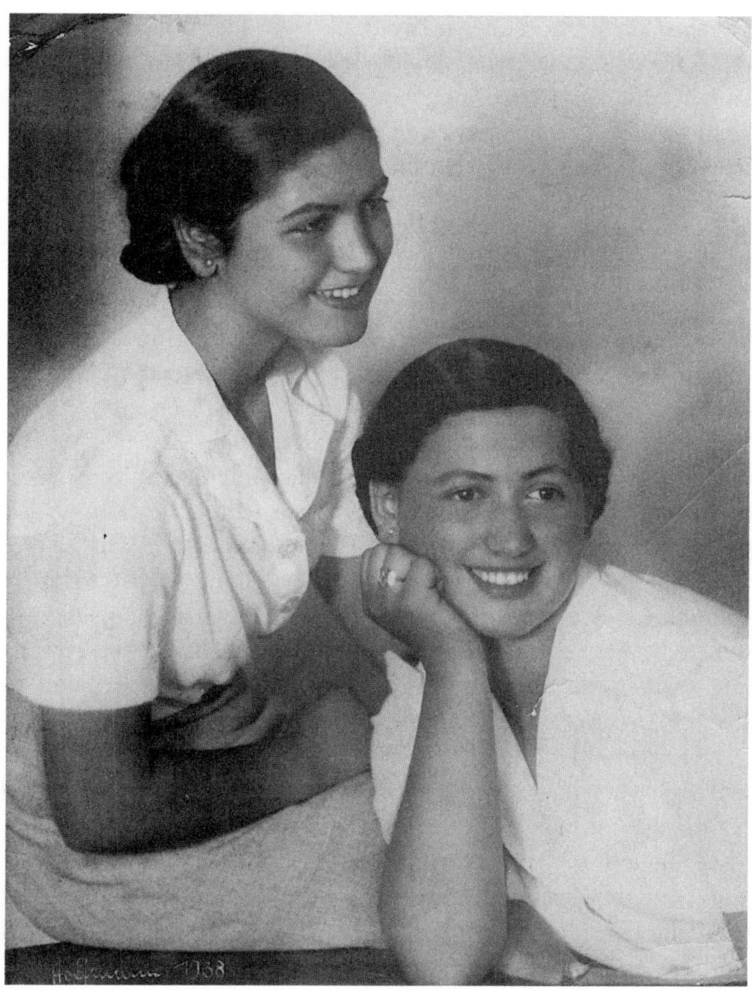

Ruth Elias (right) with her sister, Edith, 1938.

with one of the best-known dressmakers in Ostrava. Edith had a knack for fashion; even as a child she had known what looked good on her. Still, Aunt Irma had always insisted that we wear identical sailor dresses, and we dressed in this fashion until we entered high school. Even later, when the sailor outfits were retired, we still had to dress alike, so I, a sporty, casual type, had to wear the same dresses as my sister, whose whole manner and appearance were very feminine. I looked awful in ruffles and felt best when I was wearing a skirt and blouse—but that wasn't what suited Edith, so I was forced to wear the sort of clothes that looked best on her. It was enough to give me an inferiority complex; I was miserable and often felt like crawling into a hole in the ground.

I can still see Edith preparing for her first dance, radiantly beautiful in an evening dress made of light-blue organdy. She got dressed and made up at Aunt Irma's house, which had been turned upside down in the process. Father picked her up in the car, and he and Aunt Irma took her to the dance. Every young girl had to be accompanied by a chaperone. The chaperones sat to one side and watched over the behavior of the young ladies. Usually the chaperone was the girl's mother, but we refused to let Lore step into that role. On occasions like this, we missed our mother.

How proud we were of beautiful Edith! Pursued by the best-looking young men, she was admired by everyone. It wasn't long before she confided to Aunt Irma and me that she had fallen in love. She told me about her first embrace, her first kiss, and a little later about her disillusionment when the affair came to an end. But soon she consoled herself with Fredy Schöngut, a young medical student. They talked about getting married, but both sets of parents said they were too young.

Whenever I needed new piano music I would go to Buchsbaum's, a large bookstore on Nádražní Trida in Přívoz. Willi Morgenstern, who later became a well-known expert on music literature, worked in the store's music department as an apprentice. He always waited on me, sold me my first jazz scores, and told me about the latest music editions. One day he asked me to go for a walk with him. I turned beet red with embarrassment, but then I hesitantly agreed. Never confident about how to behave in the company of young men, I always heard the warning echoing in my head: You are the child of divorced parents and you must not bring shame on your family. It was a caution that had been drummed into me over and over again.

Willi and I became inseparable, sharing a truly comradely relationship. He was invited to come along on our outings and soon was treated like a member of the family. He introduced me to the best in current books, so I read the latest contemporary literature as well as the classics that had been assigned in school. Willi contributed considerably to my general education and often invited me to go to lectures with him. I remember one of these in particular. It was a so-called Utopian lecture, where the speaker explained how pictures could be transmitted and received through the air. We just laughed: How was that possible? By then we were listening to music broadcasts on the radio. I was still very young when Father bought us our first radio, a Radione, a rectangular black box with five or six plugs that were connected to earphones. We would sit next to each other, wearing these earphones. Loudspeakers were installed much later. But how could you possibly transmit *pictures* through the air?

When I was sixteen, Willi gave me my first kiss. He did his utmost to treat me tenderly, but I didn't know how to respond. And he understood. I was able to tell him how I felt about everything. He made no demands on me, and we remained friends. When he began to see other girls, he told me about his experiences with them, and that only strengthened our friendship. In spite of the other girls, I was the one he took to the movies, the theater, and concerts. We were never at a loss for things to talk about, because both of us were hungry for knowledge.

Willi knew all about my background: my life as a child from a wealthy home as well as the disjointed family relationships. He, on the other hand, came from a poor family and had to educate himself. His mother was a widow and he was her only son, a good son who cared and provided for her and would never desert her.

Around that time, my father became ill with tuberculosis and had to remain in a sanatorium in the High Tatra Mountains, where the doctors collapsed one of his lungs in order to give it a chance to heal. When he came home after several months, he had to rest a good deal and was not permitted to work hard. Lore cared for Father and nursed him devotedly. Edith and I were concerned about his health and resolved that whatever happened, we would stick by him.

From all of this, one might conclude that we were so immersed in our own day-to-day personal concerns that we took little notice of what was going on in the wider world around us. Yet not a day passed without serious family discussions about the ominous political situation. We kept up with the news of Hitler's rise to power in Germany. The newspapers and the movie newsreels were bursting with reports of new developments, and we listened to Hitler's inflammatory antisemitic speeches on the radio. Jews were fleeing Germany, many of them crossing the border into Czechoslovakia, hoping from there to continue on to other countries. They told us what was going on in Germany, yet many Czech Jews managed to convince themselves that it would not affect them. The Jewish refugees were refused permission to remain in Czechoslovakia. Some succeeded in emigrating to Palestine. Others took the risk and stayed without registering with the authorities. Those who were discovered were expelled and returned to Germany. Many Czech Jews began talking about emigrating, but each time we considered taking this step it was agreed that because of Father's illness we could not do so.

When Austria was occupied by the Germans, one of Father's cousins, Artur Wurzel, and his wife, Karla, escaped and came to stay with us. Artur had owned Café Schlösselhof on Schlösselgasse in Vienna. When we were little, we had once visited him and his wife. Now Father was able, somehow, to obtain an Ostrava residence permit for them and to rent a small apartment where they could stay.

Ethnic Germans, who had lived well in Czechoslovakia, organized and began to turn openly against the country. Czechoslovakia mobilized: Army units were stationed along the borders, and everywhere one saw and heard the slogan "We shall not surrender an inch of Czech soil." But it wasn't long before the Sudetenland was handed over to Germany. Not a shot was fired. The ethnic Germans were jubilant.

Chaos. The first Jewish refugees began arriving from the Sudetenland. They reported the same persecution that the German and Austrian Jews had described. There was one difference in their treatment upon arrival: Those who could prove that they had Czech citizenship were allowed to stay in rump Czechoslovakia; everyone else was turned back.

Ženka, who had come to work for us as a young girl, was notified by the Czech authorities that she would be deported. She was a Polish citizen, but it had never occurred to anyone in our family to suggest that she apply for Czech citizenship. She was from the same impoverished village as Aunt Irma, and that's how she had come to Ostrava to be trained and to work as a salesperson in our shops. She was not only an excellent worker but trustworthy and loyal. Although she was seven years older than I, she immediately became our friend and was treated almost like a third sister. Whatever Edith and I got and did, Ženka often got and did, too. She lived in Uncle Hugo's house, and even after Father got married and we moved out, we kept in close touch with her. It was unthinkable that Ženka would have to leave us. Father and Uncle Hugo did everything possible to get a residence permit for her, but all their efforts were in vain. Edith and I cried inconsolably, and Ženka cried even more. We felt that we were losing a member of the family.

There was one Jewish journeyman working in the factory, Artur Eichner, who, like Ženka, was a Polish citizen. He had been with us for quite a few years, and though he lived with the other workers in the employees' house in the courtyard, he was close to the family. He, too, was expelled.

Mr. Klatt, who had started as an apprentice with Father, becoming a journeyman and then foreman of the factory, and in whom Father and Uncle Hugo had placed their complete trust, began to disassociate himself from us. This man had been the beneficiary of our family's generosity and kindness, not just for himself but also for his family. He now openly declared himself an ethnic German and our enemy. I still wonder why Father and Uncle Hugo did not fire him. But perhaps it seemed wiser to keep him on. Who knew how he might avenge himself if he were let go.

The expulsion of Ženka and Artur, and Alfred Klatt's betrayal, demonstrated the gravity of the situation and had a marked effect on our mood. Yet even though we had heard the news of the surrender of the Sudetenland, seen Jewish refugees streaming out of Germany and Austria, and heard Hitler's inflammatory speeches against the Jews and the stories the refugees told about persecution—beatings, arrests, smashed shop windows, and many other things—we still felt secure in the belief that now that Hitler had grabbed Austria and the Sudetenland with all its Germans, he wouldn't attack Czechoslovakia. After all, with the exception of a few ethnic Germans among us, we were the citizens of a Czech state. The Germans had achieved what they wanted, and they wouldn't bother us any further, would they?

Nevertheless, Czech Jews were now beginning to look intensively for ways to get out. Our family had no relatives abroad to whom we could turn for help. In vain Father applied for permission to go to Palestine. Because of his tuberculosis it was out of the question to try to get there illegally; the journey would be much too arduous. There was talk of going to the Dominican Republic, the United States, or England, but these countries had no consulates in Ostrava, and to get any information about their immigration policies one had to go to Prague. When we heard about the long lines of people waiting at the consulates there and how hopeless it was to get visas for any of these countries, we gave up.

Eventually Father no longer insisted that the family try to emigrate together and concentrated instead on getting his daughters out. He wanted to send Edith and me to England, and he arranged for me to be enrolled in an English boarding school and for Edith, who was already eighteen years old, to support herself by working as an au pair for an English family. At that point Fredy, Edith's current love, said he was going to England and would send for her once he arrived there. Father bought three hundred British pounds at an exorbitant exchange rate and asked Fredy to take the money with him and to make sure it would be applied to my boarding-school fees. Shortly thereafter, Fredy sent us a letter saying that he had arrived safely and that he had invested the money. However, a little later he wrote to Edith withdrawing his proposal of marriage. Nevertheless, Father, eager to see us safe in England, continued his efforts to get authorization for our emigration. Then came March 14, 1939.

2

Going into Hiding in Pozořice

OSTRAVA WAS THE ONLY CZECH CITY to be occupied by the German army on March 14, 1939; the following day they took the rest of Bohemia and Moravia.

Around six or seven o'clock in the evening on that day, we watched aghast as wave after wave of German soldiers, some on foot, others on motorcycles with sidecars, trooped by singing, and shouting "*Sieg Heil*" and "*Heil* Hitler." Neither the newspapers nor the radio reports had warned us of a possible occupation that day, and we had been going about our daily routine unaware of the impending danger. Once the Sudetenland had been handed over, "sold out" by British prime minister Neville Chamberlain in exchange for Hitler's promise not to occupy any other countries, we hoped that his greed would be satisfied. We also took a measure of comfort in knowing that the Czech borders were closely guarded by our military. Therefore we could not understand why Czechoslovakia had given up without firing a shot.

Father telephoned Aunt Alma to find out if German troops also had marched into Brno. She had heard nothing. The evening news on the radio carried no reports of an occupation. But the next morning the radio announced that Bohemia and Moravia had been "liberated" by the Germans and that Hitler already had arrived at the Castle in Prague. President Beneš had fled to London earlier, and so had a few members of the Czech government and the secret service.

When Father arrived at the factory that morning he found Alfred Klatt standing at the door, wearing a brown SA uniform, a swastika armband on his left sleeve. Klatt said that Father was no longer in charge of the business and should leave the premises at once. We now realized how well organized the ethnic Germans in Czechoslovakia were. They had been preparing for this day long before the occupation. Father had no choice but to turn his back on his life's work. Uncle Hugo and Aunt Irma had to move out of their house adjacent to the factory. They rented an apartment in Mariánské Hory. Our two trucks and two cars were immediately requisitioned; we were told that they were essential for the business. That put an end to weekend outings. Fortunately, I had brought my accordion back to Ostrava previously, but all the wonderful records, a veritable collector's treasure, were still at the cottage, and I could not retrieve them.

Suddenly everything changed. The first edicts against the Jews were issued. I had to leave school, because it was a German school and now only Aryans were admitted. The Jewish principal was dismissed.

We were given identity cards that were stamped with a *J*—for *Jude* (Jew). Leaving the house after eight o'clock at night was prohibited. Signs reading No Jews or Gypsies Allowed went up on all government buildings, movies, theaters, restaurants, and many shops. A few seats on streetcars, buses, and trains were marked "For Jews Only." Ironically, this was often a plus: Even when it was crowded there would be seats for Jews, because no Aryan would sit in a "Jew-seat." Eventually, in 1941, all Jews had to have a yellow star bearing the word *Jude* sewn on their outer garments. Yellow is a conspicuous color, so it was easy to spot a Jew from far off. Non-Jews, whether they were Germans or Czechs, avoided us and never spoke to us on the street. Everyone was afraid of being reported.

My first encounter with the Gestapo occurred only a few weeks after the Germans occupied the country. Jews had been ordered to appear in person to turn in all valuables such as jewelry, furs, works of art, carpets, musical instruments, and radios. There was feverish activity at our house, because we wanted to give our valuables to Czech friends rather than hand them over to the Gestapo. One of our erstwhile employees, Gustav, lived in Marianské Hory, and we took turns delivering our more treasured belongings to him. Every time one of us arrived at his house, he assured us that he would take good care of our possessions and return everything to us after Czechoslovakia was free again.

Then, on the appointed day, we took the remaining, less valuable things to the Gestapo building. A long line of people had formed on the street, and we had to wait for hours before we were admitted. No one was allowed to leave the line, and when old or sick people couldn't stand up any longer and tried to sit down, they were beaten and forced into line again. When we were finally allowed to enter the building we had to stand precisely in the center of one of the black or white floor tiles, and woe to him who drifted from his spot. He would be yelled at, punched, and ordered to get back to that specific tile. We were not allowed to speak or make a sound. The steely-eyed Gestapo officers walked up and down with hard, expressionless faces. It was terrifying. I don't know what happened to our things, nor do I recall whether we were given a receipt for what we turned in. All I remember is the shouting, the yelling, and the constantly repeated epithet "*Saujude*" (Jewish swine). Naturally, the Gestapo officials did not believe that Jews would have so few valuables to turn in.

Of all the items we had to surrender, the one we missed most was our radio, but we couldn't risk keeping it in the apartment. If there had been a raid they surely would have found it, and at least one of us would have had to go to prison. The radio had been our source of reliable information about what was happening in the outside world, and we had taken turns listening to the reports about the political situation. The news in the local papers was censored and untrustworthy; newspapers had to report whatever the Nazi propaganda machine ordered them to print. We were still hoping that the occupation would be brief and that this awful state of affairs would end soon. Surely our allies would come to our aid and the exiled Czech government in London would take a hand in our liberation.

Gradually we became accustomed to these altered circumstances and tried to arrange our lives accordingly. Those who had large apartments had to share them with other families. People of my age gave lessons to Jewish children, who had been expelled from the schools. One by one, Jewish businesses and shops were "aryanized" and a "trustee" was appointed for them, usually an ethnic German. Swastikas and the word *Jude* were painted on the windows of Jewish stores. Frequently these windows were smashed. Our synagogue was plundered and the Torah scrolls desecrated. Jews were arrested, usually for no reason at all, and taken to prison, where they were interrogated and tortured. As a result, many people signed entirely unfounded "confessions," hoping they would be released. But the exact opposite happened. On the basis of these confessions, they were transferred to one of the concentration camps; they did not return. We tried to remain inconspicuous, to live very quietly, in the hope that something or someone would save us.

All the men in our family were forced to work. As Jews they were ordered to do the hardest and dirtiest jobs. My father became a street cleaner; he was out in all kinds of weather under the watchful eyes of German overseers, who didn't even permit him to take a break. We were very worried about his health.

Then came our second encounter with the Gestapo. Father, after a great deal of effort, had succeeded in obtaining permits for Edith and me to leave for England. Now we had to go to the Gestapo offices to pick up our passports and sign declarations that we would never return to the Protectorate of Bohemia and Moravia, as the German-occupied territories were called. Again the long wait in line until our turn came. Amazingly, everything went smoothly, and we were beginning to think that our chance to escape was at hand.

Many people envied us. Everybody congratulated Father for bringing it off. After all, it wasn't easy to get an exit permit from the Gestapo. But Edith and I now began to have second thoughts. How could we leave our sick father behind? What would become of him? Would we ever see him again? After two days we decided that we couldn't leave. This made Father unhappy. He and the entire family tried to persuade us to get out immediately. But we stuck to our decision: We weren't going to desert Father. However, since we had signed the declarations that we were leaving and would never return to the Protectorate, Father was now faced with a new predicament. It cost him a great deal of money to have someone at the Gestapo office destroy the documents we had signed.

Ostrava's Jews were obsessed with the necessity of emigrating. It was the predominant topic of conversation. Edith and I still wanted to get out, but only if the entire family could leave together. There were so many problems: How to get an affidavit[1] for America. How to get across the Polish border. How to transfer money abroad. There were long discussions about all this, but they always ended inconclusively because of the complications posed by Father's illness.

The Palestine Office in Ostrava was working around the clock to find jobs on farms for young people where they could get the training—called *Hachsharah*—that would prepare them for life and work in Palestine. The office also issued certificates granting people permission to go to Palestine, but these permits were few and far between because under the British quota system only a small number of Jews were allowed to enter. Consequently many

[1] Publisher's note: An affidavit (Latin for "he has sworn") is a declaration by a citizen that he has the means to ensure that an immigrant he is sponsoring will not become a burden to the state.

young people, with nothing more than a rucksack on their backs, crossed the Czech border into Slovakia. From there they hoped to travel through other countries and eventually, aboard small boats that were totally unsuited for such a voyage, sail for Palestine and enter the country illegally. The ships' captains exploited the situation by demanding outrageous prices for the trip. On arrival in Palestine, if an illegal immigrant was caught by the British authorities, he would either be interned or taken to a prison camp on the island of Cyprus. Still, this seemed preferable to confinement in a ghetto or a German concentration camp.

Little by little, our family scattered. Aunt Resi, her husband, and son had to give up their home and business and move to Vyškov, a small town where they went into hiding, passing themselves off as non-Jews. Aunt Resi's daughter emigrated to England. Aunt Regina received a coveted entry certificate, and she and her family left for Palestine. Aunt Messner managed to provide herself and her family with Aryan identification papers. This meant that she could no longer have any contact with us. Some of Father's cousins emigrated, both legally and illegally. Uncle Hugo was not feeling well; consequently, he and Aunt Irma stayed in Ostrava. When he went to see a doctor he was told that he had cancer. We were worried about him, because he would soon have to undergo surgery.

One day Father was picked up by two SA men and taken to the Gestapo for questioning. No one told us why or where they had taken him, and so, not daring to leave the house, we waited. He returned very late, past the 8 P.M. curfew. His face was ashen, and he looked sad and troubled. He said very little other than that they had beaten him, demanding information about concealed valuables. We were relieved to have him home again, but Edith and I now had an additional reason for not wanting to leave. At the same time, we were also beginning to have serious trepidations about staying; no one knew what the future held in store—perhaps it would be better to get out, after all.

September 1, 1939. Germany invaded Poland, and the Second World War had begun. The Poles fought back. Remembering that the Czechs had surrendered without a fight, we admired the Poles for resisting the German armies. But it didn't do them much good. The Germans overran and occupied Poland, too.

Up to that point many Czech Jews had hoped to escape to another country via Poland. Now this avenue was also closed. Only one border was still open: that with Slovakia. But the antisemites Josef Tiso, Vojtech Tuka, and the Hlinka Guards,[2] who held the reins of power there, were collaborating with the Nazis. Refugees who fell into their clutches were often handed over to the Germans or shot.

Emigrating was no longer possible. There was no place to go. It was too late.

A few weeks after war was declared, the Jewish men in Ostrava were ordered to report for transport to Nisko. No one knew where Nisko was, what it was, or what would happen to the men once they were there. Nisko was not to be found on any map. We heard a rumor that it was a work camp near the Soviet border. One thing seemed clear: Father must not be part of that transport. A brief family council was held, and it was decided that he should go to Aunt Alma's in Brno for the time being. Meanwhile, Uncle Hugo had been taken to a cancer hospital in Brno. The women were to stay behind in Ostrava and dispose of the household as inconspicuously as possible so that our family's departure would not be noticed. Lore and Aunt Irma would then also try to get to Aunt Alma's. Edith and I were to stay at Aunt Resi's in Vyškov for a while so that all of us wouldn't arrive at Aunt Alma's at the same time.

---

[2] Publisher's note: Josef Tiso, who was born in 1887, headed a pro-Nazi Slovakian regime, first as prime minister (from October 6, 1938) and then as president (from October 26, 1939). He was succeeded as prime minister by former minister of the interior Vojtech Tuka, who was born in 1880. Both men were executed in Czechoslovakia after the war. The SA-like Hlinka Guards were the paramilitary organization of the Slovak People's Party, the state party of the Tiso regime.

Father left for Brno, and my sister and I heaved a sigh of relief when we heard that he had arrived safely. We started packing clothes and linens, making small bundles to take to Gustav's house in Mari-anské Hory. We gave him the keys to our apartment, and both he and his wife came over to help us with the move. After dropping off the clothes, we went back to get the china and the silverware. All this had to be finished in three days, because the Nisko transport was leaving on the fourth day. By that time, we had to be out of Ostrava.

In those days it was the custom to provide a complete set of household linens, clothes, and so forth for young girls—a hope chest for the day they would marry. Aunt Irma had filled two hand-some, handcrafted chests with lovely things for Edith and me. The chests and their contents were identical, except for the ornate monograms embroidered on the damask bed linens and linen damask tablecloths. These came in all sizes, some with beautiful decorative hand embroidery. Then there were towels, batiste chemises trimmed with lace, nightgowns, and pajamas, even a dozen dish towels. Gustav consoled us each time we brought things over to him, reiterating that he would take good care of everything, that we would get it all back in perfect condition. I asked him to take anything he wanted out of the apartment after we had left. In particular, I urged him to take my piano; I already had brought my accordion to his house.

During those last hectic days in Ostrava, I took time to run over to see Willi and his mother as often as I could. Swearing him to se-crecy, I told Willi of our plans to escape. We tried frantically to think of a way for him and his mother to get out too, but there seemed to be no hope. He had no choice but to report for the transport, since he didn't want to endanger his mother by trying to escape with us. Saying farewell to Willi, the best and most loyal friend I had, would be very hard. Both of us cried, not knowing whether we would ever meet again. Willi asked me to look after his mother once he was gone. I promised, but we both knew that it was a promise I could not keep, since I would be leaving Ostrava the next day.

Willi was to report for the transport before noon. Early in the morning, I went over to say good-bye. In my mind I see him still, tall and skinny in his belted winter coat, a big rucksack containing some of his belongings slung over his back. That was all he was taking with him. Willi, his mother, and I cried wordlessly. What could we have said? Then, hand in hand, Willi and I went to the transport collection point. A last embrace, a final kiss, and my dearest friend was gone.

I returned to the half-empty apartment, where Edith was waiting for me, and we discussed our plan to take the evening train to Aunt Resi's in Vyškov. We couldn't stay in the apartment any longer; they might come at any moment to pick up Father for the transport. So we went to the train station, checked our little suitcases, and just wandered around the area. There was plenty of time before our train was scheduled to leave. Somehow we heard that some Jews were being loaded onto a train waiting some distance beyond the station. I ran to a coal pile and clambered up. From there I could see the train, watch the loading. It was much too far away to make out individuals, and I knew I wouldn't be able to pick out Willi, but this was my last chance to be near him, at least in my thoughts.

Shivering from the cold, I rejoined Edith inside the station. We decided to take a train to Brno first, to see Father at Aunt Alma's house. Once aboard the train we separated, each going into a different compartment and praying that there would be no sudden inspection of passengers. Because we had no identity papers, we would have been arrested on the spot. Luck was with us. After several hours, we arrived in Brno and headed for Aunt Alma's. Father was there with Lore and Aunt Irma, and there was a happy reunion, even though we knew that it would be brief: All of us couldn't stay there.

The following day I went to the hospital to visit Uncle Hugo. He was much worse and looked terribly ill. The dreadful surroundings and the sight of so many cancer patients left me depressed. This was the first time in my young life that I had to confront this frightful disease. And now, another good-bye. Uncle Hugo, whom I adored, would soon be transferred to the Jewish hospital in Ostrava for an operation. Would he get well? What was happening to our family? I couldn't allow myself to cry in front of him. We held each other in a long hug, and I can still hear him saying, "My Rutinko, my Rutinko." As he had done when I was a child, he stroked my hair and my cheeks, and I again felt secure and loved. He had shown me tenderness during a childhood without a mother's love, and now I was about to lose the only person who had ever understood me. I returned to Aunt Alma's house feeling shattered.

That evening Edith and I took a train to Vyškov, where Aunt Resi lived in a small apartment with her husband and son. She had been able to obtain identity cards without the telltale *J* for herself and her family. Not wanting to call attention to themselves, they lived in total seclusion and left their apartment only when it was absolutely necessary. Aunt Resi cautioned us to go out as little as possible, but it was nerve-racking to stay cooped up all day in that tiny apartment, even though she, who reminded us of our Oma, was kind and good to us.

After about a month, we received a letter from Father asking us to come to Aunt Alma's in Brno. We were glad to be leaving the almost prisonlike atmosphere of Aunt Resi's place. Again, we had to take the train and were in constant fear of being discovered. Traveling without identity cards was becoming increasingly dangerous.

When we arrived at Aunt Alma's, we found that by paying a lot of money to a priest, Father had obtained identity cards (without the *J*) for himself, Lore, Aunt Irma, Edith, and me. He also had arranged for us to live and work on a farm in a village near Brno. We looked forward to having more freedom there, without being continually hounded and subjected to oppressive antisemitic measures. The arrangement Father had made with the farmer required us to pay him not only for room and board but also for being allowed to work for him. It didn't take us long to get used to farm life; in fact, we liked it.

Pozořice u Brna (Posorchitz) was a picturesque hamlet in a hilly agricultural region. Here people lived modestly, subsisting entirely on what their farms produced. We had a house with three rooms and a big kitchen. At the back of every house was a long barnyard with stalls for the horses and the cattle, barns, and equipment sheds. Geese, chickens, and ducks, clucking and quacking, were everywhere. There was a doghouse for the watchdog, and at the far end of the barnyard, a big iron gate that was actually the entrance to the farmstead. Beyond the gate there was a steeply sloping meadow with some shrubs and hazelnut bushes growing here and there.

A wonderful dense forest was a half hour's walk away. For me these woods became a substitute for Mount Visalaja, and I used every free moment to go hiking there. Later Father bought a bicycle for me, which made it possible to go even farther and deeper into the woods. Mr. Žalman, the director of the forest service, supervised the management of these forests, which were part of the Liechtensteins' forest preserve.

The Žalmans lived in a beautiful villa in Pozořice. They were among the village elite. Other members of this group included the village priest, the doctor, the pharmacist, and the schoolteacher. Every Sunday morning, after church services, they would get together at the local inn.

During the week Mrs. Žalman, a plump, good-hearted woman, could be seen early in the morning, working in her garden. She was especially proud of her vegetables—she grew every variety imaginable, doing all the planting herself. The Žalmans had two children, Marenka and Miloš, both slightly older than Edith and I.

There were only a few stores in the village. The most intriguing of them was the grocery store, which carried not only food but many other items as well. It was dark and cavernous, and there were several adjoining rooms that contained an assortment of extraordinary goods and extraordinary smells. Pots and pans hung from the ceiling, and you could find spices, flour, wood, coal, kerosene and alcohol burners, and fuel. There were also pepper and poppyseed grinders, potatoes and onions, hairpins and curlers, needles and thread, soap and washing soda, beer and liquor, and lots of other things.

The proprietor sat behind a counter on which stood a balance scale. He used polished brass weights to weigh the rice, candy, lentils, and so forth; then he poured your purchase into a cone-shaped bag made of newspaper. He himself skillfully folded these cones in all sizes; not a scrap of paper went to waste.

We did not know if the villagers were aware that we were Jewish; we were tolerated and even made friends with a few of the locals. All in all, we had complete freedom. The young people of the village belonged to the Sokol Athletic Association, which was notorious for its antisemitism. Still, Edith and I were invited to become members and to participate in the group's gymnastics program. After a heated family discussion, it was decided that, in spite of our aversion to Sokol's views, we had better join to avoid raising suspicions.

Several other activities besides gymnastics took place at the Sokol house. A dance band met there once a week to practice, and it became an irresistible attraction for me. I went to every rehearsal and listened, totally absorbed. One day the band members asked me whether I played an instrument. I said that I did, and was thrilled to be taken on as a piano and accordion player. Father objected because he was worried that this would draw attention to our family. But young people pay no heed to danger. There were family arguments, but music was my life and I couldn't be dissuaded. Finally Father gave in; he even bought a secondhand accordion for me.

There were eleven people in the band; I was the only girl. We played on Sundays from four in the afternoon until late at night, not only in Pozořice but also in neighboring villages. Walking to these places, I carried light instruments, such as the violins or clarinets, while the boys lugged my heavy accordion. These were the happiest moments of my "undercover" life in the village. The musicians became my buddies; sometimes they would even have to protect me from harassment by drunkards.

One of the band members was Miloš Žalman, the son of the forest director. A talented bassoon player, Miloš was studying medicine in Brno. He came to visit us more and more frequently, and I thought that he was coming to see me because of our shared love of music. Soon, however, I began to realize that he was actually interested in my sister. It wasn't long before he and Edith fell passionately in love. By then, Miloš was coming to our house every day, and shortly thereafter our family was honored with an invitation to the Žalmans' home.

Once again, Father raised objections. He wanted us to lead a secluded, quiet, and inconspicuous existence in the village. But he couldn't do much with two teenagers who thought they had their entire lives before them and considered his ways to be old-fashioned. Nevertheless, we realized that we had no choice but to tell Miloš our secret and warn him not to get involved with us. It was no use. This secret forged an even stronger bond between the two lovebirds; they became inseparable.

Father also grew alarmed when Edith began to take on work as a dressmaker. She became popular with the local women for her skill and her good fashion sense. Between her work and my playing with the dance band, we got to be quite well known in the village. Father thought this attention was most unwelcome, but Edith and I, ignoring his fears and anxiety, enjoyed our freedom. I'm glad Edith was able to have this love, even if only for a short while. Her beautiful face became radiant, and she walked about as if in a dream, oblivious to the threatening clouds that gathered around us.

Czech universities had been closed by the Germans, and Miloš spent more and more of his time at our place, planning excursions into the woods whenever we were not working. He had grown up in these forests and knew every path and every tree. Each Sunday we took long hikes with him. The first leg of the trip would be by bicycle, then we'd continue on foot. There were two wooden huts used by woodcutters in the forest, and they provided shelter for us in the event of a sudden shower. Usually Miloš and Edith headed for one of these huts, while I roamed through the woods by myself or fished for trout in one of the many forest streams. Aunt Irma, who insisted that I accompany Edith and Miloš, would have been horrified if she had known that they were alone. Even in these tense times she did not waive the proprieties, demanding that I play chaperone to the lovers wherever they went. ("It's not proper for a young girl to be alone with her admirer," she would say.) We usually took a frying pan and some butter with us on these excursions, and when I returned to the hut we would start a fire and prepare the trout I had caught, using fern fronds as plates. Dessert in the summer consisted of the strawberries, blackberries, raspberries, or blueberries that we had picked. How I enjoyed those quiet and peaceful woods!

I was working for a farmer named Buchta and had to be at his place early in the morning to milk his four cows. It didn't take me long to learn how to do this, especially after I was kicked a couple of times and knocked off my little three-legged milking stool, all the milk spilling onto the straw bedding. The farmer cursed and swore. But with time I got better at it and even enjoyed watching the warm milk squirt into the bucket, forming a great pile of froth. Next, I poured the milk into a larger wooden pail. When I finished I brought the milk to the farmhouse, where it was allowed to stand for a while. Then the cream that had risen to the top was skimmed off with a big ladle. This done, I had to wash out all the pans and buckets and collect the eggs. Before we came to Pozořice, I had had no idea how ingenious chickens could be—the places they found to hide their eggs!

After these morning chores we would drive out into the fields on a wagon drawn by two powerful brown horses. Depending on the season, we gathered potatoes, turned the hay, or bound the grain into sheaves after it had been cut by scythe. In the fall there would be turnips and sugar beets to harvest in the rain and the cold. The farmer's wife brought lunch to us in the field: usually soup and delicious freshly baked yeast dumplings filled with cottage cheese, prune jam, or poppy seeds. Meat was served only on Sundays, but we really didn't miss it the rest of the week.

If it was raining too heavily to work in the fields, I helped indoors. The house had to be scrubbed, laundry had to be washed or ironed, poppy seeds taken out of the seed capsules and dried and stored. Whenever poultry was slaughtered on the farm, the feathers were saved. Later the down was separated from the feathers and stuffed into ticking to make wonderfully warm quilts and pillows.

Pozořice had a single policeman. One of his duties was to acquaint the villagers with new regulations and information. Whenever he had an announcement to make, he would tie a drum around his hips and go drumming at various locations in the village. You could hear him from far away. He kept beating his drum until at least one person from each house came out to listen to him. Then he would take out a piece of paper and solemnly read his introductory words, which were always the same: "You are hereby informed that . . ." ("*Na vědomost se dává* . . ."). He would pass through the entire village in this manner until the new information had reached every household. Every time one of these orders dealt with Jews, we were seized with fear. But when we saw that the policeman's announcements were ignored by the hardworking farmers, we began to ignore them, too. Untroubled, we continued with our daily routines.

Toward the end of April or the beginning of May 1940, an unexpected visitor arrived. Willi appeared on our doorstep. He was a changed man, emaciated, ashen-faced, but worst of all he looked indescribably sad. He had run away from Nisko and managed to cross the border into Czechoslovakia. First he had gone home to his mother, who was overjoyed to see him again, but she was also worried about him because it was obligatory for everyone in the Protectorate to register with the police. Yet how could Willi possibly do that? What would happen if they caught him without identity papers? How could he get food without a ration card? Willi realized that he was a danger to his mother and wondered what he should do under these precarious circumstances. He tried to find out what had happened to us, and when he was told that Uncle Hugo was in the

Jewish hospital in Přívoz, he immediately went to see him. Uncle Hugo, who hadn't told a soul about us, gave him our address, certain that Father would do everything he could to get Willi the necessary documents. I don't know how he managed to make the train trip to Pozořice without papers; it was an incredibly risky thing to do.

Willi's story was horrendous. After the men had arrived at the collection point in Ostrava, he said, registration began and the Nazis realized that not all the town's Jewish men had reported for the transport. So they began a house-to-house search for the missing ones. (What a lucky thing that Father, Uncle Hugo, and all the women had already left their apartments!) The train did not leave until evening. It headed eastward toward Poland. The next day it stopped, and the men were told to get off. They were in a wide-open area with no sign of a village, houses, or any form of shelter. This nothingness was Nisko. It was October and already very cold. Willi couldn't say how many hundreds of men had been brought to Nisko, how old they were, or what their physical condition was. They had been shipped to this barren place without food or water; they had to sleep on the ground, and they suffered dreadfully. It was not until several days later that some lumber was dropped off and they began to build barracks. Slowly, Nisko took form; it wasn't a village but a camp, and no one knew why or for what purpose it was being constructed. Many of the men, primarily the old and the sick, died. A few who managed to escape to Russia were caught and imprisoned. Many of those who fled died too, but a few eventually succeeded in joining the Czechoslovak Army units formed in exile, and they came back after the war. Others who escaped returned to Ostrava, but since they had surrendered their identity cards when they reported for the transport, they could not register with the police and had to leave again to avoid arrest. Staying in Ostrava would have been much too risky for these men and their relatives. And that was why Willi decided to leave, too, so as not to endanger his mother.

Whenever Willi talked about Nisko he became utterly despondent and gloomy, and we who were living fairly normal lives, even though we were undercover, couldn't imagine such terrible suffering, so we didn't understand the implications of what he was telling us. We would ask repeatedly, "Why us? What did we do?" Our only crime was that we were Jews. I felt empathy and deep pity for Willi. I wanted to help him forget the horror of Nisko, but his psychic wounds did not heal quickly. We spent many hours listening to him talk about the camp, and I must admit that it all sounded unbelievable at the time. During those hours he and I were very close. We thought that we were bound by a great love for each other, but we soon came to realize that pity is not the same as love. The bond that connected us was really a deep and sincere friendship.

Willi stayed with us for about three months. He gained some weight, his face lost its ashy gray pallor and became sunburned, and I was happy to see the brightness return to his eyes. Whenever I wasn't working, I was with him. We wandered through the woods and talked about the future, which seemed so uncertain, so unpredictable.

Through Aunt Alma we stayed in constant touch with Uncle Hugo. He wrote to her that Camp Nisko had been disbanded and those who had survived were coming back. When Willi heard this, he decided to return to his mother in Ostrava so that he could stop living the life of a hunted animal. But how could he make the long trip without being arrested? It would have been impossible to get there on foot, so he would again have to risk going by train. I walked with him part of the way to the station, which was some two hours away. Pozořice is in a famous cherry-growing region, and we passed through the most wonderful cherry orchards. It was the end of June, and the trees were heavy with fruit. Embarrassed and busy with our own thoughts, we didn't know what to say to each other. So we picked cherries instead. I don't know what was going through Willi's mind; he was silent and sad. I was thinking that I was about to say good-bye to him for the second time. Perhaps I *did* love him. Was this love?

At that moment I was acutely aware of how much I had missed by not having had my mother's love, and how difficult it therefore was for me to give and to receive love. Even though I didn't want to burden Willi with my feelings, I began to cry. We could see the train station in the distance. I couldn't accompany Willi all the way because we might have run into Germans. We stopped, and holding each other tight, we kissed for the last time. Not a word was said. Willi walked on, carrying his little suitcase. I climbed into a cherry tree and watched until I saw that he had boarded the train and it had left the station. The cherries I had been eating absentmindedly tasted salty from my tears.

Willi arrived safely in Ostrava. He reported to the police and received an identity card and a food-ration card. Like the other Jewish men there, he was again assigned to do heavy labor. A few months later, he wrote to tell me that he had met a girl named Elischka and would probably marry her. Did this news make me happy or sad? Again, I had doubts about my feelings, but after some reflection I wished Willi much happiness. He deserved it after having suffered so much. An announcement of his marriage arrived in the mail several months later.

From time to time we took the bus into Brno to go shopping. This, of course, was dangerous. First we went to see Aunt Alma, then we made our purchases. During these visits we got an indication of how the Jews in Brno were faring. They were still hoping to leave the Protectorate and to emigrate. But with every passing day their chances became less likely. The borders were sealed. They had to perform heavy physical labor, such as street cleaning and shoveling snow. Often there were raids on Jewish coffeehouses, and those who were sitting there would be dragged off to concentration camps. The uncertainty and the insecurity drove many to desperation. Jews were not allowed to go to school, own radios, or travel, and they had to be home by the start of the 8 P.M. curfew.

These and numerous other restrictive regulations drove many Jews to seek other outlets, to get involved in different activities, or to learn something new. Quite a few of the young people wanted to participate in Hachsharah, hoping that it would help them emigrate to Palestine. But there were few jobs available on farms or estates because nobody wanted to hire Jews. Some started to train for new occupations or a new trade, taking advantage of the many vocational courses that were being offered. Women learned how to bake pastries or make artificial flowers and leather belts. They took courses in specialty or machine knitting. None of them knew whether they would ever be able to use these skills, but it was a way to keep busy, to get through the long evenings.

Life in Pozořice was uneventful, enhanced only by our rare trips to Brno. We were getting ready for our second winter (1940–1941) of living undercover. Father bought skis and ski boots for Edith and me so that once snow covered the ground we could get out of the village and enjoy the splendid forests. On one of these excursions I broke a leg, and the village doctor encased it in a giant plaster cast. This physician didn't have much doctoring to do, apparently, and spent most of his time in the tavern, marginally tipsy. You could usually find him there when you needed him. Although we didn't have much faith in him, we couldn't risk going to a doctor or a hospital in Brno because we were afraid of being arrested. There was no X-ray machine in the village, but the doctor claimed that his hands and eyes were just as good. So we had to rely on his skill, and amazingly, he was right. After he took off the cast, he told me to soak my leg in red cattle salt, and within a couple of months I was able to walk again.

A similar problem arose when I had a toothache. A dentist visited the village only once a week, and if you came down with a toothache the day after he left, you had to endure the pain for the entire week. That's what happened to me. I couldn't go to see a dentist in Brno because Jewish dentists were no longer allowed to practice, and it would have been much too dangerous to go to a non-Jew. I was in agony and spent five days and nights holding a hot-water bottle against my swollen cheek. At last the dentist arrived, and his treatment got rid of both the swelling and the pain. (The drill he used was powered by a foot pedal rather than electricity.) His office was located on the floor above the tavern, and for a while I thought that was where the alcohol fumes around the dental chair came from. It turned out that they came from the dentist's mouth. But what mattered in the end was that my toothache had vanished, miraculously.

Spring 1941 arrived, and with it the cherry blossoms. We worked hard, but in this wonderful season there was always time for a hike through the woods and the flowering meadows.

During one of my trips to Brno I heard about a course in machine knitting. Because this was something that really interested me, I signed up even though it meant that I would have to go to Brno once a week. I did rather well in the course. Sometimes we would run out of wool, but I was able to buy more at the general store in Pozořice. The man who owned the knitting machines was Jewish, and he often talked to me about his son Koni, who was working on a farm for Hachsharah. Eventually, we met. He was a textile engineer, about seven years older than I. We liked each other, and before long I found that I was going to Brno not only for my knitting course but also to see Koni. My family, of course, knew nothing about this. They were quite proud of me for persevering so enthusiastically in the course. I'm sure that if Aunt Irma had known about Koni she would have saddled me with Edith as a chaperone.

Koni talked a lot about his Hachsharah friends. There were six fellows and two girls, and I was sorry that I couldn't join a similar group. One day Koni told me that he and his group had to leave the big farm where they were working because the owners no longer wanted to use Jews. The members of the group were desperate, he said, because they all wanted to emigrate to Palestine and without the Hachsharah training they could not hope to go. I suggested to Koni that he find out whether working as woodcutters in the forest could be counted as Hachsharah time. When he told me that it could, I talked to Miloš, and we developed a detailed plan. But when I proposed that the Hachsharah group live in the two wooden huts in the forest, Edith and Miloš protested. After all, the huts were their secret love nests. After I persuaded them to drop their objections, Miloš presented our plan to his father, who agreed to help. And so ten young people moved into the huts. The girls cooked, and the boys worked hard as woodcutters. All were happy to have escaped from Brno and its antisemitic laws and persecutions, and to live in this trouble-free atmosphere.

With the arrival of the Hachsharah group, our life changed. They had to pick up food in the village and keep in touch with the forest management, so not a day passed that one of them didn't come to see us. Oddly, it was usually Koni and Franta Munk who came down from the huts. Franta was attracted to Edith, but when he found out that she loved Miloš his visits stopped. After that only Koni came, and it wasn't long before everyone knew why. I was nineteen years old. A relationship that had begun as a friendship was developing into more than that.

I continued with my knitting course, and on my trips to Brno I would take along letters from the fellows and girls in the huts and bring back mail for them. Koni's parents looked forward to my visits and began to introduce me to their friends as their future daughter-in-law. It was embarrassing, but I had to put up with it. I still marvel at my foolhardy courage and the brashness with which I undertook these bus trips to Brno. I didn't allow myself to think that I might be arrested for carrying contraband items—meat, eggs, butter, and lard—to Aunt Alma. Food rationing in the cities was severe, but in the village it was still relatively easy to buy food on the black market.

During one of my weekly trips I learned that Czech Jews were being transported to Poland. Somewhat later, we heard about a ghetto that was being set up. No one knew any details; even in Brno people were only guessing. We still believed that we had some reason to hope that the war would end soon and the Germans would leave

Czechoslovakia. There was scarcely any talk in our family about what was in store for us. How could we discuss the future when no one had any idea what tomorrow would bring? We lived one day at a time. One thing was certain: There was no longer any way to get out of Czechoslovakia. We would either survive the war undiscovered in Pozořice or we would have to share the fate of other Jews.

Surprisingly, Father had begun to feel much better—probably thanks to the tipsy but talented village doctor. He worked hard on the farm, and being out in the fresh air all day long did him a world of good. Edith and I were amazed to see that Lore and Aunt Irma were beginning to get along. During this time there were hardly any of those family squabbles that used to erupt so frequently. Aunt Irma was very concerned about Uncle Hugo; he was still in the Přívoz hospital but had not yet undergone surgery. Perhaps these worries made other things seem relatively unimportant.

Heavy snow fell on Pozořice in the winter of 1941–1942. The Hachsharah group had brought their skis from home because it was the best way for them to get around. They invited us to a New Year's Eve party in one of the forest huts, and we made the climb, taking with us meat, cake, fruit, wine, and my accordion. It turned into an unforgettable evening, a wonderful time, with lots of singing and not a thought for our bitter present or uncertain future. Before leaving, we told each other that perhaps the war would soon be over and we agreed to meet again in one of the huts the first New Year's Eve after the end of the fighting. That was not to be. Only four of us survived.

Koni's visits became more frequent. We spent many happy hours together and decided to get married at the first opportunity. Aunt Irma finally became used to the idea that her two nieces were now grown up; she no longer chided us and resigned herself to leaving us alone with our boyfriends.

During one of my weekly trips to Brno I heard of the first transports from Prague to Terezin, the Theresienstadt ghetto. Despair spread among the Brno Jews, for rumor had it that Brno would be the first city in the Protectorate to be made *judenrein,* to be "cleansed" of Jews.

In March, the little group of woodcutters disbanded when they were notified that they must report for a transport. The day before Koni was to be taken away, he came to Pozořice. With sadness and foreboding, we walked up to one of the huts for the last time and said our good-byes. The thought that we might never see each other again hung over us like an impending disaster. I wept inconsolably, while Koni tried in vain to calm me. Before heading back, we looked for a spot where we could hide some jewelry and a few valuables Koni had brought from Brno. His parents knew no one there to whom they could entrust these things; we thought they would be safest if we buried them under a stately tree at the edge of the forest. After the war, the first one to come back would dig up these last remaining possessions and family keepsakes of Koni's parents.

One day I came home from working in the fields to find the rest of my family in a frenzy. The Gestapo had come to Pozořice; they had heard that there were Jews living in the village. For some inexplicable reason, the officers did not stop at our house but went to see the mayor, who urged us to leave immediately because we presented a danger to the villagers.

Who had betrayed us? Where could we go? Who would take us in? A few days later we received a notice from Brno ordering us to report for transport to Theresienstadt. Who had given them our names? How had the Jewish Community office[3] in Brno found out about us? These questions remain unanswered.

---

[3]Publisher's note: Jewish religious communities were ordered by SS headquarters to prepare lists with the names of Jews who had been targeted for "resettlement," and also to participate in the preparation of the transports. The religious communities acquiesced in this demand because they hoped that they might be able to arrange a postponement of one or more of the transports or, at least, make the whole affair more humane by having Jewish authorities participate in it.

Almost with a sense of relief, we thought: Finally, we won't have to run like wild animals anymore; at last we'll have a place where we belong. We were ordered to be at the collection point in Brno on April 2, 1942. We had a four-day reprieve.

What were our alternatives? Miloš did not want Edith to go to Terezin under any circumstances. He wanted to marry her and go into hiding with her. But because that would have been a dangerous undertaking for both of them, everyone advised against it. The deciding factor was the fear that Miloš's parents would be interrogated and perhaps tortured. They would certainly be punished severely. Edith and Miloš disappeared, but a day before we had to report for the transport they returned. Both were devastated, as were Miloš's parents. They knew that it was only for their sake that Edith was going into the ghetto.

Mr. Buchta, the farmer, brought us flour so that we could bake something to take along. We made a big batch of cookies to eat in case we should get hungry. In those last hours of freedom we thought a great deal about Uncle Hugo, who was still in the hospital. It was especially sad not to be able to say good-bye to him. On the other hand, we were glad that he had been spared all this turmoil.

Now began the job of selecting things to take along. Each of us was permitted to take fifty-five pounds of baggage. What does one take to a ghetto? Clothes and shoes for the summer and winter? One or two books? Food? Some plates and cutlery? Photographs? How quickly the limit of fifty-five pounds was reached! Once again, we had to part with things that we had acquired during our stay in the village and leave them behind in someone's care. I gave my accordion to the farmer for safekeeping. We filled a couple of suitcases with various things that we couldn't take, and the farmer promised to care for them until we came back.

The evening before our departure, many of the villagers came over to say good-bye. That's when we found out that most of them had known from the very beginning that we were Jewish. It had not been a well-kept secret at all. Even today, I wonder why we weren't turned in sooner. On April 2, 1942, dressed in three layers of clothes, coats, and wearing ski boots, each of us carrying a suitcase and a woolen blanket, we started out for Theresienstadt. Some of the villagers came to the bus stop to wave a last farewell. Through our tears we couldn't distinguish faces, but there were many. Holding Edith tightly, Miloš walked her to the bus that would take us to Brno. A last kiss, a last wave, and the village priest's hands raised in blessing—such was our parting view of Pozořice, the peaceful village in Moravia that had made one and a half years of our lives so pleasant.

When we left Ostrava, where we were born and where our family had lived for generations, no one waved to us or publicly lamented our leaving. But the people of Pozořice made us feel that they cared. A few days after we left the village, Miloš was picked up by the Gestapo and interned. Edith was never told.

This was my last bus trip to Brno. With the yellow Star of David on my chest, I no longer had to worry about being arrested by the Gestapo for traveling without a permit. This time I had their permission, and that's how we headed for the ghetto.

Because there was no intracity bus link in Brno, we had to walk to the collection point. It was a strenuous walk, loaded down as we were with all our luggage and the multiple layers of clothes we were wearing. Our destination was a large building with impressive pillars. Inside, everything was perfectly organized with legendary German order and efficiency. There was even a sleeping spot reserved for the Huppert family on the floor; it was marked with an *H.* The floor tiles were ice-cold.

Registration was carried out in accordance with a precise plan. All personal data and the last place of residence had to be declared. We had to turn in our identity cards—the authentic ones this time, stamped with the *J*—as well as our food-ration cards. Our baggage was thoroughly searched for possible contraband, valuables, or money. The Germans even inspected the seams of our clothing to make sure nothing of value had been sewn into them. The first time valuables had to be turned in, some Jews did not surrender their most precious belongings—their wedding rings. When these or other valuables were discovered now, they were confiscated and their owners were beaten and humiliated. "You Jewish swine" was the common form of address.

We spent the first sleepless night pressed together on the cold floor. Everyone complained, and Edith wept continually for her Miloš. I think I was the only one who wanted to get to Terezin quickly; Koni was waiting there for me. Looking forward to seeing him again made this dismal situation a little easier to bear.

The next morning there was another registration procedure. I received a little card that dangled on a string around my neck. My transport number was written on it: AH 4. This card and the yellow star were to be worn at all times; we weren't allowed to take them off. Whenever I was asked to identify myself, I had to say "AH 4." The transport number and our full names had to be written on our baggage with white paint. Our names were expanded: Women had to add "Sarah" as their middle name, the men "Israel." That day I became Ruth Sarah, AH 4.

Another night at the collection point was sheer torment. Many of the older people and those who were sick suffered terribly. There was only one washroom, and too few toilets; the food was inedible; and there was the constant sound of wailing, interrupted by the yelling and shouting of the Gestapo men. Most unbearable of all was the crying of the children. Only yesterday they were sleeping in their own little beds, surrounded by toys and the loving care of their parents. And now they had to lie on ice-cold tiles. Even though their parents tried to console them, the children never stopped crying. I felt terribly sorry for them. Was it their fault that they had been born Jewish?

This building was a collection point for Jews from Brno; all of them were meeting friends and relatives here. But we were outsiders; we knew no one from Brno except Aunt Alma and Koni's family. This was painful, but there was no changing the reality, so we had to try to make new friends—something that proved to be quite easy under the circumstances. Edith and I offered to take care of some of the children, to play with them and give their exhausted mothers a chance to rest. Soon we were too busy to think of our own troubles.

Before dawn the next day, we were taken to the train station. We were glad to leave this awful place. On the way, I saw Aunt Alma standing some distance away, waving to us surreptitiously. A few passersby—perhaps they were Czechs, perhaps Germans—stopped and watched our procession for a while, then they walked on. Did they know that these Jews were probably headed for slaughter? Did they feel no pity, no urge to help us? I imagine they were afraid the same thing might happen to them. Besides, it didn't pay to endanger yourself for the sake of a Jew. Escorted by SS men carrying weapons at the ready, our silent, tragic procession moved toward the train station, each of us burdened by uncertainty for the future and lost in his own thoughts. There was not much need to keep us under strict guard because those who could do so already had escaped, and we who were left had nowhere to go. No one wanted us; no one was reaching out to help us.

We boarded a regular passenger train, and within a few hours we arrived at the Theresienstadt ghetto.

3

In the Theresienstadt Ghetto

THE RAILWAY STATION FOR THERESIENSTADT (TEREZIN) was at Bohušovice, a mile or two from the ghetto. We were met by young men wearing belted raincoats, visored caps, and boots. Called *Spedition* (expediters), they showed up for every arriving and departing transport, loading and unloading all the goods shipped to and from the ghetto. The Czech gendarmes who had come with us on the train were also there, as were SS men. We had to form a column, three or four abreast, carrying our baggage. The walk from the station to the ghetto seemed like an eternity. There were old people who, unable to keep up, collapsed under the weight of their suitcases and bundles. Whenever they fell behind, the SS men struck them with the butts of their rifles. To keep them from being beaten we, who were younger, helped them; in addition to our own baggage, we carried theirs, too. It was worst for the children. They cried incessantly. One of the parents would pick up an unhappy child, but then the other parent would have to worry about the family's baggage. Here, too, the young people helped out. It was a pitiful,

One of the Theresienstadt barracks. Photographed before 1939. (Yad Vashem Photo Archives, courtesy of USHMM Photo Archives.)

heartbreaking procession: a long line of people, each with a number hanging around his neck and a yellow star sewn on the left side of his coat, carrying suitcases, backpacks, and a blanket tied into a bundle slung over his back. The SS and the gendarmes walked alongside. Eventually we came to a stone wall encircled by a big moat. A bridge led across the moat to a gate in the wall.

At the Hohenelbe Barracks, one of eleven in the ghetto, we were shown to our temporary "living area," a large room that housed between fifty and sixty people. Two mattresses on the floor for each of us were to be our abode, with about eight inches separating us from our nearest neighbor. We set about arranging things, trying to make the place feel cozy. Suitcases were positioned so that we could lean against them; backpacks served as pillows, and woolen blankets covered our belongings. At least we didn't have to drag the heavy baggage around anymore, and we could take off some of the layers of clothes. Most important, the family was still to-

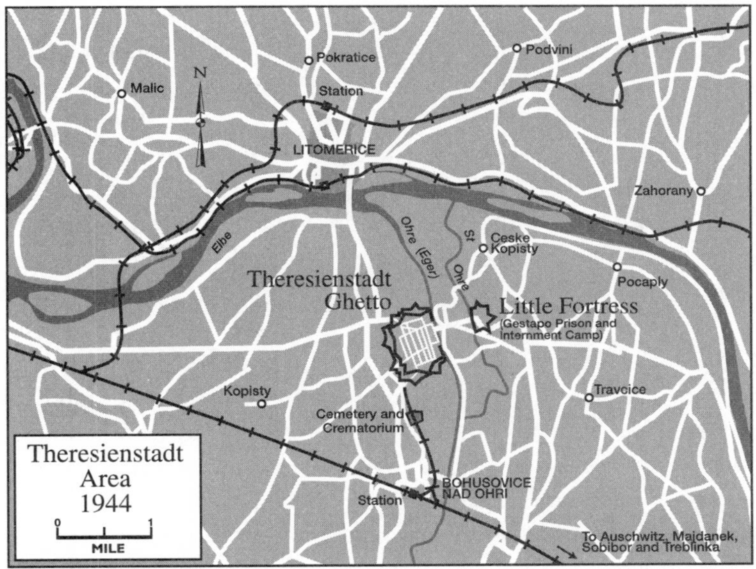

gether. After drinking a liquid they called coffee, I fell into a sound sleep. It was good to lie on a mattress rather than on those cold tiles at the collection place, even if the mattress was rather short.

The following morning the inevitable registration began again and, as always, entailed a lot of tedious bureaucracy. We were told that we were in a so-called *Schleuse*—a "sluice"—a sort of reception section; later we'd be assigned our living quarters. Until then, those who had preceded us into the ghetto were forbidden to have anything to do with us. A whole day was taken up with this registration business. Father, Lore, and Aunt Irma were despondent, and Edith and I couldn't cheer them up. Father had trouble breathing in the overcrowded, stuffy room, and although he had brought along quite a supply of medications, they didn't help. He really needed a doctor, but he was told rather bluntly that a doctor couldn't do much for him because there was a serious shortage of medicine in the ghetto.

After undergoing another baggage check for contraband and forbidden jewelry, we had our first taste of Theresienstadt food. It was impossible to swallow the stuff. We resorted instead to the reserves we had brought with us.

The next morning we were assigned to living quarters. To our dismay, we were told that Father had to join the men in the Sudeten Barracks, while the women were ordered to go to the Hamburg Barracks. We left him with heavy hearts; how would he manage to take care of himself?

Two ghetto policemen (*Ghetto-Wache*) stood guard at the entrance to the Hamburg Barracks, which was for women only; men were not allowed inside. Nevertheless exceptions were made, and although it was difficult some of the men were able to get a permit to enter the women's barracks. Each of us was again assigned two mattresses on the floor of a large room, and we arranged our things as best we could. Altogether there were about forty women in this room, which in Theresienstadt slang was called *Ubikation.* Even with the windows open, the air was stuffy and there wasn't enough oxygen.

Suddenly, unexpectedly, Koni was standing before me. I couldn't believe my eyes. Here at last was someone who was more than a friend. But how had he been able to get in? The answer was quite simple. As soon as he arrived in Theresienstadt, he was assigned to the ghetto police, whose duties included guarding the entrances of the women's barracks. In exceptional circumstances he could enter the *Ubikation,* but this was somewhat dangerous—an SS man or an SS woman might discover him there. The SS women were especially nasty. Usually they were young and sadistic, which is probably why they volunteered to serve in the SS. They conducted surprise raids on the barracks, searching for items we were not permitted to have. Not only would they go through the few things we had been allowed to bring with us, but when they saw something they liked or that seemed useful, they would confiscate it. We called them *Berushky,* which comes from the Czech *bráti,* "to take away." They were real thieves.

Edith and I hugged Koni. He said he could not stay, but he told us that he was in the same barracks as Father and had already talked with him. Now we were among the happy few who at least knew where their men were. Koni would act not only as our liaison with Father but also as a go-between for other women in the room and their men.

Each of Koni's stints as a guard at our barracks lasted four hours. While on duty he could not talk with me; that would have been too risky. But sometimes we were able to speak to each other briefly, and we were grateful for these opportunities. Not many of the ghetto inmates were that lucky.

Theresienstadt, named after Maria Theresa, the mother of Emperor Joseph II, had been a small town. The Emperor had arranged for eleven military barracks to be built there, turning it into a garrison town where many troops were stationed. The townspeople made a good living off the soldiers. A protective wall with several entrances and exits was built, and the wall was encircled by a deep moat that could be flooded whenever the town was threatened by enemies.

Now all the gates but one were hermetically sealed, and Theresienstadt became an ideal place in which to concentrate Jews. The town's Czech citizens had been evacuated, and Czech gendarmes guarded the sole exit. They were our only connection to the outside world. Some of them were hostile, but quite a few behaved decently and were willing to smuggle letters into and out of the ghetto. Sometimes they would sneak in small packages, even cigarettes, which were not otherwise available to us. These services were well paid for by Jews on the outside who had not yet been "ghettoized." If the policemen were caught during an exchange of this sort, they would be severely punished. The Jew involved would immediately be sent to the East and certain death.

The word *Osttransport*[1] (transport to the East) hung over all the Theresienstadt Jews like a sword of Damocles. In accordance

[1] Publisher's note: Altogether, about 141,000 prisoners were brought to Theresienstadt. About 33,500 of them died in the ghetto. About 88,000 were deported from the ghetto between January 9, 1942, and October 28, 1944; of these, 3,500 survived.

with the Nazis' plans all cities, in fact all of Czechoslovakia, and later Germany, Austria, Holland, and France—that is, all the lands occupied by Hitler—were to be cleansed of Jews, made *judenrein:* an utterly incomprehensible and unimaginable concept until then.

Approximately 55,000 to 60,000 Jews were crammed into Theresienstadt, where once there had lived 3,000 civilians and about 10,000 to 13,000 soldiers. To make room for more Jews, the Nazis' simple solution was *Osttransports.* Jews were loaded into freight cars like cattle and shipped to the East. None of us knew the destination of these transports; no news about them ever came back to Theresienstadt.

It's characteristic for human beings to adapt, even under conditions of great hardship. And so we soon got used to our frightful new situation. But again and again we were plagued by questions and fears: Just what was meant by "East"? What awaited us there? No one knew, and this uncertainty was frightening. Completely separated and closed off from the outside world, we still knew nothing about concentration camps, the use of gas, or the extermination of the Jews. All we had were our instincts, which told us that we had to avoid the transports to the East at all cost.

Since we had no radios or newspapers, we depended on the information that new arrivals brought to the ghetto. This information, called *Bonkes,* would race like wildfire from mouth to mouth. But by the time it reached us we could no longer tell truth from fantasy. Yet I think these "news reports" helped to keep our hopes up. One of the questions ghetto inhabitants asked most frequently was "When will the war end, and when will we be free again?"

Each incoming consignment of Jews brought new information about the situation at the fronts. The expectation that the war would end soon gave us the strength and the courage to endure. Optimists had an easier time coping with the harsh conditions than did the pessimists, who seemed to suffer more. I picked out and held on to the good news in the *Bonkes* because that was what I needed.

Many of the barracks were named after cities—Dresden, Hamburg, Magdeburg, and the like. The stone buildings were two or three stories high, each with a large entrance door that was guarded by the ghetto police and an inner courtyard that probably once had been used as a drill ground. An arcade surrounded the courtyard and provided access to the living quarters. The rooms were large and probably had been used as dormitories by the soldiers. There also were small apartments that originally had been intended for the officers; these consisted of two rooms and a kitchen with a cookstove.

But now there were no beds anywhere; all we had were mattresses on the floor and our baggage to use as pillows. At the end of each hall there was a toilet with three cubicles. These proved to be quite inadequate, given the large number of inmates who were crowded into the barracks. It was especially degrading when people suffered from severe diarrhea, brought on by the inferior food we were forced to eat and which our systems were not used to. There was but one washroom on each floor, with troughlike washstands and two rows of faucets that provided only cold water. This made things particularly unpleasant in the winter. When I wanted to wash myself and my laundry, I had to get up very early to avoid the long lines.

Each of us took care of her personal cleanliness. A plan for keeping the rooms in order had been carefully worked out. Every room had a room "elder," who was responsible for keeping things neat and organized. She reported to the group elder, who in turn was subordinate to the building elder, who reported to the head of the housekeeping department. Long live bureaucracy! But it was impossible to maintain cleanliness under such crowded conditions. The bulky suitcases and the mattresses lying on the floor couldn't be cleaned and aired every day. So it wasn't long before fleas, bedbugs, and lice moved in. These vermin caused indescribable suffering. No sooner did you fall asleep than you would be awakened by bites. We got to be quite skilled at catching and crushing the bugs, but they multiplied so rapidly that we couldn't keep up with them.

You were lucky if you knew someone who worked in the carpentry shop, because he might give you a nail or two that you could hammer into the wall to serve as clothes hooks; it was even better if you could "organize" or, rather, steal (the ghetto slang for this was *schleusen*) a little wooden board to use as a shelf, a *polička*. The *polička* had to be taken down and cleaned frequently, because it provided an ideal hiding place for bedbugs.

Theresienstadt had "self-government." All services, including food, health, transportation, security, and youth welfare, were handled by the inmates themselves. It was indeed a fabulously organized "autonomous administration." Whoever was in charge of a particular service division selected his subordinates and was in turn responsible to the Council of Elders. The men in this council were like ministers, and they were subordinate to the *Judenälteste,* the elder of the Jews, whose position was comparable to that of a prime minister. The elder and his council reported directly to the SS command and had to follow its orders and regulations to the letter. This chain of command turned out to be the best solution for the SS because all responsibility devolved on the Jews themselves. Whenever something was not done to the Germans' satisfaction, severe punishments were meted out, including deportation to the East. And for that reason, even though it wasn't easy, the Council of Elders tried hard to please the SS. But in view of the overcrowding, it was virtually impossible to maintain order, cleanliness, health, welfare, and sanitation. Given the circumstances, what the elders managed to accomplish was admirable.

There was also the constant problem of finding accommodations for the new arrivals. The departure of a transport to the East left some space, of course, but when a new shipment of Jews arrived, the old inmates had to crowd together to make room. So there was continual movement, and it was essential to keep track of all these moves, because each inmate had to be issued a food card, and the Council of Elders had to know precisely where each prisoner could be found in case he had to be notified that he had been designated for transport to the East.

It was not the SS but the Council of Elders that had the monstrous job of determining who would be on these transports. I still don't understand what criteria they used. Perhaps there is some protective mechanism at work that keeps me from going into this question more deeply. The fact is that the SS decided *how many* were to be shipped, and the Council of Elders chose *who* would have to go. Each transport usually consisted of one thousand people, but there always had to be alternates because some of those who were picked became ill, or performed a role that was important to the functioning of the ghetto, or there was some other reason they could not leave. Then people on the backup list had to go in their place. Everything was organized down to the most minute detail. Those chosen for a transport had to surrender their food-ration cards. You could not exist in Theresienstadt without one of these cards. With rations close to the starvation level, no one could afford to share his food with someone else. If someone tried to get out of reporting for a transport, he was sure to be caught. Then he'd be put on the next one.

To keep the registration figures updated, the floor elders had to report on the status of the inmates every day—the number who were ill in the "hospitals," and how many had died. Even for those who made small mistakes or committed minor offenses there was always the threat of the transports. That's how the SS kept the machinery running smoothly. We obeyed all orders to the best of our ability out of fear of being shipped east. If someone was caught in possession of a forbidden item or smoking a cigarette, he immediately received "instructions to report"—that is, he was assigned to the next transport.

Koni and his parents had arrived in Theresienstadt three weeks before we did. Koni had a friend who had access to the transport lists, and when transports from Brno and the surrounding area were expected in March 1942, and also in April, he found our names on one of those lists. As a ghetto policeman, he was able to move about freely. The ghetto police were a kind of security service that was charged with keeping order in the ghetto; of course, they carried no weapons. In addition to guard duty at the barracks gates, they patrolled the carpentry shop, the bakery, and various storage places to prevent theft. At first they wore identification bands on their sleeves; later they also wore black caps with a yellow band. Whoever had a ghetto policeman as a relative or a friend was envied by everyone else. In the beginning, tight rules of separation were the norm. Husbands were not even permitted to speak to their wives on the street, except for a half hour after work each day. In that short time it was scarcely possible to discuss important things, because everybody always talked at once. The ghetto policeman often acted as a sort of Cupid's messenger, carrying letters back and forth.

Koni told us that Father was not feeling well. He had trouble breathing in the overcrowded room he shared with some forty people. Ever since he had been diagnosed with tuberculosis, Father had been pampered and cared for by his family; separated from us now, he suffered terribly.

After fourteen or fifteen days in Theresienstadt I came down with a high fever caused by a serious throat infection. Before the discovery of antibiotics, this was a dangerous illness, particularly in the ghetto, where medicines were lacking. I lay on my mattresses on the floor, shaking from the fever. Although the doctor came to see me every day, he had nothing but a few aspirin to give me. Then my family received the dreaded notice that we were to be on the next transport east in three days. The doctor pronounced me unfit to go. The regulations then in force stated that people under the age of twenty-one who were not fit to go could shield their immediate families from the trip to the East. Koni quickly went to see Father and told him that he wouldn't have to report. However, Father said he might actually be able to breathe better in some other place. When

Koni brought this bit of news back to us, we were devastated. Father then sent a message saying that the family must stick together and that I, sick as I was, should also go. A day passed. The doctor cautioned me not to leave. Father sent another message, saying that I might get well on the transport. Only one day was now left in which we could strike our names from the list. Again Koni went to see Father, who stuck to his decision that the family should go east together. We'd all be better off there than in Theresienstadt, he said. After an intense discussion, Koni and I arrived at a simple solution. We would get married immediately. That way I would not be staying behind alone, and Father and the rest of the family could leave on the transport. As a member of the ghetto police, Koni was shielded from the transports and as his wife I would be, too.

Koni brought a rabbi to my bedside. One of the women in the room lent me a wedding ring that she had smuggled into the ghetto by hiding it under her tongue. Like every young girl, I had dreamed of a beautiful, festive wedding in a synagogue, with singing and dancing, a long white dress, and bridesmaids. And so I was terribly disappointed with the ceremony, which lasted only a couple of minutes. The rabbi recited the words of the marriage ritual, and we repeated after him, "Behold you are consecrated onto me with this ring according to the laws of Moses and Israel." Then Koni put the ring on my finger. And that was it.

This would be my last day with my family. I wanted to say good-bye to Father, and sick as I was, I went to see him. Having been assigned to the transport, he was forbidden to leave his barracks, but Koni brought him to the wooden fence. There I told him that I would not be going east with the family, that I had just been married and would stay in Theresienstadt with Koni. Father was silent, but there were tears in his eyes. Did he sense perhaps that these would be our last moments together? Too young to understand, I asked him, "Aren't you happy that I'm married?"

Instead of answering me, Father, who was a Cohen, raised his hands in the traditional gesture and began to recite the familiar words of the priestly blessing while tears flowed down his cheeks. Then he whispered only, "My Rutinko, my Rutinko." It was the last time I saw him. When I think of him, dream about him, or talk about him I always see him standing there at the fence at this, our final meeting.

Especially painful was saying good-bye to Edith. We had spent nearly the entire night standing under the arcade of our barracks, talking and weeping. Edith spoke constantly of Miloš. She wanted to stay with me, but there was no way. I still feel guilty today when I wonder why I let her go. Why couldn't I have done something to keep her there, this beautiful young woman who had only recently begun to live, to love?

The answer is that I was powerless against those who decided matters of life and death in the ghetto. Precise lists were drawn up, and if someone didn't report for the transport there would be a search that lasted until he or she was found. If the missing person was discovered hiding with someone else, that individual, too, would be sent away. If he was not found by the time the transport left, someone on the backup list had to go.

As I write this I see Edith, exactly as she looked then, clinging to me, and I see Aunt Irma, who had raised me. With Uncle Hugo still in the hospital in Ostrava, she had no one but her two nieces, who were like her own daughters to her, and now she was about to leave one behind in the ghetto. I had never had any deep feelings for Father's wife, Lore, but at this moment of parting it was hard to let her go. After all, she was part of the family and had been a good wife to our father. It couldn't have been easy for her to care for him in the atmosphere of adolescent jealous hostility that Edith and I had generated. I still see all of them standing there, crying as we said our farewells. I never saw any of them again. All were murdered. Somewhere.

Those of us who stayed behind knew nothing of the horrible, tragic things that were happening in the extermination camps. We were almost completely closed off. The Nazis were experts at keeping news about the mass extermination of the Jews from the outside world. There were rumors, but no one had any solid information; we simply didn't want to believe the worst. It was self-immunization against despair.

After my family was deported and I had recovered from my illness I, like all the other ghetto inmates, was required to work. Since there were not enough nurses, I volunteered for a nursing job; it would give me a chance to help others. I was assigned to care for the old and the sick in the hospital for incurables. This hospital was on the ground floor of the Jäger Barracks. There was no heat because there was no coal. There were no beds. The patients—each lay on two mattresses on the floor—were always cold because the single woolen blanket they had been allowed to bring to the ghetto was not enough to keep them warm. Patients received only a meager portion of food that contained very few calories, not enough to keep anyone warm. For washing, only cold water was available. There were scarcely any medicines, but there were lots of lice and bedbugs against which people were defenseless. Many of these incurably sick patients were confined to bed, could scarcely get up, and the nursing staff had the almost impossible task of seeing to it that they were washed, kept clean, and cared for. A dreadful stench hung over the hospital, because many of the patients had no control over their bladders or bowels. Having no clean bedding, they lay in their own filth. When I had night duty and some of them died on my shift, I learned to wrap the corpses in sheets and dispose of them. It was gruesome and strenuous work to transport the corpses down to the cellar that served as a morgue. The next morning I had to report the names and the number of people who had died during the night so that these data could be precisely recorded in the main registry. The Germans insisted on order above all else. I don't know how many patients, crying out with longing for their children, died in my arms. I know only that most of them died deserted and alone, without children or other relatives near them. It was my first encounter with death and despair.

We were always hungry, very hungry. There was never enough to eat. In the morning: ersatz coffee. At noon: soup, usually made from powder or some sort of turnips—with luck you might even get a small piece of turnip floating in the broth. This was the "first course"; it was followed by boiled potato or a yeast dumpling with sauce, and once a week a little hash that was more flour than ground meat. In the evening: ersatz coffee, sometimes margarine, jam, or artificial honey and a third of a loaf of bread. Fruit, vegetables, eggs? Those we ate only in our dreams.

Gradually, because of the constant hunger and the misery I witnessed day in and day out, I became depressed and asked to be relieved of working with the incurable patients. I was assigned to assist a doctor who visited sick inmates in the living quarters. We would check on sick people who had not reported for work, to determine whether they were fit enough to work or, if necessary, to transfer them to a hospital.

Given the scanty food rations, many people didn't have the strength to work. It was not easy for the doctor, who was hungry himself, to decide who should and who shouldn't work. The patient's emotional state was a key factor in his decision. Sometimes it was better for patients to be forced to work so they could forget their suffering for a few hours while they concentrated on an assigned task.

My association with this doctor led me into the various living quarters in barracks and in the houses abandoned by Czechs. Everywhere people were lying on the floor, and it was heart-wrenching to witness their misery. What could a nurse possibly do to help them? How could she cure this mass suffering? The best doctors and scientists who came to Theresienstadt were powerless when confronted by this situation. I was young and hungry, and I no longer had enough stamina to deal with all this wretchedness. Consequently, I began to keep a lookout for a different job. Through sheer coincidence, I found it.

I was passing one of the rooms when I heard the sounds of an accordion. Drawn to the music as if by a powerful magnet, I opened the door and stared at the instrument in fascination. When I was asked what I wanted, I said, "Please let me play." It didn't occur to me to wonder how the accordion had come to be there. (Actually, it belonged to Kurt Meier, an extraordinarily talented musician.) We had to turn in all our musical instruments at the beginning of the German occupation, and when we reported for the transport to the ghetto our baggage had been inspected so minutely that we couldn't have brought anything in secretly. Much later, I found out that Czech gendarmes would bring musical instruments to the ghetto gate and the inmates smuggled them inside.

Someone in the room handed me the accordion and, hesitantly, I started playing; after a while, I also sang. Others joined in, and before long we began to forget our troubles. We just sang and sang. There was one man in the room, Emil Schneider, and even though I knew that men were not allowed in the women's quarters, I was too deeply moved by the music to be surprised that he was there. Emil, it was explained, was permitted inside the Hamburg Women's Barracks because he was the head cook for the barracks. When he asked me whether I wanted to take on a hard but "belly-filling" job in the kitchen, I couldn't believe my ears. To be allowed to work in the kitchen was everyone's dream in Theresienstadt. It would make it possible for me to eat there and to give my ration card to my husband. Indeed, working in the kitchens, farm work, and butchering were the most desirable jobs in the ghetto. There were five or six central kitchens where food for the inmates was prepared. A few days later, Emil got me a job in the kitchen of the Hamburg Barracks. It was hard physical work, cleaning the huge kettles, bringing in the food to be cooked, and then carrying the heavy wooden barrels filled with soup to the place where it was dished out. This had to be done by two people because the barrels were very heavy. A strong wooden pole was pushed through the handles and then, holding on to the ends of the pole, we carried the wooden containers full of boiling hot soup to the distribution place. Long before it was time for the food to be portioned out we could see people standing in line, waiting. There were always three of us at the distribution window, each doling out a part of the meal: One ladled the soup, another passed out the potatoes, and the third poured the sauce.

Women from the food service stood in front of the window and tore a coupon from each inmate's food card. They would then tell us how many portions to pour into each dish. Whenever possible, I tried to get out of working at the distribution windows so that I wouldn't have to watch the disturbing and degrading scenes that were played out there. You could tell by looking at them that most of the inmates had been well-to-do in their previous lives, and my heart broke whenever I heard them plead, "Give me the thick part of the soup from the bottom, please." What they were asking for, of course, was a little piece of turnip to allay their hunger pains for a few minutes. I always stirred the soup thoroughly so that everyone would get a fair portion. As soon as we took the empty wooden buckets out into the courtyard, these pathetic people would pounce on them in order to scrape out the dregs with their spoons.

The word *Schleuse* (again, the English meaning is "sluice" or "lock," as in a canal) had two meanings in Theresienstadt. As I have already mentioned, the *Schleuse* was the reception area for newcomers that had been set up in one of the barracks. They had to pass through there for registration and inspection. Each person had to unpack his or her suitcases and other baggage. The SS women, the *Berushky,* went through all these possessions thoroughly and removed items they wanted to keep. Some inmates were immediately designated for transport to the East. Then registration and the allocation of living quarters began. The new arrivals were totally confused by this procedure—no information about Theresienstadt had reached the outside world. We were allowed to mail only one postcard at a time, on which we could write up to thirty words that were heavily censored: "We are well and hope you are too . . . ," and a few other empty phrases that said nothing about conditions in the ghetto. Whenever a transport arrived, no one was permitted on the streets until the new arrivals had reached the *Schleuse.* The Nazis wanted to keep old inmates from warning the newcomers about what lay in store for them. It wasn't until they had gone through the *Schleuse* that we old-timers were allowed to talk to them. By that time they had gone "through the mill" (*durchgeschleust*).

Used as a verb in another sense *schleusen* meant taking something that didn't belong to you—in other words, stealing. But that didn't mean stealing things that belonged to your fellow inmates; it meant absconding with something that was common property. For instance, if you wanted to hang up your clothes, you would *schleus* (swipe) a nail. In the ghetto there were no stores where you could buy things, so you had to filch them. You might have a friend who worked in the woodworking shop, and he would *schleus* a nail or a piece of wood for you. In exchange you would give him a potato or a piece of bread that you had *schleused* from the kitchen. And so a lively barter system ensued despite a camp detective unit that was set up to prevent these petty thefts. All we were trying to do was make our miserable lives a little easier, each of us eager to find what we urgently needed. When the soles of my shoes developed holes, I would get them back from the repair shop much faster if I brought a potato for the shoemaker. When the baker had his shoes repaired, he would add an extra piece of bread; someone else would come up with a cigarette. Cigarettes were a highly prized and costly item for which the ghetto's Czech gendarmes demanded unbelievably high prices. Smoking was prohibited in the living quarters, and if an SS man or a *Berushka* arrived unexpectedly and smelled smoke, he or she would launch an immediate search for cigarettes. Usually other contraband items were found during these searches. The punishment for this, too, was transport to the East. In spite of the constant danger, the inmates continued with their petty thefts, trying to make life in the ghetto a little more bearable. Actually, it was more than that: An extra bite of bread or an extra potato helped ward off starvation and kept one alive. To filch coal in the winter when the temperature hovered between 5° and 15° F (−10° to −15° C) was to have a little warmth to keep from freezing to death. So, *schleusen* was not stealing. It was trying to stay alive. It was essential.

Every two weeks we had ersatz lentil soup for lunch. It tasted awful, but it was thick and filled our stomachs. The "second course" was a yeast dumpling served with a sweetened blackish-brown sauce in which little flecks of margarine floated. Whenever we made these dumplings it had to be warm in the kitchen so that the dough, which we kneaded by hand in wooden troughs, could rise. One day I decided to take a little of the yeast dough for my roommate and her child. I took a handful and put it under the big oilcloth apron I wore over my work clothes. I was about to leave the kitchen when two police detectives (*Kripo*) walked in. One of them started a routine inspection while the other guarded the door. Because of the heat the dough under my apron began to rise, and the dimensions of my bosom became larger and larger. Terrified that the dough would expand beyond my apron, I gave my chest a hard thump. The dough collapsed, but only for a moment. It immediately started to rise again. The *Kripos* didn't notice. My co-workers, though, were highly amused by these antics. Finally, after what seemed an eternity, the detectives left. Instead of a handful of dough for my roommate, I returned with dough smeared all over my clothes. We were able to scrape some of it off, and she and her daughter received a little additional nourishment.

The Czech gendarmes were our only link to the outside world. Occasionally they would "accidentally" leave a few pages of a newspaper behind, and from these we sometimes were able to glean clues to the political situation. The gendarmes were poorly paid, and they were glad to pick up some additional money, either from Jews who were still outside the ghetto or from those who were inside. Almost all of us had concealed some money or a few valuables in our clothes or shoes and had smuggled these into the ghetto. We thought they would come in handy when times got tough. It turned out that the money and the valuables were essential for our survival.

Isolated, we received virtually no spiritual or intellectual support from the outside. The Nazis probably wanted to kill our spirit by keeping us cut off from the world. But if this was their plan, it did not succeed. With no weapons, the only resistance we could mount was a spiritual one, and it was extraordinarily strong in Theresienstadt.

The Nazis funneled a constant stream of Jewish scientists, doctors, musicians, teachers, painters, singers, and actors into the ghetto. They came not only from the Protectorate but from Germany, Austria, Holland, France, and later also from Denmark. So it was that some of the intellectual elite of central Europe passed along their knowledge to other inhabitants of the ghetto. It was the only way to resist the Nazis' efforts to kill our minds, our spirits.

Immediately after his arrival, each inmate was assigned a job. Everyone had to work eight hours a day to keep all the facets of the "autonomous" ghetto administration running smoothly. But after work, in our free time, there was a tremendous upsurge of cultural activity. It began with lectures to small groups; some people studied Hebrew; choral groups were formed; there were stage productions; and after the first musical instruments were smuggled in there were concerts. All this had to be done secretly. During a performance inmates stood guard outside, and when an SS man approached, the guards would give a warning signal and all traces of the performance immediately disappeared.

First an accordion, then a guitar, a violin, a viola, a cello, and other instruments were brought into the ghetto. One problem was that we had no printed music, but the musicians had memorized the scores, so they played by heart. Trios formed, and it was remarkable and incredible to hear these musicians playing from memory without making mistakes. The first concert I attended took place in an attic. People were posted at a dormer window and on the stairs to warn us in case the SS approached. The room was relatively large, and chairs had been set up for a trio, composed of a violin, a viola, and a cello. Since there were no other chairs, the audience stood, silently listening to the marvelous music. This was one of the most festive concerts I have ever been privileged to hear. People around me listened with rapt attention. Many cheeks were wet with tears.

These few hours of spiritual nourishment helped us temporarily to forget our hunger pains and our misery. We longed for another concert, a lecture, or perhaps a play. The performers viewed this as a revolt against the regime. They were using their instruments and their words as weapons against the Nazi terror.

Later the Council of Elders reached an agreement with the SS that officially allowed the Jews to obtain musical instruments and bring them into the living quarters. The result was an incredibly vital and diverse cultural program during our so-called leisure time in Theresienstadt. Working at night, the musicians drew musical staff lines on paper and wrote down, from memory, the parts for each instrument. During the day each inmate had to perform his assigned tasks, but after work many of us were able to forget our suffering for a few hours. The German authorities encouraged this and later used it to support one of their biggest propaganda lies.

In the fall of 1943, it was announced that the Red Cross was coming to inspect Theresienstadt. The Nazis wanted to show the world what a good life the ghetto Jews were leading. Theresienstadt was beautified—even the streets were washed—and playgrounds were built for the children. The Nazis produced a film called *Der Führer schenkt den Juden eine Stadt* (The Führer Gives the Jews a Town). It showed ghetto performances of plays, concerts, and lectures in halls crowded with well-dressed spectators. It was intended to give the world a picture of Theresienstadt as a model ghetto where Jews lived contented, happy lives. A Red Cross commission arrived in June 1944 (by that time I was no longer there), and right after this visit all the improvements that had been made were torn down and the sad, dreary life of the inmates resumed. After the commission left, virtually everyone who had participated in this staged event—now that they were no longer needed—was designated for transport east.

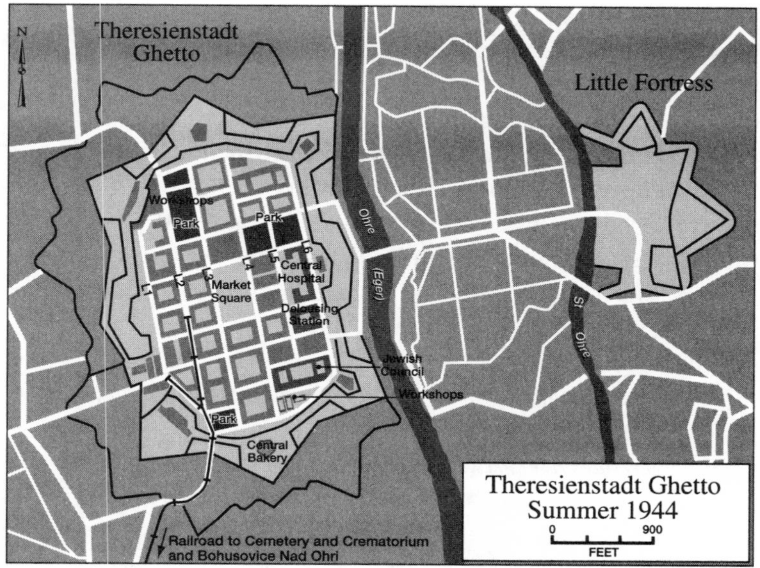

A group of artists—among them Leo Haas, Fritz "Fritta" Taussig, Otto Ungar, Karel Fleischmann, and others—were ordered to produce paintings for the SS. The Nazis dictated the subject matter. But these artists also initiated a major clandestine and illegal undertaking: They captured life in the ghetto on their canvases. While they were working, lookouts were posted to warn of surprise SS visits. When they finished, the paintings were concealed behind walls and in other hiding places. It was intended that after liberation, these paintings would testify to the realities of life in the ghetto. One day the SS arrived without warning, discovered some of the paintings, and put all the artists into "the Little Fortress," the Theresienstadt prison. There they were tortured to force them to tell where they had hidden the rest of their paintings. When they refused, two of the artists had their fingers mangled. One by one, they perished in the Little Fortress. Only Leo Haas survived. After his liberation in 1945, many of the paintings and the truth about the fate of the other artists came to light.

Various drama groups gave performances in German and Czech. A young Czech cabaret writer named Karel Schwenk wrote the words and music for satirical reviews that dealt with ghetto themes. For the finale of Schwenk's first cabaret piece, the actors stepped to the edge of the stage and, holding hands, sang a simple song that he had composed. It instantly became the Theresienstadt anthem. Everyone in the ghetto knew it and hummed it, and those who survived remember it to this day. Karel Schwenk lives on in our memory even though in the fall of 1944 he died in a gas chamber. The song went like this:

If we really want to, we'll make it through, hand in hand,
joined as one,
though times are hard, our sense of humor still prevails.
Every day we have to move, making room for others.
We're allowed to write just thirty words.
Hey, tomorrow life begins again, and the day approaches
when we'll pack our little bundles and return to our homes.
If we really want to, we'll make it through, hand in hand,
joined as one,
we'll stand on the rubble of the ghetto, someday—and we'll be
laughing.

It was no longer enough for me just to attend concerts. I longed to actually make music. Occasionally I would visit Kurt Meier to play his accordion. Often, while we were working in the kitchen, we would start singing. One day Eda Krasa, who also worked there, told me that he had joined a chorus. He had a beautiful baritone voice and we sang together whenever we had the chance. It was Eda who encouraged me to try out for the chorus. An old, damaged harmonium had been found in the cellar of one of the ghetto houses, and that's where they were holding auditions. The place was ice-cold, but I was delighted with the friendly welcome I received from Raffael Schächter, a wonderful musician and the driving force behind the musical life in Theresienstadt. I was accepted as an alto in the chorus, and we immediately began to rehearse Smetana's opera *The Bartered Bride.*

In another cellar someone had discovered an old grand piano. Since its legs were missing, it was set up on sawhorses, and Schächter, sitting at the keyboard, played and directed the first Theresienstadt performances of this opera. It wasn't difficult to find soloists among the inmates. After about thirty-five enthusiastically received performances of this work, Schächter prepared other operas, including Mozart's *The Marriage of Figaro* and his greatest achievement, the Verdi *Requiem.* These were unforgettable experiences. But because my hours in the kitchen were quite irregular, I often could not attend the rehearsals. It was a choice between eating or singing. I chose eating.

The stream of Jews coming into Theresienstadt seemed endless. My heart sank whenever we were told that another transport would be arriving from Bohemia and Moravia, and I always wondered which of our relatives would be on it. When I heard that a transport from Ostrava was expected, I became restless, wondering how I could help my relatives, should any turn up among the new arrivals. Since it was forbidden to be out in the streets when a transport arrived, I hid in a doorway, and as the people from Ostrava were led through the empty streets I stared into their faces, trying to spot a familiar one. An SS man had just passed the doorway when I made a split-second decision to join the new arrivals. (I knew that if I were caught I would immediately be sent to the East.) But no one noticed as I fell into step with the silent procession. In a whisper I asked one of the men in line to give me the tag he was wearing on a string around his neck. Wordlessly he handed it to me, and I walked into the *Schleuse.* After returning the tag, I saw a friend from the ghetto, who was working in the reception area, and told him why I had come. I also asked him to help me get out of the *Schleuse* later. Then, acting as though I too were working there, I kept a lookout for relatives until I spotted Uncle Otto, Father's youngest brother, his wife, Fanny, and their fifteen-year-old daughter Alena. They were the only members of my family who arrived in this transport. I whispered to them that they must not talk to me or show that they knew me. I was able to save some of their belongings from confiscation and to escort them to their living quarters, the *Ubikation.* But a few days later I was not able to prevent their being assigned to a transport east. Another parting.

The transports kept coming.

Uncle Emil and his wife arrived, as did Aunt Tauber, my father's cousin, who was a beautiful, elegant lady. She had tried to teach Edith and me good manners, showering us with proverbs and advice that we were too young to appreciate. Now she was weighed down with grief: Her husband had died, her son had killed himself, and her daughter had been deported to Poland—all within the span of a few days.

Father's cousins Friedrich, Emmerich, and Artur Wurzel arrived next. Artur had fled from Vienna to Ostrava, and Father had gotten him a residence permit before he was deported to Theresienstadt. Others who came included the principal of my school, Dr. Holz; my dear teacher, Grete Gross; and Aranka Wasserberger, my piano teacher. My entire childhood and my youth rolled by me like a film that faded away into the East, as if in a dream. The stream of people I loved had no end, and with each good-bye went a piece of my heart.

Willi arrived, accompanied by his pregnant wife and his mother. His wife knew of our close friendship and understood when we hugged each other for a long time. I attempted to keep them off the transport, but in vain. And so the best friend I ever had went east.

The one thing that helped me get through this difficult period was the work I was doing. But then came the day when someone arriving on one of the transports brought a newspaper published by the Ostrava Jewish Community. Glancing through it, I came upon the announcement of Uncle Hugo's death. My beloved uncle whom I had idolized, who had spoiled me outrageously, and who I thought was safe and well cared for in the Ostrava/Přívoz Hospital, had died of cancer, which had metastasized throughout his body. In retrospect I'm glad he did not have to enter the gas chambers of Auschwitz; at least he was spared this suffering.

After reading Uncle Hugo's obituary I could no longer suppress my pain. There had been too many partings, too many tears, too much sorrow in this short period of my imprisonment and in my young life. My body was shaken by an uncontrollable fit of crying, and the tears would not stop flowing. People tried to calm me, but nothing helped. Ilse Weber, my neighbor, came over, put a lighted cigarette between my lips, and ordered me to smoke it. The crying began to ease up. After that, whenever I was upset I would look for a cigarette; I was even willing to exchange bread for a smoke. I became addicted. Today I know that distracting myself with an activity, in this case the act of smoking, helped to ease my pain. But it was getting harder and harder to find cigarettes in the ghetto. Like many others, I was always on the lookout for discarded butts, which were real treasures. I would pick them up, buy or filch some paper, and soon I became adept at rolling my own.

In the Hamburg Barracks, each time a transport departed for the East those of us who were left behind had to move to make room for new arrivals. I cursed this constant moving from one spot in the barracks to another. Just as I became accustomed to a new spot and new neighbors on the floor, I would have to leave. I had always been quartered in one of the large rooms, where about forty people lived on the floor, but this time I was lucky. I was moved into one of the areas that formerly had been an officer's apartment. These flats consisted of a good-size room, a tiny room intended for the officer's servant, and an entrance hall in which there was a kitchen stove that now was rarely used because there was no coal.

I was assigned to share such an entrance hall with Helene Zuckermann and her little girl. (Anyone who wanted to reach one of the other rooms had to pass my mattress on the floor in the hall.) About twenty women lived in the larger room. There was space for only one person in the little servant's room, but Erna Traub and her sister-in-law, Ilse Weber, were squeezed into it. Both women as well as my roommate, Helene, were from Ostrava, so we had many things in common. All of them knew my family, and Erna was even distantly related to me. Her brother, Manek Weber, was married to my aunt Hanča, who used to own the Buffet Anka.

These two women furnished their *Kumbalek* (Theresienstadt jargon for tiny room) with admirable ingenuity. They created a sitting nook on the floor, using four mattresses covered with a blanket. Their suitcases formed the backs, and the second blanket, rolled up on top of the suitcases, served as a headrest. Their clothes, hanging from nails pounded into the walls (there were no closets), were covered with a piece of cloth. There were also two little shelves, but the most beautiful object in this tiny space was a guitar that hung in a place of honor on the wall. I couldn't believe my eyes when I first saw it, because at that time it was still forbidden to own a musical instrument. I had learned not to ask too many questions, but I assumed the guitar had been smuggled into the ghetto by a Czech gendarme. The women had managed to give the little room a homey atmosphere, and we passed many wonderful, intimate hours in this *Kumbalek*.

Ilse Weber, who worked long hours as a nurse in the children's infirmary, was an unpretentious-looking woman; she wore glasses and her hair was held back firmly by a wide ribbon. She dressed simply but always looked clean and neat. When she went to work, she wore her white nurse's apron with its broad straps and ties, and we were at a loss to know how she managed to keep it snow-white. She suffered with her young patients, who had scarcely any medicine or nourishing food. Completely selfless, she cared for the children as though they were her own, always trying to think of ways to bring them a little joy, whether it was by giving them more food or some other extra attention.

She had arrived in Theresienstadt with her husband, Willi, and one of her two sons, Tommy, who was then five years old. Willi lived in the men's barracks and Tommy, in the children's quarters. Ilse found this separation extremely painful, especially in the beginning, when we were allowed to see our families for only a half hour each day. Later, as regulations in the ghetto became less strict, this constraint eased somewhat.

Ilse spoke of her other son, Hanusch, with great longing. Before she was deported, she had sent the eight-year-old boy to some friends in Sweden, not knowing what fate awaited him there. Often she expressed doubts that she had done the right thing. True, she had saved him from the privation and humiliation of life in the ghetto, but she had also deprived him of his mother's love. She read us a heart-wrenching letter that she had written to him but was never allowed to send. Ilse saw her own son, her little Hanusch, in each of the sick children she cared for.

In her free time, and while she was working the night shift, Ilse wrote about what she saw, what she heard, but primarily how she felt. It is extraordinary how this outwardly simple woman was able to put into poetry, profound poetry, everything she observed. One marvels how, in that monstrous time, she managed to see so much that was ugly and yet sometimes also that which was beautiful and describe it all. In her verses she painted a nearly complete picture of ghetto life.

We would often squeeze into Ilse and Erna's little room to listen to Ilse read her poems. Later, when the guitar arrived, Ilse set several of her poems to music and sang them for us while accompanying herself on the guitar. During those hours in the *Kumbalek,* we felt our exile and the longing for freedom especially keenly.

Eventually Ilse, Willi, and their son Tommy were sent east. Only Willi survived. He and Hanusch later collected Ilse's poems in a little volume they called *Theresienstadt.*

The entrance hall I shared with Helene Zuckermann and her daughter, Evička, was directly accessible from the arcade. I still wonder why she was allowed to keep Evička with her. Usually children were assigned to the children's home so that the mothers could work. But this was not the case here. The child was living with her mother, who, consequently, did not have to work. The father, Julek Zuckermann, was a good, warmhearted, and caring husband. He was a coal carrier in one of the communal kitchens, and that gave him an opportunity to pilfer coal and bring it to us hidden under his shirt. Once we had collected enough, we were able to make a fire in the kitchen stove and heat water for washing, boil the potato peels I'd collected, or even bake a pancake with the dough or flour roux I had filched. Those rare cooking days turned into festive occasions. But one of us had to stand watch outside in case SS people passed by. When the food was cooked, it was divided among those in the *Kumbalek*, Koni's parents, and us.

Eventually the Zuckermann family was transported east, where Helene and her child perished in one of the Auschwitz gas chambers. Julek came back, blind. He lost his sight after he was shot in the back of the neck because he could not keep up with the others on one of the death marches. He was nursed back to health, but his blindness will always be a reminder of those painful times.

Until September 1942, the ghetto was "closed"; that is, one could leave one's living quarters only in groups or with a special pass. But as a ghetto policeman, Koni was able to enter the women's quarters. And so he divided his free time among the Dresden Barracks, where his mother lived, the Sudeten Barracks, where his father was housed, and the Hamburg Barracks, which was my "home." After we had been in the ghetto some six months, this closure was eased somewhat and we were permitted to move about freely on the streets. Women still were forbidden to enter the men's barracks, however. To get around this prohibition, I volunteered for the cleaning detail that scrubbed the wooden floors in the men's barracks. It was the only way I could get to see my father-in-law. Instead of scrubbing the floor, I would quickly wipe it with a damp rag so that I would have more time to spend with him.

Koni's father was a man of great personal dignity, but he was slowly wasting away. He could not cope with the suffering, the meager food, and above all the feeling that he was powerless to take care of his family. It was not long before he became ill and was brought to the infirmary. There he lay in a clean bed, but soon he lost all interest in life, and he no longer wanted to get up. After coming down with much-dreaded pneumonia, he died. Yet another parting. Each one left us a little bit older. Where did we find the strength to bear it all?

The funeral service took place the following day. Corpses from all over the ghetto were collected and placed into open hearses on a daily basis, then taken to the mortuary. Sometimes they were covered with a sheet; at other times they weren't, and often a hand or a foot would dangle down or one of the bodies might even slide off. At the mortuary the bodies were put into coffins that were then nailed shut and placed in neat rows. When we arrived for the funeral these coffins—each carrying the name of the deceased on the outside—were already set out in alphabetical order in a long row. We stood next to the coffin of Koni's father. After a short prayer, the coffins were taken away. Where to? It was said that the bodies were either burned in the crematorium or placed in freshly dug mass graves. We never found out where Koni's father was buried.

Since the carpentry workshop, located in the former riding school, could not keep up with the demand for coffins, workers from other units were called in to help. Eventually my turn came, and I, too, had to learn how to make coffins. In a huge room that had been the riding ring where horses were once trained, carpenters now trained us poor hungry creatures to make coffins. The death rate in the ghetto had increased sharply, about 150 people were dying daily, and we were not allowed to go home to our barracks until we had met the daily quota of coffins. We worked with great diligence in order to finish early. Surprisingly, the women became expert coffin makers, but we had to work quickly to keep up with the demand. The workshop motto was "Keep pace with death."

One day I was ordered to pack up my things and go to work in a kitchen outside the ghetto. I was disconsolate. Where were they sending me? Why? And why without Koni? No one seemed to know or want to tell me. Another parting—and then off into the unknown.

Those of us who had been given this new assignment were taken to newly constructed wooden barracks outside the ghetto. There we were told that a children's transport was expected and that we who were experienced in the ways of the ghetto were to perform essential services for the new arrivals. Looking at the others who had come with me, I saw that people had been chosen from each of the service divisions. Franz Kafka's sister, Otilie, was among the medical personnel. I was responsible for the kitchen. Before we started to work, each of us was given a thorough medical examination. I realized that everyone except me was unmarried. Why was I, a married woman, among them? There wasn't much time to ponder this. The children were expected the next day, and preparations had to be made.

Early the following morning Jakob Edelstein, head of the Council of Elders, arrived to inspect the new barracks. Although the members of his entourage didn't approve, I explained my situation to him. He was surprised to hear that a married woman had been picked for this job without her husband and ordered that I be exchanged for an unmarried prisoner. Overjoyed, I returned to the ghetto.

Later that day the children—they were from Bialystok—arrived. When they were asked to undress and take showers, they refused, crying, screaming, and kicking. None of the Theresienstadt staff could understand why they were behaving this way; probably just childish fantasizing, they thought. But these children, whose parents had been sent to the gas chambers, understood the incomprehensible: undressing and taking showers meant death. Eventually they were forced to comply.

After only a short time in the new barracks the children and all the ghetto personnel who had been assigned to work with them were sent east to be gassed. As I write these words I am overcome with horror: Who had to give up his life for mine?

We were afflicted by various diseases, and I still cannot understand how we got well without medication. The wooden clogs I wore while standing on the wet floor in the kitchen chafed one of my big toes and it became infected, developing into deep cellulitis. I was in terrible pain and ran a high fever that caused my entire body to shake. I was sent to the surgical department in the Hohenelbe Barracks, where Dr. Springer, a skilled surgeon, worked under the most difficult conditions. He examined my foot, diagnosed the problem, and lanced my painful toe without using an anesthetic. I screamed in pain, but the anesthetic had to be saved for more serious operations. The surgeon then pulled a piece of gauze through my toe to facilitate the draining of pus from the wound and told me to return in a week so that the dressing could be changed. I was brought back to my hallway room and I lay there, the fever still raging. The wound emitted a dreadful, putrid stench, forcing the women who passed by my mattress to hold their noses. Despite the lack of antibiotics, after a week the infection miraculously cleared up, and two weeks later my toe was completely healed.

Another time I came down with a severe case of infectious hepatitis. Since it was not possible to adhere to a special diet, there were only two options: Either I survived or I didn't. Dr. Mautner, the physician in charge of our floor, cut quite a figure. His clothes were fastidiously clean, and in spite of the adverse conditions under which he worked he always had a reassuring smile that barely concealed his despair. From his aristocratic bearing you could tell that he had seen better times. When one of us became ill, he could offer only his presence to help us get better. He was often called to attend my roommate's child, and to show him my gratitude for his kindness I occasionally brought him a potato or a little piece of bread from the kitchen. I felt awkward whenever I gave him something, but I suspect that it was even more embarrassing for this proud man to accept my gifts.

The toilets in the Hamburg Barracks were at the end of the arcade. There weren't enough of them by far, and we usually had to wait in line for a long time. When I developed a serious inflammation of the bladder (cystitis), I became desperate. My urine was bloody, and I was in great pain. No sooner had I used the toilet than I would have to line up again. It was terribly cold in the arcade, and there was a constant draft. Day by day I felt worse. Finally, Dr. Mautner was able to get me into the infirmary. What a luxury it was to lie on the wooden frame that passed for a bed in the slightly heated room. Only a few sulfa tablets, the prescribed treatment, were available, so it was primarily the warmth and bed rest that cured me.

When an epidemic of scarlet fever hit the ghetto, a quarantine section was set up in the Dresden Barracks. Koni contracted the disease and spent six weeks in strict isolation. We were able to wave to each other through a small opening in a window. When he was released, he was pale and thin.

A transport of mentally disturbed Jews arrived. I don't know how many there were, but when I passed their living quarters I was shocked by what I saw. Some were naked, others covered with only a blanket. Their hair was in wild disorder, and their bodies, just skin and bones, were dirty. Their eyes were sunk in their sockets, and all had the indescribable look of madness. It was gruesome. None of us dared to enter these quarters for fear of being attacked. The poor creatures had no control over their bowels, and the stench was unbearable. Even from outside the building you could hear them shrieking and screaming. Shortly thereafter they were transported to the East, where they met the same fate as other Jews.

In November 1943, we were told that a census of ghetto inhabitants was about to be taken. All those who were able to walk were led to an open field in a nearby valley. There the men were separated from the women. Guarded by SS troops and gendarmes with loaded weapons, we had to form rows of five. There was nothing to eat, nothing to drink, and we were not permitted to leave our row. A fine rain began to fall; it was bitter cold. Nobody counted us. Nothing, absolutely nothing happened, just thousands of people standing motionless in the cold drizzle, hour after hour. The elderly who could no longer stand and tried to sit down were struck with rifle butts and forced to get back on their feet. And then, as it was getting dark, a rumor spread: There was about to be a mass shooting or some other form of liquidation. But nothing happened. When darkness fell our premonitions turned increasingly more gloomy. Black night. Then, a murmur, the sound of shuffling feet, loud shouts, and we found ourselves dragged along by a stream of fleeing people. In panic we ran along in the direction of the shuffling feet, paying no attention to anyone who lay in our path. All that mattered was getting away, away, to save ourselves, to run, run. Finally, we arrived home—home in the Theresienstadt ghetto. We were alive. Had they counted us? Did they get the numbers right? I doubt it. But of one thing I was sure: That day, in the course of this senseless census, several hundred people must have lost their lives.

Gradually regulations in the ghetto were relaxed somewhat. We could walk freely on the streets and didn't need a pass to leave our building.[2] There was lively cultural activity, supported by the Germans, who saw this as a way of distracting the inhabitants from what was really happening. In addition to concerts and plays, there were many other activities. A coffeehouse opened, and although no real coffee was served you could order a sort of brew and there was always some form of entertainment, usually light popular music performed by singers and a jazz band, the Ghetto Swingers. Sometimes there were classical music concerts, too. One had to buy tickets beforehand in order to get in.

---

[2] Publisher's note: In the fall of 1943, after approximately 450 Danish Jews were deported to Theresienstadt, the Danish government requested permission to inspect the camp. The camp administration tried to make the camp "presentable" through extensive "improvements" (see also p. 84) and a certain degree of relaxation of the camp regulations. A commission of the International Red Cross arrived for an inspection visit in June 1944. The Nazis succeeded in large part in deceiving the commission about the real conditions in the camp.

The inmates immersed themselves in any diversion that was at hand just to keep from being constantly reminded of the horrible conditions around them. We wanted to fill each free moment with something beautiful, and therefore we plunged into these cultural activities to savor every minute of life. No one knew what awaited us or when it would all end. But as soon as we began to believe that life in the ghetto had become somewhat settled, a transport leaving for the East would rip into our illusion and we would once again be confronted by terrible reality.

There were broad meadows on the other side of the wall that surrounded Theresienstadt. One of these was called the *Schanzen,* or "earthworks." From time to time, the *Schanzen* were opened to us, and—guarded by gendarmes—we could sit on the grass, stroll in the open fields, or stretch a net between two trees and play volleyball. Mothers would take their children for walks. During those rare moments we scarcely remembered that we were prisoners. To an outside observer, we must have presented an idyllic picture of normality. Looking across the fields, we could see a village far away. But when we returned from these brief moments on the earthworks we always felt the deprivation of freedom much more keenly. The thought of having to go home to the ghetto made us shudder.

There were organized sports in the ghetto. Some of the young men had brought soccer balls with them, and soon soccer clubs were formed. A league was founded, and matches were arranged. The matches were played in the courtyard of the Dresden Barracks, with the spectators standing pressed up against the balustrade of the arcade, cheering for the players in "their" clubs. There were several of these clubs, and they had names like the Cooks, Expediters, Ghetto Police, Transportation, and so on.

Almost every day women's gymnastics lessons were given in the courtyard of the Hamburg Barracks by a former physical education teacher, and more and more women joined in these sessions to keep fit. It was surprising how many inmates, despite their hunger and privation, participated in the exercises.

All these activities helped us to forget. On Friday evenings we sometimes met in one of the barracks with a group of young Zionists to celebrate Shabbat and light the traditional candles. Our common yearning to go to Palestine brought us together and gave us a chance to affirm our belief in a better tomorrow.

We lived from moment to moment, never knowing what the next day would bring or when we'd be together again. We therefore immersed ourselves in these activities and lived every minute to the fullest. The desire for human closeness and touch, for physical love, was especially strong. It was amazing that even in our state of constant malnourishment this longing for love was so powerful. Love meant life. We wanted to experience it to the utmost and thereby prove to ourselves that we were still alive, still able to enjoy a few happy hours, to plunge into forgetfulness and savor life. It was as though we could sense that the end was drawing near but we didn't want to surrender. We wanted to grasp the few beautiful things that we had in the ghetto, to hold them tight and not let go.

Love makes you inventive. There were quiet little hiding places in the arcades, and we used every opportunity to make love in these deserted corners. People in the workshops were especially fortunate. And if one of them was your friend you were lucky, because he would let you use his workshop in exchange for a piece of bread. That satisfied both parties. When the barracks became overcrowded, ghetto inmates moved into the vacated private houses in Theresienstadt, where conditions were no different. Many young people built themselves little wooden lean-tos in the attics of these houses and lived there with their wives or girlfriends. Officially, either men or women could live in these houses, but one member of a couple had to be registered in the barracks. To build a little lean-to you first "organized" some wood and nails and a hammer. The carpentry work had to be done quickly so that someone else wouldn't come along and appropriate your precious material.

I still had some friends in the carpentry shop where I had made coffins. They gave Koni and me some wood in exchange for pieces of bread. But it wasn't enough, and we had to join forces with another couple, who contributed more wood. The four of us, longing for privacy, worked quickly to build our little room. Although Koni and I were married, we had not really lived together up to that time. Luckily we had found a corner location, which meant that only two additional walls had to be put up. We also built a bed and a small table for each couple. Our clothes were hung on nails hammered into the walls. This was a real paradise. The two beds were separated by a curtain so that we had something resembling a little room of our own. Each couple had different working hours, so Koni and I often had the "apartment" all to ourselves. However briefly, we found a measure of happiness there. And the private accommodations made us feel privileged.

This love nest was in house L 408. A large black funeral coach was parked in the broad entryway. The vehicle had four decorated columns, each topped by a little angel and connected by decorated crossbars. Funeral coaches like these, in various shapes and sizes, were quite a common sight in Theresienstadt. They were used either to carry corpses—scantily covered with a sheet—or to transport bread. Instead of horses, they were pulled by people. In the house next to ours, L 410, there was a youth center, and when the hearse was being used to distribute bread it was pulled by youths from the center.

One of the communal kitchens was in L 408. I was still registered at the Hamburg Barracks and worked in its kitchen. But when we moved into the attic of L 408, I asked to be transferred to the kitchen there. Then to get to work all I had to do was walk downstairs.

The Zuckermann family, Ilse Weber, and her sister-in-law Erna Traub were quite unhappy about my move. We had lived together for a year and had grown close. Now they would no longer receive the little additional food I used to bring them. I visited them less and less often; that still saddens me today.

I missed my co-workers in the Hamburg Barracks kitchen; we had been a tightly knit community, working hard but helping one another. We sang songs and pilfered food together. In this new kitchen I was an outsider. But after a while the other workers accepted me, mostly because our attic room was an ideal place to hide some of the things they had appropriated. Yet I never quite got used to the conditions in L 408. What I missed most was singing with Eda Krasa, a big, strong man with huge hands who always had a good word for everyone. He had a wonderful sense of humor and managed to cheer us up when we were depressed.

Koni's mother lived in the Dresden Barracks. She peeled potatoes there in order to add a little something to her meager rations. We didn't see each other very often because we worked different shifts. But when there was a soccer match in the Dresden Barracks we would inevitably meet, since Koni was goalkeeper on the Ghetto Police team.

After Koni's father died, his mother became depressed. She no longer had her husband to care for and had to share her only son's love with me. I felt sorry for her, because her whole life had revolved around her family. Now she was lonely, and Koni and I, being young, could not fully empathize with her sorrow. We were living our own lives and gave too little thought to this good woman. If only I had been more considerate in those difficult times.

The couple who shared our attic room were the Fertigs. He had been a pharmacist in my hometown and now worked in the ghetto pharmacy, where, he said, there was a dire shortage of medicines. We saw one another only occasionally even though we shared the small attic space. Although we spent the nights together, each couple lived in their own space. We had moved in during the summer, when it was very hot under the tiled roof. With the coming of fall the nights grew cold. There was no stove to heat the little room, so after we came home from work there was not much else to do except go to bed immediately and warm each other up. But despite these problems the short time Koni and I spent in our *Kumbalek* was a time of closeness and togetherness.

After almost six months, I began to feel sick and queasy in the mornings. I didn't know what was wrong, and I had no mother to ask for advice. It didn't seem serious enough to see a doctor, but by chance I ran into Dr. Mautner during one of my visits to the Hamburg Barracks. He seemed truly happy to see me again. With professional concern he asked me how I was feeling, and I told him about my problem, adding that I probably had gastroenteritis or some similar infection so common in Theresienstadt. Dr. Mautner looked shocked. "My dear," he said, "you're pregnant. You must do everything possible to terminate this pregnancy."

To whom could we go for help? A recently issued regulation prohibited abortions in the ghetto. We made desperate appeals to one doctor after another, but none wanted to take the risk; if the authorities had found out about a doctor performing an abortion, he would have been on the next transport east. A cousin of my father's, Dr. Paul Wurzel, tried to help me. Although he was a surgeon, he lacked the experience necessary to perform such a procedure himself, and he didn't want to endanger my life. He appealed to his colleagues, but none would do it, even for him. All of them were afraid.

During this time of despair Koni, his mother, and I received the dreaded slips of paper notifying us that we had been picked for transport to the East. I was two months pregnant and I had no choice but to go. Given my condition, how could I make such a trip? Where would my child first see the light of day? I made another desperate round of all the doctors in the ghetto, begging them to help me. In vain.

In mid-December of 1943, it was very cold in Theresienstadt and probably much colder in the East. How could we get hold of warm winter clothes in the short time before we were scheduled to leave? I was able to swap my winter coat and several rations of bread for a warmer coat with a fur collar. In exchange for bread, we also were able to get warm underwear for Koni and his mother.

And now the time had come. Once again we said farewell to friends and colleagues with whom we had lived and worked. Each of these partings marked the end of an era in our lives, a break with all that had gone before. The question "Will we ever meet again?" was never expressed in so many words, but it was implicit in every kiss, every handshake. Many of those who stayed behind smiled in embarrassment, just as I used to when I went to say good-bye to friends who were leaving. The embarrassment stemmed from discomfort: Their friends had to leave, and they did not. I could see it in many of the faces now, and I wanted to console them.

Koni and I had spent our last night in the attic room in a tight embrace. We had each packed a suitcase and a backpack in which there was food that friends had given us for the trip. Officially we each received a loaf of bread from the ghetto authorities. Early the next morning we went to the Jäger Barracks. There our suitcases were taken from us and we surrendered our food-ration cards. Then began the inevitable registration; they had to make sure that everyone who was supposed to leave had reported for the transport. The suitcases were stacked in front of the waiting cattle cars. Koni and I recognized ours in a large pile that had not been loaded. We decided not to go into the cars until we were sure that our suitcases had been put on board. Meanwhile, people whose names were called were chased into the cars by SS troopers shouting, "Hurry up, hurry up!" Then one car after another was closed and locked from the outside. We knew that soon it would be our turn. Watching what was going on through a crack in the window of one of the barracks rooms—something that was strictly forbidden—we saw that our suitcases were still on the platform, and we stuck to our decision not to board without them.

We hid in a closet in a corner of the room. There would be another transport in two or three days and we would leave on it if our suitcases were put aboard. We heard them call, "Everybody out to the loading ramp!" A search of the barracks ensued. SS men repeatedly passed by our hiding place. To this day I am amazed that they didn't find us. We stood absolutely still inside the closet, not moving a muscle, but our hearts were beating wildly. Had they caught us, we would have been given *Sonderbehandlung* (special treatment): an individual transport straight to death. We heard the train whistle and then the chugging as the train departed. It became very quiet. We knew that everyone had left the barracks and the nearby area. We wondered who had been forced to take our places on this transport.

We opened the closet door carefully, made sure no one was around, took our backpacks, and returned to our attic room in the ghetto. The Fertigs were happy to see us again, but they had their doubts about what we had done. We all knew that sooner or later the authorities would find out. Our action was really senseless and rash, since we knew that we couldn't survive in the ghetto without food-ration cards. In addition, detailed records were kept of all the ghetto inmates, and if we were caught it would mean *Weisung* (banishment), a word all of us dreaded even though none of us knew what actually happened to those who were banished. We could no longer move about freely in the ghetto; there was always the danger of being caught. Like hunted animals, we longed for the day when the next transport would leave and we would finally be able to get out of Theresienstadt. That happened three days later. This time Koni and I were alone, since Koni's mother had left with the earlier transport. We hoped we would see her again soon.

The registration went surprisingly smoothly. We told a Jewish clerk[3] that we had been scheduled to leave on the earlier transport and had already handed in our food-ration cards. He sent us to the train without raising any further obstacles. Our suitcases didn't matter anymore. This time we didn't even see them.

---

[3] Publisher's note: Theresienstadt had an extensive Jewish "self-government." The transport lists, among other things, were prepared in the so-called *Zentralevidenz,* a sort of resident registration office.

4

Auschwitz

THE TRAIN, A LONG LINE OF CATTLE CARS, was waiting. Young men from the transport unit were loading suitcases, and SS men were patrolling the area, rifles with fixed bayonets slung over their shoulders. A ramp had been moved up to the doors of the cattle cars, and the loading of the human freight began. They chased us into the cars, yelling, "Faster, faster, you Jewish swine!" So much for the refined sentiments of the master race. Our car slowly filled up with fifty, sixty, or perhaps seventy people. Finally, it was as full as it could get. When cattle were shipped, straw usually was spread on the floor of the cars, but for people—for Jews, that is—this was superfluous. These Jews could lie on the bare boards. But not really. There wasn't even enough room to lie down. The heavy sliding door was closed and presumably locked with chains so we could not open it from the inside. Gradually our eyes got used to the semidarkness. The car we were in was packed with old people, sick people, children, and young adults. There were two pails on the floor. One was filled with water; the other was supposed to be our toilet. An attempt was made to organize things within the car. Even when we pressed close against one another there was scarcely enough room to sit down, to say nothing of lying down. At the four upper corners of the car there were small window openings with barbed wire strung across the outside—no doubt to keep us from jumping out, as though anyone could possibly fit through such a small opening. But these little windows turned out to be useful for two reasons. First, whenever the toilet pail was full it had to be emptied. We would all squeeze into one half of the cattle car, and one of the young men did his best to pour the contents of the pail through one of those windows. I don't know how much spilled back into the car, but there was a terrible stench in that corner. The second reason was that one young man standing on the shoulders of another could look out and tell us where we were. We were heading east.

The most difficult moments came whenever we passed a village or a town and someone said, "That's where I was born. That was my home!" It happened to me when we came to Ostrava and the train passed Uncle Hugo's house, which was near the Přívoz/Oderfurt railway station. So close and yet so far.

All this time the children were crying, and the sick were moaning. The water in the pail was gone in no time, and everyone was thirsty. We arranged things as well as we could for the night. Half of the prisoners stretched out and tried to sleep, while the other half crowded together standing up. It was bitterly cold that December night, several degrees below freezing, and being crowded so close together at least helped us to keep warm. We tried as best we could to help the sick and the children, but all we had to offer them were kind words. These didn't do much to alleviate their misery.

Small children clung to their mothers, who tried desperately to console them. In the midst of all this anguish, we suddenly heard a mother singing to her five-year-old daughter:

Eine rosa Krinoline kauf ich dir, mein Kind,
wenn wir zusammen auf deinen ersten Ball gehen werden. . . .

I'll buy you a pink crinoline, my child,
when you and I go to your first ball together. . . .

It was a simple tune, but for us it was heart-wrenching. Choked with emotion, we all joined in. In later years, whenever I heard that song I would picture them again, that mother and her child. Both were gassed.

Was it one night, or was it two that we spent in the cattle car? Was it a year? An eternity? The time dragged on endlessly. At some point in the late afternoon the train stopped. The doors were ripped open and we faced a terrifying pandemonium: shouting, yelling, barking dogs. A brief glance showed countless lights at regular intervals; there was no time for a better look.

The Nazis were shouting: "Get out, out! Leave everything behind! Get out! Faster, you swine! Line up in rows of five! Faster, faster!" The horrible barking of the dogs grew louder and louder. We obeyed blindly, jumping down from the cars; there was no time to think. The old and the ill fell and were beaten with clubs by SS men holding dogs on leashes. Children screamed and cried. Men wearing odd, gray-and-blue striped suits that looked like pajamas and flat caps made of the same material were walking around among the SS men. They were silently watching the spectacle; evidently they were forbidden to talk to us. I mustered some courage and asked one of them, "Where are we?"

Without looking at me, he said, "Auschwitz."

That meant nothing to me. It was the name of one of many towns in Poland. I didn't know how deeply *Auschwitz* would be engraved into my very being, so indelibly that it could never be erased.

Our pitiful human column in rows of five, flanked by SS men with their rifles at the ready, began to move. Not a word was said. Totally intimidated, we moved forward like automatons. Koni and I had only one thought: Stay together; don't lose sight of each other. The column came to a halt in front of a large building, and we were ordered to undress. Undress? Here we were, women and men and children all together. We couldn't do that! But when the SS men

A typical arrival of a transport at Auschwitz. This photograph was taken about 1944. (Yad Vashem Photo Archives, courtesy of USHMM Photo Archives.)

used their whips, we obeyed. It was shortly before Christmas, and the temperature hovered between 10° and 14° F (−10° to −15° C). Then the men were separated from the women, and we were led into a large room where showerheads were attached to the ceiling. Ice-cold water poured down on us. There was no way to avoid the downpour, since we were crowded together like sardines. We cursed. But I still wonder today if this was the same room where, instead of water, Zyklon B (cyanic acid) gas issued from the showerheads. There was no soap; there were no towels. When we came out, we were sopping wet. They threw some clothes at us. There was no sign of my fur-trimmed winter coat that had cost me so much bartered bread. Instead, I was handed a flimsy dark-blue silk dress and a lightweight coat; no underwear, no stockings, just wooden clogs. Before we were led into the shower room, we had to bundle our own clothes and shoes together and turn them in. We never got them back.

After I put on the "elegant" dress and the coat, I went to look for Koni. But all the men had been led away. None of us knew where they had been taken. Many of the women began to cry, calling for their husbands, sons, or fathers. We tried to console one another, but we knew that we were doing so with empty phrases. A young woman was standing off to one side, crying. When I walked over to her, I heard her murmur, "Where is my Erischek? They took my Erischek away. I want my Erischek." Her name was Ruth "Houština" Nassau. I tried to comfort her, telling her that we were all in the same boat, we all missed our men. Nothing helped; she continued her lament. It wasn't any easier for me; I missed Koni just as much, and I didn't know what had happened to him.

The women and children were taken to a huge wooden barracks. Inside it was lined on both sides with three tiers of wooden bunk frames. There were no mattresses. Each of us was given a thin blanket with which to cover ourselves. Thus equipped, we climbed into our beds. It was terribly cold, and we were freezing. Three of us huddled together in one bunk so that we could cover ourselves with three blankets and warm one another. Houština was still crying "Where is my Erischek?" until she finally fell asleep.

In the morning a disgusting brew they called tea was served, and we pounced on it like a wild mob. Except for a few drops of water that had fallen into our mouths during the shower the previous day, we had had no food or water since Theresienstadt. I can't explain our unbridled behavior in any other way except to say that animal instincts had taken over. All of us had come from the same social milieu; we were quite civilized and peaceful people. From now on, our instinct for survival would dictate our behavior.

After this breakfast, registration and the numbering process began. We had to hold out our left forearms, and each of us was tattooed with a number. At first we did not understand why, but gradually it dawned on us: They no longer considered us to be human beings. We had been loaded into the railroad cars like cattle and, like cattle, we were now being branded. The numbers on our forearms marked our depersonalization. From now on I would no longer have a name. Whenever I was asked to identify myself, I was supposed to reply, "Number 73643."

Nor was the number tattoo the only identification mark we had to carry. Each prisoner also had to wear a colored triangle sewn onto the upper left side of his or her clothing. Beneath it was the number of the tattoo. Political prisoners wore red triangles, criminals wore green, "asocials" wore black, and Jews wore red triangles with a yellow triangle superimposed on the red to form a six-pointed star. In matters like this, superlative order prevailed in Auschwitz![1]

Once all the formalities had been taken care of, we had to line up in rows of five again, and our human column—this time composed of only women wearing flimsy, lightweight, ridiculous clothes—moved out of the camp. We arrived at a gate guarded by the SS, the entrance to another camp. Once again we were carefully counted, and after all of us had passed through the gate an SS man and a prisoner wearing a green triangle came to look us over. They ordered all the young women to step forward; that included me. We were led to a large wooden barracks that had the number 6 above the entrance. Henceforth it was called Block 6. The female prisoner responsible for the block was called the block elder. She welcomed us with a few gruff words and showed us where we were to sleep. Houština and I were lucky to be assigned places on the third level. It was warmer up there, and we couldn't be observed closely from below.

We still knew nothing about what had happened to the men, and there was no way to ask anyone. Besides, either no one knew anything or they were unwilling to give us even a hint. Then, toward evening we heaved a sigh of relief when the men, dressed in the gray-and-blue striped prison pajama suits, were brought into the camp.

---

[1] Publisher's note: The author's experience in this regard seems to differ from that of the general triangle-marking system used in Auschwitz/Birkenau, in which the colored triangles were printed on the left side of a rectangular piece of white cotton that bore the prisoner's number, which was printed on the right. The yellow triangle typically was sewn under the red, second triangle assigned to most Jews.

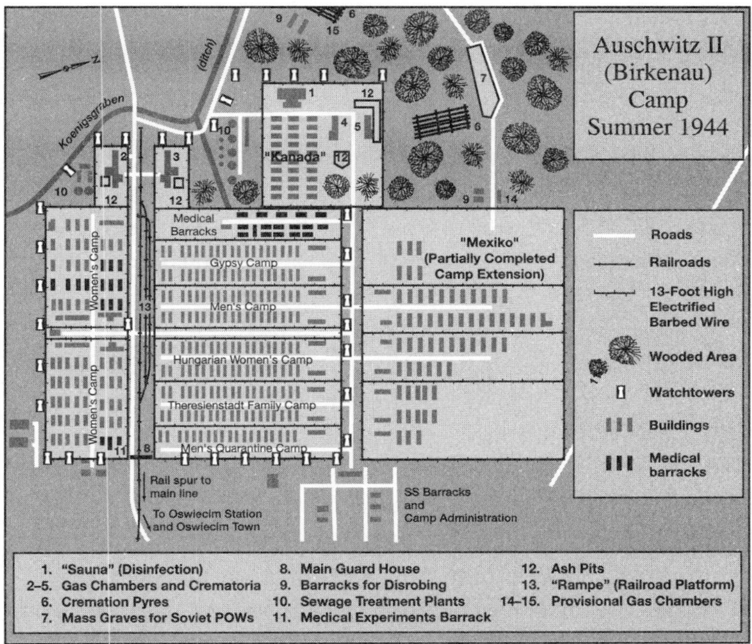

The family camp, Birkenau BIIb,[2] was one of many camps in Auschwitz, but it was the only one that housed both sexes. All the other camps were either just for women or just for men. The camp consisted of two rows of large wooden barracks called blocks. The women's blocks were on the right side of the camp, and those for men were on the other side. Men and women had communal washrooms and toilets. The so-called *Lagerstrasse* (Camp Street) ran between the rows of barracks, and after work we were allowed to get together there with the men for half an hour. Each barracks had a large entrance door. Once you went through it, there were two rooms on each side; these were the private domain of the block elder and her

[2] Publisher's note: The Auschwitz concentration camp consisted of the main camp (Auschwitz I); Birkenau (Auschwitz II), the actual extermination camp where the gas chambers were located; Auschwitz III (Monowitz); as well as a number of subcamps.

deputies. The common prisoners were not allowed in there. Inside the barracks were these wooden three-tiered bunks. Because the camp was overcrowded, five of us had to squeeze into one bunk space that had no mattress and originally was intended for three people. A benchlike structure, a "chimney," about two feet high and wide, built of bricks and concrete, extended along the entire length of the block. Its hollow center could be heated from both ends. But there was never any heat in this chimney, because there was no fuel.

The barracks were surrounded by a high-voltage electrified barbed-wire fence. Searchlights placed at regular intervals lit up the camp all through the night. On the other side of the barbed-wire fence was a strip of land between two and three yards wide, and then came the electrified barbed-wire fence for the next camp. There were guard towers at each corner of the camp. The guards worked in consecutive shifts; the camp was continuously watched, so no one could escape. If a prisoner approached the fence, the guards would shoot at him. And if he managed to reach the fence, he would be killed instantly by the high-voltage electricity. Many preferred to die in this way rather than endure the horrible life in the camp. We gradually became inured to these deaths, our feelings dulled, and after a time we almost considered it an everyday occurrence: "Have you seen so-and-so?"

"Oh, she went up to the fence yesterday."

"Went up to the fence" came to be a common phrase that was accepted without comment.

Our daily routine went something like this: Early in the morning—we had no watches to tell the time—a loud bell rang, waking us. We immediately had to present ourselves for *Appell* (roll call), lining up in rows of five in front of our barracks. The block elder stood off to one side, and everybody waited for an SS man to arrive to receive her morning report. Standing stiffly at attention, she had to account for the number of prisoners who were present and able to work as well as the number who were sick and remained in the barracks. Then all of us were counted by the SS man, who also went into the block to count those who were inside. He went from block to block, counting and taking notes while we stood there in our skimpy clothes—freezing in the deep snow of winter and, later in the year, getting drenched in pouring rain—until the number of the living, the dead, and the sick had been precisely determined. Sometimes this took hours.

After roll call, breakfast was served. The complete meal was either hot "tea" or ersatz coffee; we called it dishwater but swallowed it greedily nevertheless because it warmed our freezing bodies a little. Then came the order: "Get to work." At first we were escorted out of the camp in rows of five, again carefully counted at the gate, and then led to a rock pile that was about a half hour's march away. There we had to move heavy rocks from one spot to another. The following day we had to carry the same rocks back to their original place. It was totally senseless work, and we soon realized that they wanted to kill us not only physically but also spiritually. We were extremely hungry and weak. But anyone who could not continue to work was whipped by the SS men or kicked by the Kapos.[3] To avoid such punishment, we marshaled all our strength and continued to drag the rocks back and forth.

I still wonder where we found the will to go on. Our nourishment consisted primarily of water. At noon we had watery soup with, if we were lucky, a few cooked turnips. After work we were marched back to camp. Again we lined up in rows of five at the entrance gate to be counted. After that, there was another roll call inside. And again the endless standing and waiting until all the numbers tallied. Then at last we were free to have supper. It consisted of tea or ersatz coffee, about 10½ ounces of bread, and sometimes a little margarine, artificial honey, or jam. When I first arrived I divided

[3] Publisher's note: The word comes from the Italian *il capo* (boss); these were prisoners who were assigned overseer functions by the German camp administration. The Kapos were chosen mostly from among the criminal prisoners and were generally feared because of their brutality.

my bread ration, eating half of it in the evening and leaving the other half for breakfast. I carefully put the second half under my head at night to keep it from being stolen. But one night this little piece of bread that meant so much to me vanished. The instinct to survive had turned some of the prisoners into thieves. That's how low we had been pushed. We knew that once we lost our strength and our will to live, it meant the end. And this instinct for self-preservation was so strong that many people stole bread to stay alive.

After supper the shrill camp bell sounded again, signaling the start of "visiting hour" on the *Lagerstrasse*. We were allowed to meet the men on the street and talk with them. After twenty or thirty minutes that horrible bell rang again, and everyone had to return to his or her quarters. No one was allowed to leave the barracks for the rest of the night.

Women were strictly forbidden to set foot in the men's barracks, just as the women's barracks were off-limits to the men. At first, while we still had some stamina, we wanted to be with our husbands for more than those few minutes on the camp street, and preferably in a somewhat private place. Need made us resourceful. We discovered the washroom. Here, in the early-morning hours, water dripped sparsely from the faucets into halved steel drums. This was an ideal meeting place, so couples were often seen clinging to each other in tight embrace, oblivious to the people around them. It was an expression of the desperate drive to get as close as possible to a loved one and to give each other a sense of security and belonging, a desperate desire to fill our hopeless lives with love. Love signified life, and we all wanted to stay alive.

We were young, and we wanted to live. We wanted to talk with our loved ones and give them courage, to hold each other tight, to be as close as we could to each other, and to prove that we weren't alone. Who knew how much longer we would be able to express these feelings. Life and love are intricately intertwined. We longed for love, for an embrace, and for physical closeness, for a long desperate kiss that was often mixed with tears. To give expression to these feelings we needed a little hiding place, and that's what the washroom offered us, since it was used by both men and women. But we had to be careful not to be discovered. Some of the prisoners therefore stood guard to warn us in case an SS man approached.

The constant odor of burned flesh was all around us. Family camp BIIb was near the crematoria, and we could see the smoke coming out of the chimneys. Rumors had it that people were being gassed and bodies were being burned there. With time we developed a defense mechanism: We knew that the rumors were true, but we refused to believe them. We simply rejected the possibility that there was a Nazi policy to annihilate the Jews. Were sane people capable of gassing other human beings? Who could even conceive of such a thing? Would God permit it? The outside world couldn't just stand by and watch—surely someone would help us.

As soon as I arrived in the BIIb family camp, I went to the hospital block to look for a doctor—the doctors were prisoners, too—who would be willing to terminate my pregnancy. But again I was rejected. Nobody wanted to perform an abortion, because the punishment for doing so was severe. I had no choice but to hide my condition as well as I could and wait to see what the future would bring.

The September transport from Theresienstadt had arrived three months before we did. No one knew why no "selection" had been made—in other words, why those who were fit to work had not been separated from those who would die—at the arrival ramp. Everyone who was on that transport was allowed to live, and all of them had been put into the family camp. If I am not mistaken, our camp was the only one in Auschwitz that had children. There was a special block for these children; it was headed by Fredy Hirsch, a German Jew. He had been working in Czechoslovakia and was deported to Theresienstadt and from there to Auschwitz. He was young and handsome, a fine athlete who took care of the children in an extraordinary way. Without writing materials, textbooks, or toys, Fredy and his assistants set up a system for teaching the children.

They invented games that were adapted to the circumstances. Those of us who weren't working in the children's block couldn't understand how Fredy and his helpers accomplished this impossible feat. Everybody, whether child or grown-up, loved him; and he loved his many children.

At the end of February 1944, all of us were handed postcards to be sent home. I didn't know whom to write. Besides Miloš there was no one left, and I was afraid it would cause problems for him if I wrote. So I gave my card to someone else. We were told to postdate the cards by one month—that is, to put a late March date on them. Why? In Auschwitz you didn't ask questions; anyway, you never got any answers. In Auschwitz it was either blind obedience or death.

After the evening roll call on March 5, we were ordered to return to our barracks immediately. There was to be no "evening promenade." Following supper all the barracks were closed, and we were forbidden to look out or go outside. Disobedience would mean getting shot. We did not know what the Germans were up to, but we assumed that something terrible was about to happen. Then we heard the shuffling of many feet and orders being barked by the SS, and we concluded that prisoners were being led away.

The next morning, when the doors finally were opened, we saw to our horror that all the people from the September transport had been moved to the adjacent camp. No one knew why. After work we went over to the barbed-wire fence, but no one was moving about in the neighboring camp. The inmates probably had been forbidden to go outside. We were filled with apprehension about the fate of our friends and fellow prisoners with whom we had shared our lot for three months.

Following the evening roll call, we were shut into our barracks again. Although we were tired after the day's hard work, none of us could sleep. Something dreadful was happening. Suddenly we heard the sound of many motor vehicles approaching. For a while there was no other sound. Next came the terrifying clamor of bark-

heard singing, very soft at first, then louder and
e Czech national anthem, "*Kde domov můj?*"
omeland?). Then, much louder, "*Hatikvah*"
n anthem. The louder the singing, the more we
were about to be gassed. These songs were their
o the prisoners who were left in the family camp.
minutes, five thousand of our comrades went to

y, the birthday of Thomas Garrigue Masaryk, the
ident whom we had revered and who had openly
hy for the Jewish people. The next day, at the
we saw no sign of life in the neighboring camp,
ll coming from the chimneys and the smell of
stronger than ever. A month later, the postcards
soners had written from Auschwitz, the cards
dated the end of March, arrived at their destinations. On each card was written: "My dear ones, my family and I are well. We are in good health and send you our best regards."

By the fifth month of my pregnancy the changes in my body had become visible. I didn't want anyone to notice and tried to hide my condition as best I could. Nobody in Auschwitz could predict what the next day or the future held in store. All of us lived under immediate threat, but because of my pregnancy my prospects were much worse.

The Germans had set up a workshop in one of the barracks to make one-inch-wide braided leather bands that, I was told, would be used as machine-gun slings. I managed to get assigned to this lighter work, where I could at least sit down instead of dragging rocks back and forth. Here I was no longer exposed to cold, snow, and rain, and I did not have to expend quite so much energy.

Koni was ordered to push wagons loaded with rocks along rails that had been laid down throughout the camp. The prisoners had to move these wagons with their bare hands. Obviously, given the starvation rations, their strength was quickly depleted. But the SS men made no allowances for this, and they beat the inmates with their whips and clubs to make them work faster. When someone could not go on, he was clubbed to death. Every prisoner longed to be assigned to easier work and tried to get out of having to push the wagons, and after a while Koni was able to get a less strenuous assignment, something having to do with the service sector in the camp.

Koni and I got together every evening after work on the camp street. Gradually, during these meetings, we began to feel a sense of estrangement, and after a while we scarcely had anything to say to each other. Even though it was his child I was carrying, Koni didn't seem at all interested in my condition. Why didn't he have a single word of encouragement for me, a little consolation? How I longed for some understanding and sympathy. Why did he leave me to myself at this difficult time? His indifference was hard to bear. I began to wonder whether we could ever have a life together after Auschwitz, and I became convinced that if we survived we should separate.

There was a professional hangman in the camp. Up to that time I did not know that a Jew would do this kind of work; nor could I fathom why anyone would choose to become an executioner. We called him Henker Fischer, Fischer the hangman. He was a brawny, robust man whose appearance alone inspired fear, and we all tried to avoid him. He had a room to himself in the block diagonally across from Block 6. One day he asked me to come to his room. I didn't want to have anything to do with him; I was afraid of him, and I had no idea why he should want to talk to me. But he asked me again, and this time it sounded like a threat, so I hesitantly went to see him. It was strictly forbidden for women to enter the men's barracks, but since there was no SS man nearby I took the chance. It was difficult to know which was worse, to run into an SS man or to disobey Henker Fischer's order. When I got to his room, he asked me how many months pregnant I was. He then gave me a piece of bread and an onion and ordered me to eat them, right there in front of him. I had never before eaten a raw onion, but I knew that it contained vitamins, so I readily did what he told me to do. And then, much to my surprise, he suggested that I come to see him every other day to get something to eat. He said a pregnant woman had a responsibility for the development of her child and had to eat nourishing food. Even hangmen could be human, I supposed.

The family-camp orchestra, which was made up of six men, played in the women's block. There were violins, an accordion, a clarinet, and percussion instruments; they rehearsed twice a day. Since there was no printed music, they played from memory. Some of these men were superb musicians. All seemed content with their assignments, because being in the orchestra meant they did not have to do hard physical labor and could conserve their energy. Sometimes some of the SS men came to listen to the music. If they heard a player make a mistake, they smacked him.

On certain occasions, usually in the late afternoon or in the evening, the musicians were hurriedly called together to play. We had learned that when this happened something dreadful was imminent, and we were afraid. If a prisoner was caught committing some minor offense—a theft or an act of disobedience, for example, or often for no reason at all except pure sadism—he was brought to Block 6. The musicians were then told to play, and the women were ordered to watch. The chimney door, which was about sixteen inches above the floor, was opened. The prisoner being punished had to take off his pants and stick his head inside the opening. Then the music started. The poor man was given twenty-five lashes with the whip, sometimes as many as fifty, which rained down on his buttocks full force and without mercy. I don't remember ever hearing one of the victims utter a single cry of pain; the music wouldn't have drowned out his cries. We saw only the twitching of his tormented body. These proud men didn't want to give the Nazis the satisfaction of hearing their screams. Most of them, supported by one or two fellow prisoners, walked away bloodied but with their heads held high. While the whipping was in progress, the SS people laughed and talked to one another. And the orchestra played.

Drunken SS men sometimes made unexpected appearances in our block; the door would suddenly be flung open, and they would roar in on their motorcycles. Then the orchestra was ordered to play, and the SS men would sing along while they continued to drink, their mood getting ever more boisterous. Young Jewish women would be pulled from their bunks, taken away somewhere, and raped. Raping Jewish women wasn't considered *Rassenschande* (race defilement), therefore it was allowed. Whenever one of these horrible spectacles began, I was glad that I lived way up on the third tier. The SS men didn't bother to climb up there in search of young women; the pickings in the lower bunks were good enough. Those of us who were in the upper tiers pressed our bodies against the wall, hoping that we wouldn't be picked. Any woman who refused to go with the SS men was savagely beaten, so no one offered any resistance. I cannot describe the pitiable state of these poor women when they came back to the barracks.

We were infested with fleas, lice, and bedbugs. The bites made our bodies itch, but we didn't dare scratch, because it was easy to get an infection, and that would lead to fever. With a high fever you couldn't report for roll call and work, and going to the infirmary meant almost certain death; the corpses that were piled up every day in front of the hospital block made that clear. The beds in the infirmary were merely wooden frames, with no sheets or other bedding. There were no medicines, no bandages, no antiseptics—the camp doctors had nothing but their bare hands with which to treat the sick. Doctors and nurses could only stand by helplessly as the prisoners died.

So if we were sick, we were careful not to admit it. During roll call we'd bravely stand there, and with the help of friends drag ourselves to work. Everything possible was done to keep the sick in the dormitory blocks, to protect them from "hospitalization."

Our hunt for fleas, bedbugs, and lice was endless. They reproduced so quickly that not even our well-devised measures to annihilate them could keep up with their proliferation. And if you did get hold of something resembling soap it was sure to be stolen. This so-called soap was a light-green substance that neither foamed nor cleaned nor disinfected. To wash ourselves we had to get up while it was still dark outside, because that was the only time water dripped from the faucets. Later the pipes would be empty. Often when we went into the washroom we would find men there, since that facility served both sexes. With our feelings of modesty already dulled, we felt no shame in taking off our clothes to wash ourselves. Cleanliness meant good health, and that meant avoiding the infirmary. During the winter we used snow instead of soap, later we used sand. If you rubbed yourself with sand and then rinsed it off, you at least had the feeling of being clean. There were no towels—why would anyone need a towel?—so our bodies dried on their own. There was no way to wash our things, since each of us had only one dress and no change of clothing. All we could do was shake our dresses thoroughly and hope that many of the lice would drop off. But these little creatures had a way of clinging to the seams of our clothes as though they really liked it there. It was a part of our daily routine to search the seams for the lice and kill them. But by the next day a new generation of the vermin had triumphantly moved back in.

We often suffered from diarrhea and dysentery, and one of our biggest problems was finding scraps of paper, since there was no toilet paper and no newspaper. I still don't know how we managed. We were always hungry and people slowly wasted away. Their bones began to protrude and their eyes sank deep into their sockets—they were turning into veritable living skeletons. Called *Muselmänner* (Muselmen), they moved apathetically from one place to the next, dragging their feet because they no longer had the strength to lift them. They had stopped thinking. Like animals, their only interest was food. When the snow melted, the search began for the first green weeds poking out of the soil. We were always happy to find one of these, pluck it, and then hold it in our mouths for hours at a time while we imagined that the little leaves were driving away our hunger.

With the gassing of the prisoners of the September transport, the number of inmates in BIIb had shrunk by half. But the German extermination machinery functioned with precision. There was no need to worry that the camp would remain half empty. In May the prisoner population was replenished by the arrival of three more transports from Theresienstadt, which brought in about 7,500 people—including entire families. We, the "veteran" inmates from the December transport, who had been here for five months already, wondered whether our turn to be gassed had now come. Those in the September transport had been in the camp for six months before they were sent to the gas chambers. Would that happen to us in June? Each day brought increasing fear.

Somehow our survival instinct was reawakened, and we drove these dark thoughts from our minds, busying ourselves with other ideas and activities. We talked about food constantly. Every day after work we ate the meager supper that had been provided, devouring our entire daily bread ration. Then a few young women would get together up on the third tier and start "cooking"—that is, we talked about all the various foods and dishes we had known back home. These conversations were like self-inflicted torment, but they gave us a feeling of having eaten our fill. We cooked in our imaginations for hours at a time, even though most of us were too young to have had much experience with actual cooking. This cooking also affirmed the ties to our families and strengthened our will to survive, to hold out so that we could hope to see our families again.

The Nazis wanted to kill our minds even before they killed us physically. Completely cut off from the outside world, we had no news reports, no newspapers, books, or other intellectual sustenance. We were forced to pass our days apathetically and to do our work like automatons. On Sunday, a day of rest, we devoted our time to personal cleanliness, hunting lice, and having discussions. We talked not only about food but about many other things. Sometimes these discussions even turned into little lectures. This was our spiritual and mental nourishment, a ray of light piercing the dark days. Often we would start to sing, trying to remember the lyrics of a folk song or a popular tune—putting our brain cells to work to keep them from atrophying. We knew intuitively that if we gave up spiritually and intellectually, we would be giving up all hope of survival. Actually, we developed a very strong survival instinct, and I think this guided our steps, decisions, and actions. Our reactions became purely instinctive, aimed only at preserving our lives. All our senses developed into a system of defense and warning that had one goal: survival.

One night we were awakened by the penetrating howl of the camp sirens. Someone had escaped. From Auschwitz! It seemed incredible. The entire camp was hermetically closed off by the most modern techniques: high-voltage fences, barbed wire, and an intricate system of guard towers. We immediately had to report for roll call and were counted and recounted. The rumor spread that a man from camp BIIb, our camp, had gotten out. We were glad. If he succeeded, he could tell the outside world the truth about Auschwitz. Perhaps then we would be liberated.

The SS men made us stand there at attention the entire day, without food or water. The counting of the prisoners was repeated endlessly, but we were quite willing to submit to it all for the sake of the brave man who had escaped. We didn't know who he was, but to us he was a hero. At the same time, we began to realize that his escape would have consequences for us. How would we be punished? Maybe they would send us to the gas chambers even sooner?

Late that evening we were ordered back to the barracks. We fell asleep hoping that the escape had succeeded. Up to then, escape attempts from Auschwitz-Birkenau had always failed, and as a warning the bodies of the would-be escapees had been strung up in plain view. But this time the man, whose name turned out to be Lederer, made it. He reached Czechoslovakia and sneaked into Theresienstadt. There he told the leaders of the ghetto about the family camp and the gas chambers in Auschwitz. But the postdated postcards from the family camp had just arrived in the ghetto, giving the impression that the writers were still alive. Lederer pleaded with the ghetto elders not to send transports to the East, but no one believed him.

Lederer was aided in his escape by a young SS man who supplied him with the uniform of a high-ranking SS officer and accompanied him until he reached safety. The SS man was later arrested, charged with treason, tortured, and shot.

A group of Gypsies arrived and were put into the adjacent camp, which henceforth was called the *Zigeunerlager,* the Gypsy Camp. After they had been there for a short time, all of them were gassed. I shudder just writing these lines, which sound so matter-of-fact: "All of them were gassed." Just think what lies behind these words. Every one of these victims was a human being—a child, father, mother, husband, or lover. And each had his own life story. What crime had they committed—what had they done wrong? Why did they have to be gassed? Their only offense was that they were born Gypsies.

After the Gypsy camp was liquidated, Jewish women from Hungary were moved in. Some of the inmates in the family camp spoke Hungarian, so—at a safe distance from the electric fence and the guard tower—we talked to the newcomers. They described the European political situation and offered opinions on our chances for liberation. The information was not encouraging; none of them could foresee the end of the war. I was already in my seventh month, and my condition was quite obvious. Only God and Josef Mengele, the dreaded camp doctor, knew what would happen to me.

One day, while standing near the fence, I suddenly heard a man's voice calling to me from the other side. "Catch!" he said. "This may save your life!"

A small stone came sailing over the fence. Attached to it was a little gold chain and a medallion of St. Anthony, "the saint who helps those in need." To whom had this medallion belonged? Whose life didn't it save? On the other side of the fence I saw a man wearing a clean, ironed prison uniform with a green triangle on his chest: a criminal, perhaps even a murderer. Most of the men who wore the green triangles were German convicts who had been sent to Auschwitz to serve out their sentences. They often had jobs that enabled them to go into other camps. Known for their sadism, they were feared, and we all tried to stay out of their way. Who knows what impelled that man to throw this gift over the fence to me? Was it compassion for a pregnant woman in this grim place? I couldn't even thank him; before I had a chance to pick up the necklace, he had disappeared. From then on I clung to the medallion, my talisman, convinced that it would save my life. I would love to know what made the man with the green triangle do this. But now I understood something my father had told me when I was a child: "Always look for the good in everyone, Ruth; even a murderer can have some good in him." In Auschwitz, next to the electrified barbed-wire fence, Father's words seemed suddenly to be infused with meaning.

Sometimes prisoners from other camps would come to our family camp, bringing us news. Usually these were people whose work gave them certain privileges. It was through them that we first heard about the gassing of prisoners. They also told us about the air raids on Germany, and they said the country was in urgent need of workers. This news was like a tiny spark of hope, and it spread like wildfire. If we could become forced laborers, perhaps that would be a way to survive. But on the whole we were skeptical, because deep down we all felt that the only way out of Auschwitz led through the gas chambers.

One day Mengele and his retinue came to the family camp. (I can't call him "Doctor" because a beast like Mengele does not deserve the physician's title.) When he left we heard terrible rumors about his medical experiments and his "selection" process.[4] But who could conceive of deeds like these? As before, a kind of self-protection made us reject such thoughts. It wasn't long, however, before we found out firsthand that the rumors were true.

Soon after this first visit Mengele and his cohorts came again, and the dreaded word *selection* spread from one end of the camp to the other.

"Take off all your clothes!" they ordered. A long line of naked women formed, and one by one we had to walk past Mengele. I was far back in line, but I saw him standing there, legs akimbo, facing us. He looked each prisoner up and down and then indicated with a gesture of his hand the direction in which she was to go. His face was immobile and he showed no trace of emotion. Only his hand moved: right, left, right, left. Life, death, life, death. He knew precisely what his hand motions signified, but we did not. We could only guess. Instinctively, we felt that we were witnesses to an act of utter madness.

I saw that healthy young women were being sent to one side and the old, the sick, children, and mothers with children were ordered to the other side. Slowly the line moved forward. I was desperate, and I knew I had to do something. If Mengele saw my eight-month-pregnant belly he would certainly send me to join the old and the sick. How could I save my life?

Slowly, very slowly the line moved closer to Mengele, closer to life or death. Suddenly I had an idea. I asked a few of the women standing behind me to pass me in line. Maybe the man in Mengele, after seeing their young bodies, would overlook me. What I asked them to do didn't present them with additional risks, so the women readily agreed. And with his infamous gesture Mengele di-

[4] Publisher's note: In the course of the selection that Mengele performed in the family camp at Auschwitz-Birkenau, more than 3,000 men, women, and young people were selected as "fit to work." The number of Jews who remained in the camp and were subsequently murdered came to about 7,000.

rected all of us—including me—to the side of the young and healthy.

We were forbidden to approach or talk to the prisoners in the other group. I still remember those desperate scenes: daughters being separated from their mothers, sisters from sisters. Some tried to get together again, but this was impossible under the close scrutiny of the SS. People cried in despair. The young men were taken to a departing train, and we could only stand there and watch. I couldn't make out whether Koni was among them, but I felt sure that he was in one of those cattle cars.

A few days later, escorted by SS men carrying rifles, we were marched to the women's camp of Auschwitz. All the old, the sick, the children, and mothers with children—those who had been selected for death—stayed behind in the family camp. We said farewell to them with our eyes. I saw Koni's mother standing there, looking desolate. It was good-bye forever. A week after the selection, the family camp was liquidated. No one survived; all were gassed.[5]

Six months had passed since our arrival in Auschwitz, six hard, terrible months. Many prisoners who had been with us from the start perished in the family camp. And those of us who were still alive were only shadows of our former selves. Nevertheless, we had adapted to life and the daily routine here. Now, filled with dread of

---

[5] The sequence of events: The following is the chronology for the liquidation of the family camp:

July 2, 1944	Selection by Mengele
July 7	A transport of 1,000 male prisoners departs from the camp ramp; Koni is among them.
July 9	Women who are fit to work, including the author, are transferred to the women's camp.
July 11	The 3,000 prisoners left in the family camp are gassed.
July 12	The family camp ceases to exist; 4,000 additional prisoners are murdered.
July 14	The women's transport for Hamburg departs; other prisoners are shipped to Stutthof.

the future, we were leaving the "safety" of the family camp. Where were they taking us? Our nerves were strained to the breaking point. We no longer believed any of the Nazis' promises. Automatically putting one foot before the other, we finally arrived at the Birkenau women's camp after what seemed to be an endless march.

The camp's old, established residents, Slovak and Polish women, welcomed us like Furies, screaming, hitting, and cursing us. We couldn't understand why. Weren't they prisoners, too? Why this brutality?

Once again we were ordered to undress. They handed us "new" clothes, dresses that had broad bands sewn in the shape of a cross over the front and the back. On the inside under these bands the cloth had been cut so that you could not remove the bands without having the dress come apart. The crosses marked us as prisoners.

After we got dressed, we were led to a huge pile of shoes; we fell on these like wild animals, hoping to get a halfway decent pair. The rule of the jungle prevailed: It was survival of the fittest. Because of my ungainliness, I wasn't very nimble. But I glimpsed a pair of leather ski boots at one side of the pile, bent down quickly, and grabbed them triumphantly. One of the prisoners began to punch me, trying to take my hard-won booty away from me. But I held on tight. Having shoes would help us to stay healthy. Without them, we would have to make do with wooden clogs or walk barefoot. In the rain and mud, that meant certain death.

Next we were led to the most degrading living quarters I had ever seen. The bunks resembled cages, and there was so little space between them that we could get in only by creeping. Once inside, we could not sit up. We had to get in feetfirst and then inch in the rest of the way. To get a little air, we kept our heads near the open side. Five of us were shoved into one of these cages, which was big enough for three at the most. We couldn't get much rest because an argument broke out whenever an inmate moved in her sleep or wanted to go to the latrine. When she came back, her spot was occupied and she had to spend the rest of the night on the bare floor.

The next day routine camp life began, with one difference: We didn't have to leave the camp to go to work. First we went through still another precise registration—after all, order had to be maintained. During roll call a child began to cry. My blood froze. A Kapo ran into the block and in one of the cages he found a small child lying in a basket, crying bitterly. In the family camp, the baby's young mother, a Mrs. Braun, had cared for her blond, curly-haired daughter with utter devotion. Somehow she had obtained sleeping pills, probably from one of the doctors in the hospital block, and had given one of the pills to the child. All through the selection, therefore, the infant had been fast asleep. She was still asleep when someone took the basket from its hiding place in the block and handed it to the mother, who was overjoyed to have her baby back. No one had noticed the little basket that Mrs. Braun brought with her into the women's camp. But the effect of the sleeping pill wore off, and that's how the bestial Kapos discovered the baby. Mrs. Braun dashed over to the basket, picked up her little daughter, held her tightly to her bosom, and with tears running down her cheeks she sang a lullaby. Shortly thereafter they came for her and the baby. They took them back to the family camp, where they were put to death in the gas chamber.

During the afternoon roll call, column after column of women returning from work passed us. They were pitifully emaciated and had trouble staying on their feet. They didn't really walk; rather, they shuffled along while the Kapos constantly ordered them to move faster. I tried to find a familiar face among these women, but in vain. Each of us had changed so much in appearance that we were scarcely recognizable. Then suddenly I saw a woman in one of the columns timidly waving to me. I thought, surely she couldn't have meant me. But after the roll call, just as I was about to return to my cage, she came up to me and said, "Rutinko, Rutinko!" No matter how hard I tried I couldn't identify her.

"Rutinko, don't you know me? I'm Ženka!"

Our Ženka, our loyal Ženka, was here in Auschwitz! We embraced and tearfully told each other what had become of our families. After she was expelled from Czechoslovakia, Ženka went back to her hometown of Skoczow, near Bielsko. When Skoczow and Bielsko were made *judenrein,* the Jews were deported to various ghettos. She was taken to Lazy and then to Auschwitz. Even though she had severe psoriasis—her entire body was covered with scaly red patches—she had passed two of Mengele's selections. At one of these she was taken aside; she was sure she would be sent to the gas chambers. But instead Mengele called over several other doctors and gave them a lecture on severe psoriasis. All the while Ženka had to stand there, naked, listening to Mengele's explanation. The minutes seemed like years, but in the end he sent her to the right—the side that meant life.

The following day we were taken to another block, and again we were ordered to undress and line up. I was all the way at the back, unable to see what was going on at the front. As the line moved forward, I saw to my horror that each woman was being given a gynecological examination. Several tables had been set up, and the women had to lie on them with their legs spread apart. The SS women, who certainly were not doctors and were not wearing rubber gloves, inserted their hands into the vaginas of the prisoners. I felt this would mean certain death for me—they would surely see that I was in the last month of my pregnancy and would send me back to the family camp, just as they had done with Mrs. Braun. This time I lost all hope of surviving. I'd hidden my talisman on the golden chain under my tongue so that no one would find it and take it away from me. Now, in my hour of need, I called on it to save me.

A young woman named Helenka, who was standing in front of me, whispered, "Ruth, I've hidden a little diamond watch my mother gave me. It's in my vagina; what should I do?"

I whispered back in Czech, "Just push it farther up so they won't feel it."

When my turn came, I lay down on the examination table without saying a word. But after only a few minutes, I was back on my feet again. They had allowed me to rejoin the others. Later I realized that this vaginal examination had nothing to do with the state of our health. It was a search for contraband. By the way, they didn't find Helenka's watch.

Again we were loaded into boxcars. Many of the prisoners were crying as the train began to move. But as we got farther and farther away from Auschwitz our terrible premonitions began to fade, and we thought, We're moving away from the gas chambers, away from certain death. So we weren't overly worried about where we were going. Could any place be worse than Auschwitz?

Toward evening the train stopped. The doors were pulled open, but this time there was no shouting, no barking dogs. This was not a trap; we were in Hamburg,[6] on our way to the area called Freihafen. There we were housed in an enormous warehouse at the America pier. Clean wooden bunks and clean blankets awaited us and, even though it was already late, we were given food: tea, bread, margarine, and—we could hardly believe it—half of a smoked herring for each of us. Herring! I hadn't eaten anything like it since I'd left home. What a wonderful flavor. Even now I always associate smoked herring with Hamburg/Freihafen.

I woke up during the night because the baby was pressing on my bladder. In the dark, on my way to the bathroom, I bumped into several cots, waking some of the tired women. They swore at me, saying, "Watch where you're going. You're stumbling around as if you were blind!" How could I watch where I was going when it was totally dark? When still another woman complained, I lost my temper and snapped at her, "How can I see my way in this pitch-black darkness?"

"Are you crazy," she said, "there are lights on everywhere."

---

[6] Publisher's note: Of the approximately 3,000 former Theresienstadt prisoners in the family camp at Auschwitz-Birkenau who had been selected as "fit for work," about 1,000 men were transported to Schwarzheide and Blechhammer concentration camps on July 7, and 2,000 women were transported to Stutthof and Hamburg on July 14, 1944.

It turned out that I was suffering from night blindness. Our prisoner-physician, Dr. Gold, confirmed it. She told me that it was caused by vitamin deficiency. When I asked her whether it was a reversible condition, she didn't give me a clear-cut answer. I sensed that she had some doubts. In the morning I saw only shadows at first, but during the course of the day my sight gradually returned, only to disappear again in the evening. Crying didn't help; all I could do was resign myself to my fate.

The next morning (there was no roll call) we were loaded into trucks and taken to the workplace. The reports that had made the rounds in Auschwitz were now verified: The Allies were bombing Germany, and young workers were needed to clear the rubble. When we arrived at a bombed-out refinery, each of us was handed a shovel, and we began to remove the rubble around us. It was hard work, but at lunchtime we were given a passably good soup. After work we waited for the trucks to take us back to our quarters. Standing on the shores of the Elbe River and watching the water sluggishly flow by, we were gripped by homesickness, for the river has its source in Czechoslovakia. It runs through Bohemia, past Theresienstadt, and empties into the North Sea at Hamburg. One of the girls asked the soldiers escorting us whether she could climb down the embankment and go swimming in the river. Surprisingly, permission was granted, and in groups of ten the girls went swimming with all their clothes on. It didn't occur to any of them to swim to the other shore, to escape. After all, we were in enemy territory. Where could we possibly go wearing dresses marked with crosses, with numbers tattooed on our arms, without an escape plan and without a goal? Only two groups of ten managed to get a swim in before the truck came to take us back to the Freihafen warehouse. The next day swimming in the river was forbidden.

Dr. Gold, our physician—small, pleasant, always smiling—helped wherever she could. But her help was largely symbolic because medicines and bandages were scarce.

Helenka tried to retrieve her hidden watch but couldn't do it. By now our sense of humor had returned, and when one of the girls asked her, "Helenka, what time is it?" she raised one of her legs and said, "Look for yourself."

It was good to be able to laugh again. In the end, though, Helenka had no choice but to ask Dr. Gold for help. Dr. Gold very skillfully removed the watch, using an ordinary scissor, its sharp points wrapped with bandages.

Unfortunately, I was not able to stay in this relaxed atmosphere for more than three days. Early in the morning of the fourth day, before we went to work, an SS man appeared in our quarters and asked whether there were any sick women. Lisa, our block elder, without thinking, told him, "No sick people, but two are pregnant."

"Lisa," I yelled at her, "why are you reporting us?"

"Ruth," she said, "you can't go on doing this heavy physical labor. Think of your child. You have to take care of yourself."

Up to that point I hadn't known there was another pregnant woman in our group. Berta Reich was in her ninth month. She had not yet gotten over the loss of her three-year-old son Pavliček. Here we were, two strangers, who at this crucial moment felt that we had known each other for ages. Berta was petite and therefore looked as though she might give birth at any minute.

All the other prisoners (by now they had become our comrades and friends, having gone through so much with us) left for work; there was no chance to even say good-bye. We two pregnant women stood there, alone and forsaken. I begged the SS doctor to let us go to work, too; I said the hard work wouldn't hurt us. It was no use. "We don't need pregnant women here," he said. "We have no means to deliver children and to care for them. You'll have to go to the maternity hospital first and after you give birth you'll be brought back here."

We believed his reassuring words and readily went along with him. But, of course, we had no choice but to follow the Germans' orders. The SS doctor first took us to a German headquarters building. He locked us into an empty office, and we were kept waiting there for a long time. At last another SS man came in and informed us that he would be our guard and that we would be leaving immediately. When I asked where we were being taken, there was no answer.

A woman who later turned out to be a midwife also accompanied us. Berta and I, wearing our cross-marked dresses, were told to walk in front of them so that the SS man could keep an eye on us. He had slung his rifle over his shoulder; there was no need to carry it at the ready. After all, how could two such conspicuous prisoners escape? We were given some food for the trip: bread and a piece of wurst. Wurst? We hadn't had any for two and a half years and had forgotten that wonderful taste!

At the railroad station the SS man bought four tickets, but I wasn't able to hear the name of our destination. Actually, the journey was quite luxurious. No cattle car this time—instead we sat in a separate closed compartment. No other passengers dared to enter this compartment because we really looked quite forbidding.

Throughout the trip Berta and I talked to each other in Czech, speculating on where they might be taking us. When we arrived at a large station—BERLIN, the signs said—we got off and the SS guard steered us toward an UP staircase. We were going to another track. I caught sight of an escalator nearby and, following a sudden impulse, I pulled Berta onto the moving stairs. A great commotion erupted behind us. The SS man and some of the passersby shouted, "Stop them! Stop the prisoners! Catch them!"

To this day I don't understand how I could even have thought of escaping. It was an impromptu idea that came out of my yearning to be free again; I was like an animal trying to get out of a trap. But how far could we have gotten? Who would have helped two Jewish women? After all, this was enemy territory. We had proof of that almost instantly: Several strong pairs of hands grabbed us and held us until the SS guard arrived.

After this unlucky escape attempt we boarded another train and again sat in a closed compartment. In a way, I enjoyed this part of the journey. I watched the beautiful landscape go by—meadows, trees, flowers; I saw little houses in which families lived free lives, and an inexpressible longing overwhelmed me. When would I again be able to stroll through a green meadow? When would I be free again like the people who lived in those houses?

For two and a half years I hadn't seen the beauty of nature, and now I lapped up the fast-changing landscape like a parched traveler coming out of the desert. I felt sad when dusk came; I wanted to keep on looking out of the window for hours more. When we got off the train, it was already quite dark, and there was no sign at the station to indicate where we were.

Ordered again to walk in front of the SS man, we set off on a seemingly endless march into the night. I don't know how long we walked; we were both dead tired and longed to reach our destination. But suddenly all our weariness disappeared. We were approaching the typical setting of a concentration camp—the barbed-wire fence, the guard towers, and the heavily guarded gate. So this was to be our maternity hospital!

The guard took us to the office of some SS women, who had to determine what to do with two pregnant prisoners so late at night. They locked us up in one of the washrooms. Tomorrow they would decide what to do with us. Because of the air raids, strict blackout measures were in force throughout Germany; it was forbidden to turn on any lights. And so we were shut into the dark washroom. Since I suffered from night blindness, I wouldn't have been able to see anything even in dim light. Berta was quite distraught. Groping about, we began to explore the place. There were various wash basins both at floor level and higher up, and the stone floor was covered with wooden boards. We decided to lie down on one of these planks. Overcome by weariness, we fell asleep. But I woke up again almost immediately, feeling that insects were crawling all over me. At the same time, Berta screamed in horror. We had no choice but to spend the night walking back and forth just to keep the bugs away. Early the next morning Berta identified them as nothing more than big, fat, well-fed cockroaches.

I don't know what made us do it, but during that sleepless night we decided to tell the Germans that we were sisters. We knew that the SS man who had brought us here had no identification papers for either of us, and besides, we were now just numbers; we were no longer human beings.

Even in daylight I could only dimly make out the dimensions and layout of the washroom. Had they forgotten about us? Had no one been informed of our arrival? An SS woman who came to unlock the door was amazed to find us there. "How dare you stay in here!" she yelled. Furious, she took us to an office staffed by other SS women. There, once again, we were registered.

At this point Berta said she was due any day, perhaps any hour. It was what we had decided she would say the night before. The SS women ordered her to go to the infirmary; I was to go to one of the blocks. I begged them to let us stay together since we were sisters, and for some reason they changed their minds. We were both sent to the infirmary. There we found out that we were in the Ravensbrück concentration camp for women. This didn't mean anything to us, but at least it explained why SS women were in charge here. We were given something to eat, much like the food we had had in Auschwitz. It didn't matter; we just wanted to get some rest. Assigned to a single wooden cot, we instantly fell asleep.

The next morning we went outside to look around. The inmates were all wearing blue-and-gray striped prison uniforms. Like Auschwitz, Ravensbrück was made up of large barracks surrounded by a barbed-wire fence. There were loudspeakers all over the camp, constantly carrying announcements, but Berta and I paid them scant attention. Our thoughts were on where we would have our babies and what would happen to them and to us.

But that afternoon we heard an announcement that made us perk up: "All pregnant women are to report to the office immediately so they can be taken to the maternity hospital."

This announcement was repeated, again and again. When we arrived at the office we were surprised to see many other pregnant women waiting in line. Our experience in Auschwitz had taught us to be suspicious, so we stayed in the background to see what was happening. Fragments of conversations reached us. Some of the women said they were happy to get away from Ravensbrück, glad to deliver their children in decent surroundings. These women probably had not experienced the hard lessons we had learned at Auschwitz. We didn't trust the good nature of the SS women, and with every passing minute I became more alarmed.

We were getting closer to the head of the line. In response to another sudden hunch, I whispered to Berta to pretend that she had gone into labor; having had a baby, she knew what to do.

A sign on the door of one of the offices read: LAGERKOMMANDO (Camp Administration). Without thinking twice, I boldly knocked on the door. A voice said, "Come in," and I entered the inner sanctum. The woman commandant sitting at her desk, surprised to see a prisoner walk in, asked me what I wanted. Without batting an eye, I tried to appeal to her feminine sympathies. "My sister and I are being sent to a maternity hospital along with the other women," I said. "She's already started to go into labor. It won't take long before the baby comes—this is her second child. It's impossible for her to travel in this condition. I'm sure that you, as a woman, understand and that you'll let me stay here with her in her critical hour. Then, later, we'll gladly follow the other women."

I really don't know where I got the courage to make this little speech. After a moment's hesitation, the commandant called in an SS woman and ordered her to take us back to the infirmary. On our way there I saw that the women supposedly headed for the maternity hospital were being loaded onto trucks. After Auschwitz, I always associated trucks carrying human cargo with the gas chamber. And, indeed, that was the destination of these poor women who were going so trustingly to their death.

Berta and I spent another night in the infirmary. Early the next morning an SS doctor came over to our cot. He began to examine Berta and, of course, found no trace of dilation; in other words, it was obvious that Berta had told a lie the day before. But in spite of her fear of punishment, she stuck to her claim that she had had labor pains but they had stopped during the night. We were escorted back to the office, and there it was decided that we would immediately follow the other women to the maternity hospital.

An armed SS man took charge of us and led us to a prison van called a Green Anton. Everybody in the Protectorate had been afraid of the Green Antons, because they usually picked up people for interrogations at Gestapo headquarters. We climbed in. The door was closed from the outside, and we sat in the dark, not knowing where they were taking us. In Auschwitz, vans like this drove people to the gas chambers, so we thought this would be our last journey. We cried and said farewell to life. Imagine our surprise when the van stopped, the doors were opened, and we found ourselves standing in front of a railroad station. We were going to live, after all! Then we heard the SS guard ask for three tickets to Auschwitz. We had scarcely left that hell, and now we were going back there. It was clear that the maternity hospital the other women from Ravensbrück had been sent to was nothing other than the Auschwitz gas chambers.

This time there seemed to be no way out. What could two pregnant women under the watchful eye of an armed SS guard do? While I was thinking about all this, I found myself looking at the two superimposed triangles on Bertha's chest, the yellow one that marked us as Jews sewn on top of the red one. Suddenly it hit me: What if I removed the yellow triangle? Would the guard notice? It was no sooner thought than done. In the lavatory, while the SS man waited outside, we removed the yellow triangles from our dresses and flushed the yellow scraps down the toilet. When we came out, the guard didn't notice a thing, and we felt that we had at least accomplished something. From now on, with each of us marked by a red triangle, we hoped the SS would consider us political prisoners.

I have no clear recollection of what the railroad station looked like or how we got from the station to Auschwitz. One question dominated my thoughts: What would the next hour bring? Transports like ours, consisting of only one or two individuals, were immediately sent to the gas chamber. For what seemed an eternity, Berta and I walked along in front of the SS man, not taking any notice of our surroundings. Our nerves were stretched to the breaking point, and when we spoke to each other it was only about our impending death. We reached the camp around noon and were taken to a large office where there were several desks but only one SS man on duty. Why wasn't anyone else there? Perhaps they were at lunch. Was that good or bad? There wasn't much time to wonder. Our guard, raising his right arm, said, "Heil Hitler!" and, clicking his heels together, he reported in a stentorian voice, "I am delivering two pregnant women who do not belong in Ravensbrück. Heil Hitler!"

As befits a proper German he stood there, erect and motionless. Then, clicking his heels again, he did an about-face and left the room.

Suddenly it occurred to me that since we had removed those yellow triangles it was no longer obvious that we were Jews. Couldn't I claim that I was a political prisoner? Might that help us?

The SS man at the desk called out, "Name?"

He was asking for my name, not my number. Had he asked for the number tattooed on my arm, he would immediately have realized that I was Jewish.

"Jarmila Novotná," I shouted. It had come to me out of the blue, the name of a famous Czech soprano, and it sounded authentically Czech.

"Father's name?"

"Karel Novotný," I replied instantly.

"Mother's name?"

"Marie Novotná."

"Is your father Jewish?"

"No," I lied.

"Mother Jewish?"

"No."

"You are not a Jew?"

"No," I said firmly. Since I was intended for the gas chambers, anyway, what could they do to me if they caught me in a lie?

Berta gave similar answers, having had some time to think up a fictitious name for herself.

The SS man picked up the telephone and dialed a number. My heart stopped beating. I knew the next few seconds would determine our fate: life or death?

"I need an escort to take two pregnant women to the infirmary in the women's camp," he said.

When we heard him say "the women's camp," both of us knew we weren't being sent to the gas chambers. The tension eased. We had received a reprieve, a moment's grace. But for how long? In these crucial moments the thought of the lucky medallion under my tongue supported me, giving me a little confidence.

Again we had to march in front of an SS man, his rifle at the ready. The *Krankenbau* (infirmary) was located off to one side of the women's camp. It was not separated from the other barracks by barbed wire. This time we were not shoved into cages; instead, we were put into a block similar to Block 6 in the family camp. Here, too, a heating chimney that could be fired from both ends ran the length of the block and was used as a bench. Here, too, there were three tiers of shelves that served as beds without mattresses. Berta and I were each assigned a place on the lowest tier so that we didn't have to climb up, something that would have been quite impossible in our condition.

The patients as well as the medical personnel in the infirmary were prisoners. They bombarded us with questions, which made it impossible to keep up our masquerade as "politicals." Where had we come from, how and why had we arrived as an "individual transport," and why hadn't we been taken directly to the gas chambers? Slowly our secret leaked out, but they found our story beyond belief. All of them were convinced that any transport leaving Auschwitz could have only one destination: the gas chamber. If I am not mistaken, Berta and I were the first prisoners who left Auschwitz and then came back to the women's camp alive. Our story created a sensation and, as word of our experience quickly spread, more and more women came by to listen to us. We told them about Hamburg, how we had cleared the rubble at the bombed refinery, and about the Ravensbrück women's camp. What we said probably gave some of the prisoners hope for survival.

Even Mengele heard about us. He appeared in our block and ordered that we be brought to him. We stood at rigid attention; this was the second time that I had been in such close proximity to him. He began to interrogate us, asking endless questions: Where were we during the selection? Where was he standing at the time? Where were the other doctors standing? What else had we observed there? It probably was inconceivable to him that he, who was all-powerful in determining the fate of the Jews at Auschwitz, had overlooked two pregnant women during the selection process.

Finally he said, "First you will deliver your babies, then we'll see."

What did he mean by that? It certainly didn't sound good.

Mengele came by every day, not just to see us but to visit the infirmary, which was his domain. There were many human guinea pigs among the sick people in our block, young women who were forced to undergo fiendish operations. It was horrible to see them being taken away for Mengele's experiments. Rumors about the operations had spread quickly, and the women resisted with all their might. But in vain. Though weak, they were relatively healthy when they left the barracks. When they came back, they were in a pitiable state, screaming and weeping. All had about them the wild look of madness. We were young and didn't know much about medicine or what exactly had been done to these women. But we saw that they were suffering horribly. For a long time afterward, they were not able to speak. Their fellow prisoners could at most comfort them with words. And every day when Mengele came by we trembled, not knowing who his next victim would be.

Mengele was an attractive man. A perennial little smile showed the gap between his front teeth. Immaculately dressed in jodhpurs, he wore a cap bearing the SS insignia and carried the obligatory riding crop, constantly slapping it against his gleaming black boots. Whenever he spoke to me he was very polite, giving the impression that he was personally interested in me. It was hard to believe that his little smile and courteous behavior were just a facade behind which he devised the most horrific murderous schemes.

Women prisoner-doctors worked in the hospital barracks under the direction of a Slovak doctor, an exceptionally beautiful woman. She reported to Mengele and the other SS doctors. There were also assistants who took care of the routine work. Each patient was responsible for keeping herself clean, as far as that was possible. The one great luxury the infirmary offered us was a washroom with running water at one end of the block. It was for the exclusive use of the prisoners, so we didn't have far to go, and we didn't have to stand in line.

There were several smaller blocks near ours, but they were off-limits to us. It was rumored that the twins who had been picked by Mengele for his experiments were housed there, along with the twins who had arrived at the family camp in the September transport. Mengele had claimed the twins for his experiments before the rest of the people on the transport were sent to the gas chambers.

Prisoners in the hospital block were not made to stand outside for roll call; instead, we were counted twice a day inside the block. Each morning the bodies of those who had died during the night were placed outside the block door; after all, corpses had to be counted, too. It was all done very punctiliously; everyone—the living and the dead—had to be present and accounted for.

One day Ženka appeared in the infirmary. Dear, faithful Ženka, my only connection with home and the only person in this horrible place who was close to me. How did she find out that we had come back? Probably everybody knew, our return had caused a sensation. From then on she stopped by every day following the afternoon roll call, even though she was hungry and exhausted from work and needed to rest and gather strength for the next day's hard labor. She was on the verge of despair because she had received no news of her family and had heard nothing of her two sisters. Every afternoon we tried to console each other, talking about our families and our hope of seeing them again.

By now I was nine months pregnant, and I knew that the baby might come any day. At home I had overheard conversations about the beautiful layettes it was customary to prepare for the arrival of a baby: diapers, embroidered outfits, a crib, a cradle, and many other things. With a prison dress as my only possession, how could I prepare anything in this wretched place? I worried about where I could get a diaper, how I would wash the child, how I would care for it. Where could I get a bit of cotton, a little piece of soap, and warm water?

Berta tried repeatedly to prepare me for the imminent delivery. The loss of her son Pavliček had been a profound sorrow for her, and now she was worried about the future of her second child. Her doelike brown eyes were infinitely sad, and I never saw her smile. Her belly was getting huge, and we expected her to deliver at any moment. Her feet were badly swollen, and she had difficulty getting about. We both had only one wish—to get it over with. At the same time, we also wanted to delay the moment, because pregnant women got a supplementary food ration in the infirmary—an extra portion of soup! It's difficult to describe how much that meant to us. We got our first portion at noon, then the second one late in the afternoon. I suppose you could hardly call the warm water with some turnip floating in it soup, but it helped fill our stomachs for a while. Whenever I received that second portion, I felt quite uncomfortable, sensing the hungry looks the other prisoners gave me as I began to eat, but I couldn't share the soup because there was scarcely enough for one. I took the bowl back to my cot so they would not have to watch me eat.

My bunk was on the lowest level. This made it easier for me to get into it, but it also had the disadvantage of making me more visible.

The shelves of the second tier were so close that there was only enough room to sit bent over. If you wanted to sit up, you had to put your head outside and hang your feet over the edge; at least your feet were resting on the ground, which was not the case in the middle tier. There your feet just dangled, nearly touching the head of the person on the lowest level. Occasionally the entire framework of bed shelves collapsed, the lumber and the prisoners crashing down on those below. That once happened to Berta, though miraculously she was not hurt because the woman on the shelf above her was so emaciated that she weighed practically nothing. At the time, we thought the shelf collapse would surely induce Berta's labor. But nothing happened, and Berta continued to waddle about with her enormous belly.

On August 3, 1944, instead of turnip soup for lunch we were given cabbage soup, probably made with sauerkraut. It was a disgusting concoction, and I slurped it down with a combination of aversion and ravenous hunger. That afternoon Ženka came to visit me as usual, and I complained to her of a stomachache that I blamed on the awful soup. But Ženka, Berta, and some of the other inmates were sure this wasn't a stomachache but the beginning of labor. I pooh-poohed it.

"It's from the soup," I insisted. "Besides, Berta is much bigger than I am, so she's sure to give birth before I do. I still have two or three weeks to go." Unconsciously, I probably wanted to put off the fateful hour.

It was getting late, and Ženka reluctantly went back to her block. All the while, Berta tried to help, giving me good advice and telling me how to handle myself. But there really was nothing she could do for me. She stood there, unsuccessfully trying to hide the tears that ran down her face. I also cried. I was afraid, terribly afraid of what lay ahead. The cramps were coming more frequently, and at last I had to admit that they were labor pains. How, in my loneliness, could I give birth to a child?

Since I was night-blind, Berta had to tell me when the lights were turned off in the block. As long as the lights were on, I could make out shadows, but after that I could see absolutely nothing. The contractions were tearing me apart. After running around helplessly, Berta finally plucked up her courage and went to the block elder to tell her that I was about to have the baby and needed help. I did not scream, because I didn't want to wake up the whole block. With every contraction I dug my fingernails into the wood of my cot and then I bit the wood. I couldn't lie down; nor could I walk around because of the night blindness. Berta tried to reassure me, to encourage me. Again and again, she said the pains would go away; I didn't believe her. I wanted to call for help, to appeal to someone by name. Back home, when a patient was in great pain she would cry out "Mother!" But this one simple word that meant so much and brought so much relief was foreign to me. If only I could have called out "Mother!" and if only my mother could have stood by me in this difficult hour. What had I done that I should have to suffer like this? "Mother, Mother . . ."

The block elder and another woman arrived, and they sent Berta away for the time being. The woman accompanying the block elder was a professional midwife, a Polish prisoner who worked in this capacity in the women's camp. Czech is similar to Polish; therefore, we understood most of what we said to each other. The midwife led me to the chimney bench and told me to lie down. She had placed a rough woolen blanket on the bench so that I would not have to lie on the bare concrete. Now she sternly ordered me not to get up. With every contraction, I writhed in pain. The midwife was constantly murmuring something, and I could hear a strange rattling. She told me she was praying while fingering her rosary. Was that supposed to ease my suffering? Her rosary? Was there no other means, for God's sake? I prayed to God as I had learned to do at home. But where was God? Did He exist, and why was He permitting me to suffer like this? Unable to ask my mother for help, I implored God: Please help me.

It was the midwife who helped me. Even as she was praying, she gave me directions, telling me how and when to push. But she was also lamenting that she couldn't perform a normal delivery, that she had no way of sterilizing anything, not even the scissors that would be used to cut the umbilical cord. Moreover, there was no warm water to wash the baby, no cotton, no soap, no baby clothing, no sanitary napkins, and no towels—nothing.

I didn't understand everything she said; I felt like a helpless animal. Nothing interested me; I just wanted to get this terrible time behind me. What did I care about sterilization and hot water? If only these terrible pains would stop. Then the bearing-down contractions started, and soon I screamed and felt the baby leave my body. Even before I was aware of the enormous relief, I heard the baby's first cry. My child! My child was crying, and I could no longer keep back the tears. Sobs shook my body. This was no postpartem hysteria but an expression of despair at the fate of my child. I think that even in those first brief moments of my baby's life, my maternal instinct stirred.

Where was that happy moment when the doctor tells the young woman that she is the mother of a beautiful baby? I scarcely heard the midwife tell me that I had given birth to a healthy, well-developed girl. Given birth? What for? Why?

The midwife cut the umbilical cord with the unsterilized scissors and handed the baby to Berta. "Go to the washroom and wash this child," she told her.

"With cold water?" Berta asked.

"You have no choice, unless you want to hand it to the mother all bloody," the midwife replied.

"Aren't there any diapers?" Berta asked. "No blanket to wrap it in?"

The midwife laughed a cynical laugh. "How long have you been in Auschwitz? Or do you think we're in a private clinic here?"

Once the afterbirth had been expelled, the midwife ordered me to lie down on my cot. She covered me with the blood-soaked blanket on which I had lain during the delivery. The naked baby lay next to me. So that she would not have to lie on the bare boards, I tucked some of the dirty blanket under and over her little body. There was no way to sop up the blood that was flowing between my legs. Berta brought me a dirty rag. I used it to keep the blood from seeping onto the wooden planks and from there onto the floor. In Auschwitz, even dirty rags were much prized and in great demand.

The baby began to cry, but I had nothing with which to soothe her. Berta gave her a few drops of water, and later when we got some ersatz coffee it became the first warm drink my child tasted. A woman in our block came over to my bunk and shyly handed me a stolen nightgown she had been given by a friend who worked in the *Kleiderkammer* (the clothes depot, where the clothes that had been confiscated from prisoners were sorted). The woman suggested that I tear it into four parts to make diapers for the baby. How generous of her to give away this priceless treasure that she could easily have bartered for bread. I was glad, because the blanket under the baby was already quite wet and there was a bad smell coming from our cot.

The baby cried and cried, and we didn't know how to quiet her. Berta tore a square piece of cloth from each of the diapers. She took a bit of bread and chewed it until it was mush; then she put this into one of the little squares and dipped it in soup. That's how she fed the little one. It was an improvised pacifier, and the baby stopped crying for a short while.

As usual, Mengele came by for his daily visit and saw that I had given birth. He looked at the baby for a long time, and after some reflection he directed one of the women doctors to tightly bandage my breasts. In my naïveté I did not immediately think he had anything evil in mind. But when I heard him give the order that I was not to breast-feed my child I was horrified. Why was he doing this? Why couldn't I nurse my baby? What was he trying to do? One of the prisoners knew. She said, "It's another of Mengele's experiments; he wants to see how long a newborn infant can live without being fed."

This woman must be out of her mind. Could a human being think up such a thing, much less carry it out? Impossible. I told her to keep quiet, to stop saying such dreadful things.

Mengele returned the next day, stopping at my cot to check the bandage around my breasts and to examine the baby. He asked me politely how I felt and whether the baby was crying. Six days passed; each day he came to see me, and each day he asked the same questions. I shuddered before each of these visits.

The morning after the baby was born I felt my breasts filling with milk, the bandage getting damp. The baby was hungry and cried, but I was forbidden to feed her. My breasts became swollen with milk; I probably had milk fever. I lay there in my own filth, unable to think. Ženka and Berta did everything they could to alleviate my suffering, while the child cried and screamed. Berta tried her improvised pacifier again in an effort to soothe the baby, to still her hunger. She washed the little girl in cold water and rinsed out the flimsy scraps of linen that served as diapers. Despite these efforts, the baby and I gave off a penetrating smell caused by various bodily secretions. I dragged myself to the washroom, but even with the best of intentions, without soap, warm water, or a towel, I couldn't keep myself clean. On top of everything else, we were having very hot summer weather; everyone perspired, and the lice, bugs, and fleas were much worse than they were in winter.

What name should I give my child? Each name that came to mind reminded me of someone in my family. So I gave up, and the baby had but one name: "my child." My child, you were born with such a lovely little body. Your legs are soft and pudgy, and they have tiny creases. What beautiful, clear features you have. Dark hair and little fingers with such small fingernails. When you first saw the light of day, you were a pretty baby. Now, for three days, your crying has not stopped. Your pale skin turns red when you scream, and your lovely little face is distorted. Am I imagining it, or is your face getting smaller? Your legs thinner? Oh why, my child, are you not allowed to drink your mother's milk? If you could, you would fill out and not wither so quickly. Is your voice getting weaker, your crying and screaming gradually turning into a whimper? My child, how can I help you in your suffering? How can I keep you alive? Please don't leave me.

I caress you and would gladly take your suffering upon me, but even that Mengele does not allow me to do. Are you suffering a lot, my child? You're much too young to endure all this, to understand it. Can anyone really understand?

Is it really a human mind that has thought this up? Or was it the mind of a fiend?

In the few days you've been on this earth, my child, you have already had to endure so much torment. You haven't committed any sin, yet you are being punished so severely. How can we put an end to this misery? Is there anything that I as your mother can do? Do I have the right to even think of ending both our lives? How can you and I live through this? When will the pain end?

Here, my child, take this pacifier made of bread soaked in coffee; maybe it will alleviate your hunger. You have scarcely any strength left to suck on it. You're already six days old, and still I see no way out of this terrible plight. Oh God, please let us both die.

My child, you've turned ashen-gray, just a tiny skeleton covered with skin. You can't even whimper anymore. And all those bedsores. Are you still breathing? Come, Mengele, examine my child. Feast your eyes on her! Is your medical curiosity finally satisfied? Now do you know how long a newborn child can live without food, you devil in human form! Perhaps God will finally hear me now. Neither the baby nor I am able to go on living. Please take us, dear God, I implore you!

The next morning, punctual as ever, Mengele arrived and said, "I shall come early tomorrow morning to fetch you both. Be ready at 8 A.M."

Why not today, Mengele? Why do we have to endure this torture another day? Come, my child, we'll spend our last hours close together. Your little body is already blue and covered with sores, but we have to make it through till tomorrow. Tomorrow we'll go to the gas chamber together. But you know, little one, I wanted so much to live a little longer. I'm still so young, only twenty-two, and now I must die. I want to say good-bye to my loved ones. I won't ever see them again, and up to now it was this family tie that helped me to bear the tortures and humiliation. I want to *live, to live!* Have I gone mad? Why am I screaming? I can't help it. I must scream, for tomorrow I will no longer be able to scream. I never learned how to pray. Are there any prayers for people in a situation like this? Will no one help me?

A woman prisoner is standing near my cot. Is she a doctor perhaps?

"Why are you yelling like that," she says harshly. "You're disturbing the others."

"My child and I are going to the gas chamber tomorrow," I scream at her. "But I want to live."

The woman, Maca Steinberg, a prisoner like me, was a Czech Jew. She asked me how I knew that I was going to be gassed tomorrow. I started telling her my story haltingly, and soon the words were tumbling out, and I began to feel better, grateful to have found someone who would listen.

Maca had already heard the story of the two pregnant women who had come back to Auschwitz from Hamburg, but still she listened patiently to me. Then, as she turned to leave, she said, "I'm going to help you. Be patient."

A strange feeling of peace overcame me. I sensed that Maca was someone who did not make empty promises. When she returned, she said in that harsh voice of hers, "I've brought you a hypodermic syringe containing some medicine. Inject it into your child."

"What's in the hypodermic?" I asked.

"Morphine; it will kill the baby," she said matter-of-factly. I shuddered.

"But I can't be the murderer of my own child!" I screamed. "Won't you give her the injection?"

Maca's voice was the voice of an angel. "Ruth, you're young," she said. "You must stay alive. Look at your child. She cannot live; in a few hours she will die, anyway. But she must die before Mengele comes to pick you up. If the child is still alive when he gets here, he'll take you both. I've sworn the Hippocratic oath, and it is my duty to save human life—your life. I must not kill. You must do it to save your own life. Quickly, do it. Do it now."

With every word she spoke, my resistance ebbed. I could no longer think rationally. Maca kept talking. After a while I had no strength of will left. I did it. I killed my own child. Mengele had turned me into a child murderer.

I could hear the death rattle in the baby's throat, and I took her in my arms and pressed her tightly against me for the short time that we still had together. Her breathing became weaker and weaker. It didn't take long, but it seemed like hours. This is our last night together, my child. Perhaps you could have lived. Now you have stopped breathing. Are you at last free of this torment that has been your brief life? You won't have to suffer anymore. Why didn't Maca bring a dose of morphine for me, too? I want to go with you, my child. I do not want to live. How can I possibly go on living with this burden of guilt?

A new day has begun and you, my child, lie dead in my arms. Your little body is getting colder, and I can't keep you warm anymore. Soon they will start to collect the corpses of those who died during the night. They will take you away, too. Where to? Now they have picked up the bodies and you are no longer with me. They took you away from me, and I am alone. Still, I have to go on living. But why? For whom? A terrible dullness and indifference have overcome me.

When Berta woke up in the morning, she knew nothing of what had happened during the night on the cot next to hers. We looked at each other without speaking. No one, not even Berta, could console me. She could only give me support by being near me. I became completely apathetic. Having done this terrible deed, I didn't care what Mengele would do with me.

When he arrived, he asked, "Where is your child?"

"She died last night," I said wearily.

"Died? I want to see the body." He went outside to the pile of corpses. But not even he, all-powerful man that he was, could find the body of a tiny infant in the huge pile of corpses. When he came back to my cot, he said, "You're really lucky. You will leave Auschwitz on the next transport."

I didn't know what he meant. Why hadn't he sent me to the gas chamber? It would have been better if he had!

It was only thanks to Berta and Ženka, who stood by me, firm as rocks, that my will to live gradually returned. Berta said she would need me when her time to deliver came, that I had to help her just as she had helped me, that she would have to go through the same suffering and pain, and that we had no one to depend on except each other.

Maca stopped by every day. She was a dentist but had been assigned to the hospital block of Birkenau to delouse the prisoners. Lice spread typhus. When a typhus epidemic broke out in Auschwitz, the SS people were afraid they would catch it, too, and they ordered a delousing operation for the entire camp. The prisoners, their clothing, and their living quarters were dusted with some sort of white powder, and for a short time we had some relief from the constant itching and scratching.

I eventually found out that Maca came from Frýdek, a small town near Ostrava. Her husband, a lawyer, had been sent to Nisko, where he perished. She had been in Theresienstadt and, like me, had been deported from there to the family camp in Auschwitz in December 1943. At the selection in the family camp, Maca was among the young women who were judged fit for work and she was sent to the women's camp of Birkenau. But at that time the SS needed medical personnel for the hospital block in the women's camp, so, when the rest of us went to Hamburg, Maca—separated from her friends—had to stay behind.

She was a beautiful, graceful woman, with warm intelligent brown eyes; even in her prison clothes she had an air of elegance. She lived in a small room of her own in a nearby block, not in the crowded dormitories. There was no dental clinic in Auschwitz, and I have no idea what people did when they had toothaches. The kind and good-hearted Maca helped whenever she could.

When she first came to my cot, she didn't know how she could help me. But after I explained my situation she went to a Polish medical orderly who worked in the women's camp infirmary and told him my story. She pleaded with him to help save me. This man risked his life to steal the morphine. Maca then stole a hypodermic needle, and that's how she was able to bring me the death-dealing drug. What Maca did was extremely dangerous. How could she have explained what she was doing in another block after the lights had been turned out?

Maca was also at Berta's side when her contractions started, and she and I decided that we would spare Berta all the agony I had had to endure. Maca immediately obtained more morphine and stole another hypodermic syringe. Berta gave birth to a boy, but she never saw him alive, because he was given the morphine injection right after he was born. The baby died a few hours later. When Mengele came by, he was told that Berta's child was stillborn. Once again, his scientific curiosity was left unsatisfied.

Mengele told Berta that she would be leaving Auschwitz on the next transport. This time we believed him, because he now saw us as strong young women who were fit to work in the German weapons industry or to clear rubble in the bombed-out fatherland. Strong, young, and fit to work—what irony! Emaciated, weak, and totally despondent is what we were. True, we were young, and that helped us slowly to get over the traumatic experience we had just been through. Gradually, the apathy that overcame me after the death of my child faded. My sense of obligation to stand by Berta—in other words, the need to concentrate on something outside myself—helped to restore my will to live.

Even though Berta and I were now healthy again, we were allowed to remain in the hospital block. Who knows why. I really can't explain it, but both of us were glad. Had we returned to the women's camp, they would have put us back into those cages; here we had more roomy bed shelves, although there still were no mattresses. In the women's camp we would instantly have been assigned to work—

probably moving rocks, which we were in no condition to do. But in a concentration camp we learned never to ask why, because we wanted to remain as inconspicuous as possible to avoid being selected for special treatment. So Berta and I, with nothing to do, had our nagging hunger uppermost in mind. Although we were allowed to move about freely, we rarely left the hospital block to go into the women's camp; we didn't want the Germans to find us and send us to work.

One side of the hospital block bordered on some open land where trains arrived and people were unloaded. Before long I realized that these were arriving transports. Each time I saw one of these transports, I knew that while the women's orchestra played, people were being selected for death.

One day in October we heard a rumor that transports were arriving from Theresienstadt. I ran behind the block to a spot from which I could watch the unloading without being observed by the SS guards. I made out the typical clothes of the men from the Theresienstadt *Speditionsgruppe* (expediters), belted raincoats and high boots. Suddenly I saw a familiar figure: Eda Krasa, with whom I had worked in the Theresienstadt kitchen and who had persuaded me to try out for Raffael Schächter's chorus. Eda was tall and strikingly handsome. When I saw him, I yelled in a panic, "Eda, you're healthy! Eda you're healthy! Eda, Eda!"

I was too far away for him to have heard me, and the orchestra's playing drowned out my words. But even if he had heard me, he wouldn't have known what I meant. After all, who among these new arrivals had any inkling of what lay in store for them? No human being in his right mind could have imagined the Nazis' extermination policy.

"Eda, you're healthy," I continued screaming, unaware that I was getting closer and closer to the barbed-wire fence. Suddenly I heard, "Stop, or I'll shoot!" It was the guard in the watchtower. I turned away, shaken and sobbing. Nobody could calm me. How many of my friends from Theresienstadt were being gassed at that very moment? The evidence was not long in coming. The cremation process had already begun. Smoke poured from the chimneys, and the smell of burned flesh spread over Auschwitz.

Someone said, "That was the Czech transport from Theresienstadt."

Like that, so simply, as though this didn't involve human beings, families, mothers, fathers, and children. Yes, "that was the Czech transport from Theresienstadt," and it contained most of the Jewish cultural elite of central Europe.

Ženka came to say good-bye. She was being shipped off to do forced labor, probably clearing rubble in Germany. Only a short while before we had found each other under terrible circumstances, and now we were to be torn apart again. I told her, "Ženka, be strong. Hold on."

One evening a toothless, wrinkled old woman woke me from my sleep. I looked at her in surprise; what did she want? Who was she? Then she said, "Rutinko, Rutinko, don't you recognize me?"

No matter how hard I tried, I couldn't identify her. She looked like no one I knew.

"But, Rutinko, it's me, your Aunt Hanča!" she said almost reproachfully, embracing me.

It was indeed Aunt Hanča, Father's once beautiful, elegant, rich sister, who had owned Buffet Anka on Ostrava's main street, but who now looked so miserable.

She had married Manek Weber, who was several years younger than she. After Hitler occupied Bohemia and Moravia, both of them were able to obtain Aryan identification papers, but because too many people knew them in Ostrava they moved to Prague and lived there in seclusion. In spite of that, Manek was picked up during a street raid; his identity card was found to be a fake, and he was immediately deported to Theresienstadt without having a chance to say farewell to his wife. However, she found out what happened to him and couldn't bear to think that he was suffering and hungry. She located a Czech gendarme who did guard duty in Theresienstadt and paid him a lot of money to take hot meals and cigarettes to Manek in the ghetto. I had met Manek frequently on the street in the ghetto; he always looked clean and well nourished. But he never told me that his wife was sending him not only food but also cigarettes. Manek was one of the privileged inmates who had a pass that enabled him to go in and out through the ghetto gate to the vegetable garden beyond the embankment. The fields were SS property, and it was strictly forbidden for ghetto inmates to eat anything that grew in those fields or take anything back to the camp with them. This prohibition was not observed and the more adept prisoners ate and filched things. But when someone was caught, he was assigned to the next transport to the East. And that's what happened to Manek, who was caught stealing a kohlrabi.

The gendarme who had been taking the food to Manek had been under surveillance and was arrested. Meanwhile, in Prague, Aunt Hanča had had no sign of life from her husband and didn't know what had happened to him. In 1944, she was arrested and they found that she was carrying a false identity card. She was imprisoned and then taken to Auschwitz. There she ran into Ženka in the women's camp, and Ženka told her about me. When I first saw her, I wasn't able to conceal my shock at her appearance, but all she could say was, "Where is my Maneček? Can't you help me find him?"

After ten months in Auschwitz, I knew the answer, but how could I tell this broken woman about the gas chambers? My feelings probably were already brutalized, because I remember thinking, Aunt Hanča, soon you, too, will go the same route as your Maneček.

Nevertheless, I tried to console her, to reassure her, even though I may have sounded insincere. The day after her visit a selection took place, and she disappeared from her block. I never saw her again.

In early October, Berta and I were ordered to prepare for immediate departure. No one told us where we were going. Since we had nothing to pack—the clothes we wore were all we had—our preparations were minimal. I again hid the little necklace with my talisman under my tongue. There wasn't even enough time to say good-bye to Maca. We were taken to the ramp, where cattle cars were waiting for us. To our surprise we saw that men wearing the striped prison clothes were being loaded into boxcars at the rear of the train. A prisoner working at the ramp told me that these men had come from Theresienstadt. I couldn't believe it; I thought that all of them had been gassed. Then I saw the Germans' logic. Of course! They needed all the workers they could get in Germany to clear the rubble from the bombed-out buildings and to help out in the armaments industry, so they had selected these relatively strong and healthy prisoners to do that job.[7]

Berta and I joined a large group of Hungarian-speaking women from Hungary and the Carpathian region that had belonged to Czechoslovakia before the war.

Auschwitz lay behind us.

---

[7] Publisher's note: On October 8, 1944, a total of 500 prisoners were taken from the Auschwitz II concentration camp to the Taucha Kommando, which belonged to the Buchenwald concentration camp.

5

In the Labor Camp

ONCE AGAIN WE WERE HERDED INTO railway boxcars, but this time a surprise awaited us inside. Wooden benches had been set up in the cars! Was it possible that we, who had been treated like cattle all along, would now be allowed to ride the train sitting on benches? My amazement increased when an SS man carrying a rifle with fixed bayonet climbed into the car with us. Why weren't the guards just cramming us in and locking the doors from the outside as before?

There wasn't enough room for all of us to sit on the benches, so we took turns. While some of us sat, the others slept on the floor. Many of the Hungarian women cried, bemoaning their fate. Until very recently, they had lived normal lives. Only two or three days ago they had been with their loved ones, had gone with them through the selection, and then they were separated. They couldn't understand what was happening. Overwhelmed by worries about their families, many of them cried out for their fathers, mothers, or husbands. Berta and I looked at each other in silence. We knew only too well where those relatives were.

Each of us had been given an extra piece of bread, but none of us knew how long the trip would take or how long the bread ration was supposed to last. Many months in Auschwitz had taught us to be suspicious and never to save a piece of bread for the next day: Some hungry prisoner might come and steal it. Berta and I therefore ate our entire ration. It had been a long time since we had had the wonderful feeling of having enough to eat.

Evening came, and now it was our turn to stretch out on the floor of the boxcar and go to sleep. The SS man who was in the car with us pulled out his supper—a chunk of bread, wurst, and cheese—and began to eat heartily. My mouth watered at the smell of real wurst, and no matter how I tried I couldn't take my eyes off his food. He noticed that I was staring but made no effort to offer us anything. After he finished eating, he too lay down to sleep. He was lying next to me, and I pushed myself as far away from him as I could. But suddenly I felt his hand on me. Like a crazed woman I jumped up, stumbling over the others lying there, trying to get as far away from him as possible.

It wasn't until the following evening that the train stopped and we were let off. We didn't know where we were, but at least we were not at Auschwitz. Wherever we were, it couldn't be as horrible as that place had been.

We had a long walk ahead of us, and it had gotten dark as we wearily plodded along when suddenly my foot struck something. I bent down and picked up a big iron horseshoe. Horseshoes bring good luck! I began to feel confident that I would survive, and I held on to the horseshoe as though it really had protective power. This was my second talisman. The little golden chain with the medallion had become a permanent fixture under my tongue. It saw the light of day only at mealtimes. And now, the horseshoe. When people are completely at the mercy of others, they will cling to little things. Maybe it's all nonsense, but such beliefs give support and helped me enormously to get through the most dreadful times.

At last we came to a gate and saw the outlines of barracks surrounded by barbed wire. So here we were, in yet another concentration camp. Were there gas chambers here, too? We were led to a newly constructed barracks that had wooden bunks only two tiers high. And wonder of wonders! There were straw sacks and clean blankets on these bunks. The barracks itself was not large and had been subdivided into smaller rooms by wooden partitions. About twenty bunks lined the walls in each of the rooms. A large iron stove stood in the middle. What luxury! We couldn't believe our eyes.

Then an SS woman appeared. She was the head guard for the women prisoners. She was gaunt, between thirty-five and forty years old, with piercing, icy gray eyes and a bestial expression. Her face was flattened, sallow, and so ugly that later I wasn't at all surprised at her sadistic behavior. Her voice reminded me of the squawking of a crow—it had no human inflection. In general, the Germans took it for granted that everyone knew the language of the "master race," so she didn't care whether the Hungarian women understood her or not. Some ten guards reported to her. Perhaps some of these subordinates would have been more humane, but all of them seemed to be afraid of their brutal boss.

By now I had spent more than two and a half years in concentration camps. In Ravensbrück and Theresienstadt I had come to know how the SS women behaved, beating us and screaming at us like Furies. It was plain to see that they took satisfaction from this inhumane behavior. When two of them were on duty together, they would compete with each other in their brutal and abusive treatment of the prisoners. We tried to stay out of their way as much as possible.

Now the head guard addressed us. This was a labor camp, and we were here to work, she said. Anyone who tried to shirk work or committed sabotage would be punished severely or put into the bunker—a dark, windowless room where there was no food or water. Sometimes days would pass before such an offender was let out. By then she was either half crazy or dead. The senior guard gave us a detailed schedule that we had to adhere to. But she still did not tell us where we were or what kind of work we would be doing. After she left, we dropped onto our luxurious straw sacks, dead tired.

A camp barracks at Taucha, near Leipzig, in 1945, after liberation.

The next morning, after a wonderful night's sleep, we were informed by the camp commandant that we were in Taucha, near Leipzig, a labor camp satellite of the Buchenwald concentration camp. He must have noticed that not all the women understood what he was saying, because he asked, "Is there anyone here who speaks German?"

I impulsively raised my hand, and from that day on I became the camp interpreter.

After the inevitable roll call, we were led out of the camp, where we were joined by a column of male prisoners. At a nearby factory each of us was assigned to a department. Work began. Formerly this had been the HASAG Works, a plant that manufactured lightbulbs. It had been converted to produce an antitank rocket launcher called a Panzerfaust, which resembled a bazooka. German foremen showed us what to do, and soldiers stood guard as we worked.

At roll call one morning shortly after I arrived in Taucha, the camp commandant asked me to step forward. "Pick four girls," he ordered. "You will be taken by truck to another workplace."

My heart skipped a beat. After nine months in Auschwitz, being driven off in a truck could only mean that we were going to the gas chamber.

"Sir," I said, "please pick the girls yourself. I don't want this on my conscience."

Never having seen the Auschwitz gas chambers, he couldn't possibly have understood the reason for my reluctance. He chose four strong, good-looking girls from among the Hungarian women, who still looked well nourished because they had only recently been deported to Auschwitz.

The rest of the women left camp in rows of five, while we stayed behind. We had no idea where we were going. A short time later, a truck covered with a tarpaulin drove up. Beside the driver's compartment there was a long oval tank filled with brown coal. Later we found out that because gasoline was not readily available in Germany, most cars and trucks ran on coal gas. The five of us, guarded by an armed soldier, climbed into the truck. Nobody said a word during the trip. At last the truck stopped and the soldier ordered us to get out.

We were facing a large rectangular building that gave no indication of what it contained. The soldier herded us inside. I entered an enormous room and stood stock-still in amazement. Was I caught up in a dream? There were shelves all along the walls, four or five rows of shelves, and on each were piled loaves of bread. *Bread!* I couldn't believe my eyes. Could this be real? Could this much bread exist in any one place at any one time? My stomach screamed with hunger; I wanted to grab one of the loaves and eat it in one sitting. No, not eat it but, rather, rip into it with the few teeth I still had. But I had learned the hard way to be careful, to avoid provoking unnecessary beatings by the guards.

We were ordered to take five loaves on each arm and to load them onto the truck. On the way out of the building we had to pass a woman who was keeping track of our trips. She pushed buttons on a little calculator each time we passed her, but she didn't count the loaves we were carrying. Suddenly I had a daring thought: What if, "by mistake," I were to carry out twelve loaves of bread instead of ten?

I tried it. With a pounding heart, I took twelve loaves and walked by the woman and through the door to the truck. I had no idea how I would get the two extra loaves out of the truck later, but I knew that this was a chance to ensure survival. If I had bread to eat, I might remain alive. So I learned to steal—in the literal sense of the word. I wouldn't have stolen so much as a crumb from my fellow prisoners, who had barely enough food to keep them alive, but stealing from the Germans was another matter. The more bread I could take into the camp, the more would be distributed to the prisoners. I told the other girls, "Carry out ten loaves three times and then every fourth time, take out twelve." It wasn't long before we turned into an efficient gang of thieves. When the truck was fully loaded, the baker's wife called us back in and gave each of us the most beautiful, the most prized gift I have ever received in my life: a loaf of bread. How can I explain to anyone who has not been in a concentration camp what that loaf of bread meant to me? I had to keep a tight rein on myself not to break down in tears. Today, if you were to give me the largest and most beautiful diamond on earth, it would not make me as happy as I was then with my loaf of bread. I immediately walked up to our soldier guard and said, "Each of us has just been given a loaf of bread by the baker's wife. I wanted you to know that, because we'd like to take this bread back to our barracks."

"Yes, yes," he nodded. "I saw her give it to you."

On the drive back to the camp, we had a feverish discussion: How to get the bread we had stolen into the prison blocks. We were wearing skirts and hip-length jackets over our blouses, all made of the same gray-and-blue striped material. As we began to unload the truck, I saw that our guard was deeply immersed in conversation with an SS woman. I took off my jacket, threw it over my shoulder, and concealed a loaf of bread under the jacket. The soldier didn't notice. I ran into the barracks and hid the bread under my straw pallet. Then I raced back out to continue with the unloading. In this way I managed to take several loaves into the block. So did the others. When we finished the unloading, I told the soldier that we would now take our gift loaves inside, and he said to go right ahead.

The bread we brought into the camp was stored in the food depot, which was supervised by Rosa, a political prisoner. She was German and, as I recall, a communist. Under her direction the food depot was a model of order and neatness. The German camp administrators relied on her completely: all in and out shipments were always correctly and precisely entered in her record books. I didn't know much about Rosa the first time we came back from the bakery and unloaded the bread. I couldn't have known that everything would be monitored so carefully. After the bread had been neatly shelved, Rosa came out and reported to the soldier the number of loaves she had received. She must have made a mistake, he told her, since he had brought less bread into the camp than she reported receiving. Rosa's feelings were hurt. How could he say that? Her calculations were always precise! We five just stood there, looking innocent. We knew why there was a surplus.

Once we were back in the block each of us devoured a whole loaf of bread. What opulence, what joy, what a wonderful feeling not to be hungry anymore. When the other inmates came back from the factory, we began to distribute bread to them. Unfortunately, there wasn't enough for everybody, but we consoled those who didn't get any with assurances that they would be luckier next time.

The Taucha labor camp actually consisted of two connecting camps. Entering through a common gate one came first to the women's camp; after that, one arrived at the men's camp, which was separated from the women's camp by a barbed-wire fence. However, the latrines at one end were accessible from both sides. The men's latrines were separated from the women's by a wooden wall. Here we could sometimes talk with the men. There were prisoners from Poland and the Protectorate in the men's camp. All the Czechs had come from Theresienstadt. In the women's camp there were also Gypsies, who were housed some distance away from us. A camp kitchen prepared meals for both the men's and the women's camps, as well as for the SS and the guards. Prisoners worked in the kitchens under SS supervision. Not far from the kitchen was a large dining room that had a stage at one end, but this room was never used for meals. Another barracks served as sick bay, where Alex Herrmann, a Czech doctor who had come from Theresienstadt, cared for patients. He was the doctor for both camps. Taucha differed from Auschwitz in at least two significant respects: Its barbed-wire fence was not electrified, and there were no gas chambers.

The barracks for the German staff of the camp were to the right of the entrance gate, some distance away from our quarters. As I recall, the camp commandant and the women guards were members of the SS; all the other Germans were Wehrmacht personnel. There was an air-raid shelter in the camp, for the exclusive use of the Germans. Prisoners were strictly forbidden to enter the shelter, since it really didn't matter if they were killed by bombs. In Auschwitz there had been no air raids, but in Taucha they were an almost daily occurrence. First a warning signal and later the full alarm would sound, but by then the bombs were already falling. When the Germans heard the warning signal, they would run down into the bomb shelter. The prisoners were ordered into the barracks and forbidden to look outside. But I couldn't bear to stay cooped up, so

I watched with delight as the Allied planes first marked their targets with smoke bombs; then the bombers dropped their payloads on the marked spots. We could hear the detonations; each one sounded like the joyful pealing of bells to us. Instinctively, we knew that the end of the war was near, and that these daily raids were not restricted to Taucha and Leipzig. Bombs were falling on all of Germany. Of course, we had no exact information about the status of the war, and the uncertainty we felt was depressing. We could only speculate on when the fighting would end and how and by whom we would be liberated. The nighttime raids were particularly beautiful and exciting. Naturally, there could be no thought of sleep. We would stand in front of our block and look up at the sky. Instead of the smoke bombs that were used in the daytime, the planes at night dropped multicolored flares to mark their targets. The sky looked like a Christmas tree, and we were elated not only because Germany was being bombed but because it was a fantastic spectacle. None of us was concerned with the people who lay buried under the rubble, any more than the Germans had worried about how many Jews they had gassed. It was surprising that the camp was not hit by a single bomb, even at night.

I don't recall ever having felt fear during these air raids. What more could possibly happen to me? All they could take from me now was my life. Once out from under the shadow of the gas chambers, our spirits and our will to live gradually returned. We were no longer under the strict surveillance of the SS, no longer subject to their cruelties and those of the Kapos. The girls who worked in the factory never talked about having been punished or exposed to the kind of SS sadism I had experienced in Auschwitz. But it troubled them that they were producing antitank rocket launchers for German soldiers to use against our liberators. Some tried to sabotage the production, but that never worked, and if they were caught they would be sent into the bunker.

Occasionally a German—but never a soldier or an SS man—working in the factory would secretly pass a cigarette or a piece of bread and wurst to one of the girls, who then feared that he would demand that she reciprocate with some sexual favor. But even though the possibility of this was sometimes mentioned, sex was never forced on the women. The Germans in Taucha were afraid of committing *Rassenschande* (race defilement), a crime that was severely punished under the law.

Berta was appointed block elder. This meant that she no longer had to leave the camp to go to work. She always kept herself and her block clean and neat, and she never said a mean or sharp word to anyone. The girls were very fond of her. I say girls, but among us there were quite a few married women who only recently had been separated from their husbands. This separation was painful, and after work at night their conversations always dwelled on the same topic: their young husbands. They didn't know what had happened to their men, so they cried for them and tried to console one another. They had been in the camps for a relatively short time and therefore didn't know enough to expect the worst. It seemed quite natural that these women would try to comfort one another with caresses and physical closeness. But when we found out that there were three lesbian couples in our block, it upset us considerably. None of us thought of putting an end to these affairs, however. Living in such unnatural circumstances, we did not feel that we had the right to pass judgment. Each of us yearned for closeness, belonging, and love.

After I lost my child I was completely isolated emotionally, and desperately needed a reassuring touch, a consoling word, and understanding from someone who was closer than a friend. But I had no one except Berta. And though she sympathized with my need, she could not console me. In my darkest moments my thoughts turned to Koni. But I was immediately overcome with bitterness at his behavior in the family camp when I was so miserable and he failed to give me the support that I so desperately needed.

I could understand the yearning for life in Auschwitz in the shadow of the gas chambers, but I could not then, and cannot today, understand how one human being can abandon another in need. All of us had to drop our masks in the concentration camps, and our real selves came to light. No one could pretend to be what he wasn't; everyone had to show his true character.

I now felt a certain indifference because I had no one to love, and I often wondered about the why and wherefore of life. I found one answer to the question "Why go on living?" in the hope that my sister, my father, and other close relatives might still be alive. I had to survive in order to see them again. But when I thought of Auschwitz, I was no longer sure I ever would, and I was overwhelmed by hopelessness. The answer to the question "Wherefore?" came from my work on the truck. Life took on meaning because of my stealing. How absurd that sounds! But by stealing I could help my fellow prisoners. They now suffered less from hunger, and I knew that if I were to give up, their bread-ration supplement would stop. I grabbed at these straws and, feeling stronger because we were eating better, I began with all my might to work—and to steal.

We soon realized that we were trucking not only bread into the camp but that we actually constituted the camp's primary transport squad. We brought in all the essentials: not only rations for the prisoners and the German staff but also coal, ammunition, tools, nails, and many everyday products for the Germans. Once a week we took dirty clothes to the laundry and then brought the clean things back to camp. Since we usually drove to Leipzig to do this, we called ourselves the *Leipzig-Kommando,* the Leipzig Work Detail. Everybody else called us that, too.

Whenever we were ordered to load coal onto the truck at the railway station, we drove there without the truck bed being covered by the tarpaulin. Often it rained or snowed, and we would freeze. We were given huge shovels to load the coal into the truck—really hard labor that usually is done by men. I don't quite know how we managed to do it. The work did have one advantage: Although we froze on the drive to the station, we quickly warmed up once we began shoveling. When the truck was full, we had to sit, overheated and sweating, on top of the pile of coal for the drive back to camp. I still marvel that none of us caught pneumonia during this, the winter of 1944–1945. The coal-loading once a week was our hardest job. The coal we brought back had to make do for the truck, which ran on coal gas; for the kitchen; and for the living quarters of the Germans. We soon discovered that we could kick pieces of coal off the truck as we passed our living quarters. Later, on the way to our blocks, we would collect these chunks and eventually we would use them to make an occasional fire in the barracks stove. We got to be so skillful at this that we would pick up enough coal to last a whole week of cold evenings. Most important, though, was that once the iron stovepipe was hot enough, we could "iron" the seams of our prison clothes to kill the lice that were hiding inside them. On "heating day" in our block, girls from all the other blocks lined up to iron the lice in their seams, and we had the wonderful feeling that by stealing the coal we were helping our fellow prisoners cope with the infestation of lice.

After finishing our shift on the coal detail, we scrubbed the truck clean and headed for the laundry. But first I would ask the guard for clean clothes for the five of us. We received these from the clothes depot and were able to wear clean outfits on our drive to the city the next day. It was mostly the German wash that was sent to the laundry; only a few pieces belonged to the prisoners. We had no underwear, no stockings or socks, and we wore clogs instead of shoes. Soon we began to steal some of the underwear that belonged to the SS women. We gave Berta a set of stolen underthings, and after three years of imprisonment I finally came into possession of a nightgown to wear. What luxury!

Whenever we were sent to pick up flour, sugar, and other groceries, the five of us worked with enthusiasm, because not only did we have the chance to get out of the camp but we were also helping the other prisoners. By then we had developed some proficiency at stealing and we were gradually adding new techniques to our repertoire. We stole a sewing needle (a truly valuable item) from the clothing depot and obtained thread by unraveling the edgings of our blankets. We cut up a linen shirt that we had stolen and sewed five little bags with drawstrings at the top. One of us would poke a hole into a sack of sugar with a sharpened sliver of wood and fill up these little bags while the rest of us surrounded her to keep the guard from seeing what was going on. Then we concealed the bags under our clothes. Sugar contained calories, which gave us strength. In this way after each of our trips we always brought back something that had to be distributed immediately. It wouldn't do if these luxury items were discovered during a search of the barracks. That would have meant the end of our profitable operation.

Sometimes we were taken into farm fields, where we pulled carrots from the frozen ground and loaded them onto the truck. Tears came to my eyes the first time I bit into one of these unwashed carrots; almost three years had passed since I had eaten anything this wonderful. At last our bodies were getting some of the vitamins they needed so badly. I even regained normal vision. Of course, the carrots were intended for the Germans. They were much too good for the prisoners! As with the coal, we pushed some of the carrots off the truck as we drove through the camp with our valuable load. It was good to see the women inmates rush over to pick them up, though not everyone managed to get one. Frequently, we harvested onions and hauled them into camp. Each time, we went through the same distribution routine.

I had been in Taucha for about three months when I developed an abscess in my left armpit, and in no time at all it turned into a huge swelling with many smaller abscesses. At first I didn't want to report to sick bay because I was afraid of losing my job. Instead, I went to see Dr. Alex Herrmann, to whom I had often slipped some of the stolen bread. I begged him to help me so that I could go on working. He found that I was running a high fever. My arm was purplish-red and swollen. His diagnosis: blood poisoning. He forced me to stop working and to report to the hospital block. But the hospital personnel had no medicines or painkillers. There was absolutely nothing they could give me.

Alex saw only one way out: He would have to cut open the abscess to allow the pus to drain, in the hope that the septicemia would then disappear. He carefully explained this to me, warning me that he had no anesthetic but that this was the only way to save my life. The incision had to be made immediately. Alex boiled his only scalpel in a kitchen pot to sterilize it. I don't remember how many people had to hold me down, but I'll never forget the dreadful pain as he cut into the boil. Then he cleaned the wound as best he could and made a bandage out of strips of paper, which were instantly soaked through. The flow of pus seemed endless. I lay on my pallet, sick once more, and all the misery of my past and my present inundated me. But thanks to Alex and Berta's loving care I was free of fever within a few days, and ready to go back to work. Meanwhile, my companions on the Leipzig detail had taken on another girl to fill in for me, since the four of them couldn't do all the work in the allotted time. They had told the girl that as soon as I was well again she would have to leave. Working in the Leipzig detail was one of the most sought-after jobs in Taucha.

Rosa, the woman in charge of the food depot and the bread stores, continued to be puzzled by the overage of bread and talked about it with the guard who reported how much bread we brought with each load. Listening to them argue amused us at first, but soon we began to worry that our ongoing theft would be discovered. We had no choice but to let Rosa in on our secret. When we told her what we were doing, her reaction was one of horror and disgust, and it took us a long time to convince her that she, who was also a prisoner, should see things from our perspective. We pleaded with her to put herself in the place of the hungry inmates, but obviously this was not easy for her, since she had had plenty of bread to eat all along. The German camp administration had ordered Rosa to distribute a specified ration of bread to the prisoners every day. As a German, she had been raised to strictly obey all rules and regulations and never to violate them. It took us quite a while to persuade her that the camp administration would never notice if she distributed a third of a loaf instead of a quarter. Still, we were afraid that Rosa would not be able to live with this lie and that she would report us to the administration. We had to assure her over and over again that this well-intentioned stealing would remain a secret between us. It was no use. Then someone had an idea. Notwithstanding the contradiction this presented to her communist background, Rosa was also very pious and God-fearing, so we told her that her good deed would be observed and her charity recorded in heaven, and that she would be remembered and protected for all eternity. That did it. Thereafter she dutifully doled out a third of a loaf for each prisoner. But she was not fully convinced and continued to feel that she was an evildoer, a sinner, and every night she prayed for forgiveness. I still feel good today about what we did, especially when we found out later that toward the end of the war prisoners in the other camps received only two or three thin slices of bread a day.

Whenever we brought bread back to our quarters, we cut it up—with a stolen knife, of course—and hid the pieces under our blouses until the prisoners came back from the factory in the evening. Then we would run to the latrines, which the men had to pass on the way to their camp. Standing close to the wall, we'd throw pieces of bread to them, and they eagerly caught them. We had to be very careful not to be caught by the SS guards.

In the evenings, while we were resting, trying to gather strength for the coming day, we often had discussions about this and that. We had no books, no newspapers, nothing that might satisfy us intellectually. But during the course of my long imprisonment I had learned that becoming indifferent and allowing oneself to lose interest in the world around one was like a self-imposed death sentence. Whenever we saw this happening to someone, we tried to pull her out of her apathy by giving her something to think about and involving her in our discussions. All this developed into a lively activity that I called psychological or spiritual resistance. We knew that the

Nazis wanted not only to kill us physically but to annihilate us intellectually and spiritually. Only by keeping our minds active could we prevent them from accomplishing this. And therefore we would gather together in the evenings to listen to other prisoners give talks. We cooked imaginary meals, as Berta and I had done in Auschwitz, and we exchanged recipes. We discussed school subjects, books, music, and sports. Or we simply sat around and gossiped about camp happenings.

There was a woman in Taucha, perhaps forty years old, who did not join in our conversations. I frequently gave her a piece of bread, which she accepted, looking ashamed but grateful. After a while I found out that she had once been a physician but that she had not practiced for several years before her imprisonment. As a hobby, she had begun to study astrology, the occult, and hypnosis. Because we had never seen or participated in a hypnosis session, I asked her if she would hypnotize one of us. She agreed enthusiastically. It would give her something worthwhile to do in this bleak camp existence. True, we were thinking more of entertainment than science. But gradually we came to recognize this woman's knowledge and ability.

After a short search she found a seventeen-year-old girl who, she believed, would make an excellent subject to serve as a medium. When she began the hypnosis, we had to remain absolutely silent in order not to disturb the subject. Many of the prisoners asked questions of the medium during the session and presumably received detailed answers. I never tried to ask any questions; I was afraid I would hear that some of those I loved were no longer alive.

The following Sunday (we did not have to work on Sundays), when the SS guards and the soldiers were resting and no unwanted visitors were expected, the woman doctor proposed another hypnosis session. We were all for it. There was complete and tense silence, and after a few minutes the subject fell asleep. Suddenly the door to our room was opened and the head guard walked in. The blood froze in my veins, but the quick-witted doctor explained the situation to the guard, asking her not to wake the girl because that would frighten her. "Would you be interested in getting news of your loved ones?" she asked the SS woman. "If so, touch the hand of the subject and ask her something."

At first the guard hesitated; you could see indecision in her unattractive face, then she reached out and touched the girl's hand. The girl, still in a deep hypnotic trance, became highly agitated and screamed, "Go away, you're my enemy! Go away! Go away!"

We were terrified. How would the SS woman react? I should emphasize that the girl herself could not see who had touched her because she was facing in the opposite direction. The doctor took the girl's hand, calmed her down, and asked the guard to try again. This time the girl remained calm as she began to answer the guard's questions. She said she saw a youth in a uniform, a Hitler Youth uniform—the head guard's son. For the first time we saw a trace of emotion flit across the SS woman's face. But it vanished as soon as she saw us watching her. She must have realized the position she had put herself in, because she turned around and left the room without saying another word.

One day the doctor suggested that I bring her a piece of paper, some ink, and a sliver of wood. She wanted to do something for me, she said, in appreciation for the bread I had been giving her. It all sounded a little ridiculous, but I felt sorry for her and went along with her peculiar request. Finding a sliver of wood was no problem, but getting paper and ink, that was more difficult. Eventually I found both.

The doctor ceremoniously dropped a few blots of ink onto the paper and with the sliver of wood she wrote my initials in one corner. Fascinated, I watched and wondered what would come of all this. Next she folded the paper, pressing it together firmly. After some time had elapsed, she unfolded it and stared at it as if she could see something there. All I could see was one big, blurry inkblot. She then began to tell me about various things that had happened in my past. I smiled inwardly, because I was sure that she had heard about these episodes either from me or from the other prisoners. But I perked up when she said, "You will meet a widower in this camp, and you will marry him after your liberation."

Poor old woman, I thought. All this occult stuff has gone to your head. I was all of twenty-two years old, and my idea of a widower was an old man with a long beard. I was convinced that I would never marry again, and even if I did, it certainly would not be a widower. Sad to say, although we tried everything possible to take care of the doctor, bringing her extra food and encouraging her, she became increasingly apathetic, lost her will to live, and died there in Taucha.

On one of our trips we went to a cheese factory where we were supposed to load cheeses packed in cardboard boxes onto the truck. The driver drove the vehicle into the factory through a large entryway, and we began loading. Since it was stormy and snowing outside, the driver decided to close the entrance door to keep out the icy draft. The next thing I knew one of the girls, and then another and another, reeled and fell unconscious on the floor. I, too, began to feel dizzy, and I called out to the driver to open the door to let in fresh air. I cannot recall what happened after that.

When we five Leipzig detail girls regained consciousness, we saw that we were back in camp, in the hospital block. Alex was bending over us, looking concerned; he told us that we had been overcome by coal gas. And then something incredible happened: The head guard came in carrying a can of milk for us. Milk! It had been almost three years since I had seen or drunk any milk, and I had forgotten how it tasted. I would gladly have gone through another coal-gas-poisoning experience just to get more milk.

The winter of 1944–1945 was bitterly cold. Wearing our flimsy prison clothes, we sat in the truck bed without protection from the tarpaulin, which was put up only for the bread shipments. With our backs against the driver's cab, we tried to shield ourselves from the cold and the wind, squeezing close together for warmth. The soldier who accompanied us also rode in the back of the truck, but he was wearing a sweater, a coat, earmuffs, a warm hat, and gloves. In contrast, our hands and legs froze, and when we came into a warm place they itched and hurt terribly while thawing out. But, we told ourselves, that was the price we had to pay for our "rewarding" work. Those who worked in the factory didn't suffer from the cold, but they were always hungry.

We hardly talked to the soldier guard. Whenever we arrived at one of the larger factories to load the truck, he would ask us not to run away. But where could we have run in our prison clothes, and to whom could we have appealed here in the middle of enemy territory? We would have been turned in and shot. Who would have been willing to help us? We thought of the soldier as an older man—he was about forty—and we took comfort in the fact that he was from the Wehrmacht and not the SS. Yet we were certain that if we had tried to escape he would not have hesitated to shoot us; those were his orders. At the various firms where we picked up goods, the Germans who worked there always gave us a wide berth. Our clothes made it obvious that we were prisoners and consequently "enemies of the Reich." It was forbidden to approach or talk to us. They stared at us with curiosity, as though we were creatures from another planet.

At exactly ten o'clock each morning a bell would sound in all the factories, signaling a half-hour break. For the German workers this meant it was time to eat; for us it meant only time to rest. There were loudspeakers in all the factories, and at that hour they carried recorded classical music. Starved for a little culture, we would sit in a corner or on some steps and listen. Most of the time the interlude would begin with Wagner and finish with Wagner, the pride of the Germans. Ever since, I have refused to listen to Wagner because his music brings back memories I want to avoid. They also played the music of other composers, often melodies that were familiar to me. Involuntarily, I would hum along. Sometimes the music made me cry, because it reminded me of home, of my studies with Aranka Wasserberger, my piano teacher, and the record collection on

Mount Visalaja. One day the soldier who was guarding us asked me, "What's that they're playing? Who wrote it?"

I told him what it was and who composed it, and from that time on, whenever there was a morning music break he would ask me to identify the various compositions. "How come you know so much about music?" he asked one day.

I told him briefly about my studies. "If you like music so much," he said to my surprise, "you can come to scrub the floor in my room after work and I'll let you listen to music on my radio. I'll expect you at five o'clock this afternoon."

I was terrified. Why would he want me to come to his room? What did he expect above and beyond the floor scrubbing? The girls and I frantically discussed how I could get out of this predicament, but we couldn't think of a way, so I had no choice but to go and clean his floor. The moment I appeared, the soldier tuned his radio to a music program and left. I heaved a sigh of relief, scrubbed the floor until it was clean, and then disappeared. From that day on, I washed that floor twice a week, and gladly, because as soon as the soldier left I would begin to search for news broadcasts on his radio. As a result, I was well informed about the international political situation, if only from the German perspective. I immediately reported what I had heard to Alex, who passed the information along to the prisoners in the men's camp. This was the first time during my long imprisonment that I was able to listen to news reports instead of being dependent on rumors whispered by other inmates. Now I could hear directly about the "victorious" retreat of the German armies.

Except for the prisoners who worked in the HASAG factory making Panzerfaust antitank weapons, our Leipzig detail was the only group that left the camp. We got to know the surroundings and could see what was happening beyond the barbed wire. I regularly told Alex where we had been, whom we had met, and what materials we had trucked back to the camp. We would often meet prisoners of war or drive by their camps. Twice we transported ammunition and weapons back to the camp, and I immediately told Alex where these were stored. In this way an underground movement was created, with Alex acting as the liaison between the men's and the women's camps. This surveillance was very important to us. It gave us a sense of security and a certain degree of pride: At least we were doing something and not just letting things happen to us. We made plans with Alex for our liberation, and we talked about the assignment each of us would have when that day came, whom we would let in on our secret plans, and if and when we could start thinking of escaping.

In addition to Alex, three other men worked in both the men's and the women's camps. Actually, only two of them were men; the third was at most thirteen or fourteen years old. These three were designated electricians and were in charge of the electric power supply for the two camps. Bobby, the oldest, came from Vienna and was a trained electrician. The other two, Erich and Polda Huppert (brothers who came from my hometown, Ostrava, but were not related to me) had never before worked as electricians or in any related line of work.

When Erich and Polda arrived at the selection in Auschwitz from Theresienstadt in October 1944, Erich was told to state his profession. Some instinct prompted him to say that he was an electrician by trade, and he was sent to the side that meant life. But he didn't leave the selection site right away, because he thought that his little brother, Polda, might be sent to the other side, the death side. The moment they asked Polda his age, Erich spoke up: "He's seventeen and a good electrician." Polda was also sent to the "good" side, where quite a few men, representing all sorts of trades, were already gathered. They were informed that they would be sent to a labor camp. A bit like cattle being branded, each received a stamp on his forehead indicating that he would be working at a trade. They were told to preserve the stamp carefully. Every man knew it was his visa out of Auschwitz, and they scarcely dared to go to sleep for fear that the stamp might get rubbed off or disappear during the night.

Erich took care of his little brother and was like a father to the boy, never letting him out of his sight. Bobby, the real electrician, taught the brothers how to do minor electrical jobs, and they soon turned into his indispensable assistants.

The high-voltage power station for the camp was located in a small building in the women's camp. This was Bobby's domain, and no one else was allowed to enter the place. I would knock on the door whenever I had some bread to bring to them. Since the electricians were often called to fix things in the kitchen, from time to time they received food there, too. Polda was always the first to get his portion—the boy was still growing and needed it more than the others. Bobby fell in love with a pretty young Hungarian woman, Babika, and they spent many a happy hour in the little power house.

I gave Bobby the same information I passed along to Alex, because he too was able to move about freely in both camps. Our hope grew that the war would soon end, and this gave us the strength and the will to survive. Having lived through so much horror, we could not give up now.

On New Year's Eve, the last day of 1944, the Leipzig detail had its hands full bringing food and wine into the camp for a celebration the Germans were having. The five of us had been busy with our feet for the past few days, kicking as much coal and as many carrots as possible off the truck. Knowing that the Germans would be busy, we decided to organize our own celebration. We already had bread, carrots, and coal, and with a little extra effort the five of us were also able to steal a teapot, sugar, and some jam. Having provided for the evening's physical nourishment, we now had to think of some sort of entertainment. In our block there were women from various countries, and now they were asked to present something that was typical of their homeland. I had also stolen a red pencil to be used by our "performing artists" as lipstick.

It was dark outside when we heard singing coming from the German quarters. This was the signal for us to begin our celebration. We started a fire in the iron stove, and once the heat spread, our good mood expanded and permeated the block. After a lovely dinner, we started our international program. There were Hungarian, Slovakian, Czech, Polish, and French songs and poems. Since no one had offered to do anything German, I decided to sing a song from a German operetta, slightly adapting the words to suit our present circumstances:

Es steht hier ein Häftling in Häftlingstracht,
von draussen her wird er streng bewacht.
Seine Heimat, ach, die ist so fern,
seinen Weg erhellt ihm gar kein Stern.
Rings um ihn her alles schweigt,
eine Träne ihm ins Auge steigt.
Und er fühlt, wie's im Herzen frisst und nagt,
wenn der Mensch verhaftet ist,
und er fragt und er klagt:
Hast Du dort droben vergessen auf mich,
es sehnt doch mein Herz nach Freiheit sich!
Bitte, oh bitte! Ich flehe Dich an!
Mach, dass ich bald nach Hause geh'n kann.

Here stands a prisoner in prisoner's garb,
Outside his jailers keep constant guard.
His homeland, alas! is far, quite far,
His road not lit by a single star.
Around him all is dark and still;
tears fill his eyes against his will.
He feels his heart being gnawed and torn
by the misery of captivity.
And he asks and pleads in a voice forlorn:
Have You, up there, forgotten me?
My heart yearns to be free!
I beg you and cry unto you, Lord above!
Let me go home soon to those I love.

I was singing this song, standing with my back to the door, and couldn't understand the odd signals some of the inmates seemed to be giving me. After I finished, I suddenly heard a man's voice behind me say, "Well now, what sort of show have you got going here?"

It was the camp commandant, an SS man. We had been so sure that once the Germans started their celebration we wouldn't be receiving visits from them! I still don't know what gave me the courage to ask, "Sir, did you like the song? Would you like me to sing another one?"

Without answering he turned and walked off. But when he reached the door, he said, "Report to my office tomorrow morning at ten!"

Our New Year's Eve celebration was over. Everyone wondered what would happen to me the next day. An order like the one given by the commandant generally signified some sort of punishment. The women tried to give me advice, and everyone wished me well. The next day I went to the commandant's office, my head held high. I was resolved not to let him see my fear. After all, the end of the war and our liberation seemed so close at hand now. When I walked into his office I was surprised to hear him say, "Within ten days you will put together a full-length cabaret performance. The dining-room block with its stage are at your disposal. There will be a piano brought in to accompany the singers."

"But sir," I said, "I've never done anything like that before. I have no idea how to do it; how do you put a cabaret program together?"

"That's your problem. I just gave you an order. If you don't obey, I'll send you to the bunker."

As soon as I got back to the block the other prisoners gathered around me, and I told them what the commandant had said. We tried frantically to come up with a cabaret program. Then an idea occurred to me. I would involve our fellow prisoners, the Gypsies! Although I had not worked with them in the factory, I had gone to their block from time to time to talk with them and to take them bread. I didn't understand the language they spoke among themselves, but most of the time they seemed good-humored despite their hunger and misery. When things looked desperate, they would sing and dance, and I would watch enthralled. I was welcomed because I never went to their block without taking some bread, and because most of the Gypsy women came from Germany and spoke excellent German we had no trouble understanding one another. After I told them about my encounter with the camp commandant and my concern about producing a decent show, we exchanged a few ideas, and in no time we had put together a cabaret program. There were to be songs in various languages and a few sketches prepared and performed by my block mates. Then the Gypsies would do some of their traditional lively dances interspersed with tap dancing. The piano accompanist would be a Polish prisoner, a woman who in her former life had played for silent films. The prospects looked good.

As paradoxical as it may sound, this marked the beginning of ten wonderful days. All our spare time was taken up with rehearsals. It was a demonstration of the friendship and comradeship that bound us together. Nobody wanted Ruth of the Leipzig detail to be locked up in the bunker—perhaps because that would have meant a loss of bread for everybody—so the women and girls did their utmost to make things work. This brief period gave purpose to life in the camp and offered our strong will to survive a chance to make itself felt.

On the day of the performance we walked into the dining room and found it filled with SS people and Wehrmacht soldiers. Were there really that many Germans in Taucha? The show went off without a hitch. Each of us did her best so that no one would be punished. The costumes were everyday prison garb, and there was no scenery, but the piano was given a place of honor at the front of the stage. And then, at the conclusion of the first number, a miracle: The Germans began to applaud—faintly at first, then the applause grew stronger, louder. Soldiers and SS men and women were clapping for political prisoners and Jews and Gypsies. And they were aware whom they were applauding. Listen, you supermen, I thought, we have managed to show you that we're human beings, and that despite your rule of terror we still have our pride. And now you are applauding us. Thank you for giving us the chance to show you that you haven't succeeded in breaking our spirit.

Bombs continued to fall on the area surrounding the camp, and we also began to hear artillery fire. The front was getting closer. Our thoughts kept turning to our imminent liberation; we could think of nothing else, and those who worked in the factory as well as those in the Leipzig detail began to neglect their work. Nobody knew how we would be freed or what the Germans were planning to do with us. But one thing was clear: It wasn't going to be easy or simple. We were on edge, each of us eager for some certainty, and this restless longing wasn't limited to the prisoners; the SS and the other Germans felt it, too. It was obvious that they had begun to relax their strict rules. They were less sure of themselves. The daily screaming and shouting at prisoners had practically stopped, and the SS women now hardly ever came by to inspect our things.

In February 1945, the camp commandant ordered me to get another cabaret program ready within fourteen days. This time I was much more self-assured and I told him, "Unfortunately, we don't have enough female performers. But I'm sure there are some talented people in the men's camp, and with their help we could put together a good program."

To my surprise he said, "Come to the dining-room block with your performers this evening at six. We'll see to it that the men are there, too, so that together you can rehearse to put on a good show."

Evidently the commandant wanted us to do this show as a distraction from the frequent bombardments and to put a damper on the restlessness among the Germans and the prisoners. For us this was a unique opportunity to get together with the men and to talk to them about the situation in camp and the possibility of an escape attempt.

When we arrived in the dining room, seven men, most of them Czechs who had left Theresienstadt in October 1944, were waiting for us. One of them was Arnost Horner, whom I knew well from my days in the ghetto. We wanted to hug each other, but we restrained ourselves because the Nazis were watching us closely. Instead, we stood some distance apart and spoke to each other in Czech. Our conversation had nothing to do with the upcoming performance; rather, I inundated him with questions about mutual friends in Theresienstadt and what had happened to them.

Before he could answer, I glanced at the stage. Two men, wearing prison clothes and boxing gloves, were boxing! What a comical scene. I burst out laughing. How did these men have the strength to box when they must surely be suffering from hunger like the rest of us? It turned out that one of them, a Pole, was the camp barber. He had two assignments: to give haircuts to the Germans and to give the male prisoners their camp hairdos. In Taucha all the male prisoners had a two-inch-wide strip shaved down the center of their skulls so that they had hair only on the sides. We called that strip the *Reichsautobahn* (Reich superhighway). It was like a mark of Cain, and made any escape attempt almost impossible. In the course of his work, the camp barber went into the living quarters of the Germans, where he frequently was given a piece of wurst and bread. That answered my question about his fitness. I asked Arnost Horner who the other man on the stage was.

"Don't you know him?" he asked. "That's Kurt Elias from Theresienstadt. He was the coal carrier for the camp kitchen. He played soccer on the kitchen team."

"Please introduce us; I want to ask him what he can contribute to our program," I said.

When Kurt came down off the stage, sweaty and breathless from boxing, Arnost introduced us.

"Can you take part in our program?" I asked.

"I could sing," he said, and we decided that he and I would do a duet only the Czech prisoners would understand. The words of the chorus went like this:

He: *If you will be my sweetheart,*
I'll bounce you on my knees all day long.
She: *We'll make a lovely couple,*
and I'll whisper sweet words of love in your ear.

The accompaniment was quite simple, and the pianist learned it in no time. It was a catchy melody, and soon everybody in the dining room was swaying in time to its slow waltz tempo. During the rehearsals the Gypsies once again excelled. Their lively, vivacious dancing and singing were infectious. They contributed the most to the program and really made the evening.

I told the camp commandant that we would need at least three more rehearsals. He agreed. Actually we didn't, but it was an excuse to get together with the men again. Naturally, we brought lots of bread to these rehearsals, hiding it in the toilets and telling the men to pick it up there.

A prisoners' dress rehearsal was scheduled for 6 P.M. the day before the performance. That morning we had to drive to Halle on the Saale River to load carrots onto the truck. Although carrot days always were hard work for the Leipzig detail, we were already enthusiastically talking about how many carrots we could sneak to the men. But as we were passing through the suburbs of Halle, a full-scale air-raid alarm sounded. The first bombs were falling on the city. Our driver stopped the truck, and we were herded into an air-raid shelter, a cellar that was already crowded with people. As soon as we, our driver, and the soldier with the fixed bayonet on his rifle stepped inside, everybody else in the shelter moved aside in terror, giving us room to stand there in relative comfort. These good citizens probably had never shared an air-raid shelter with prisoners, and they were afraid of us "criminals." The doors of the cellar had barely closed behind us when the bombs began to fall nearby. Those were terrible moments. We were tossed around by the concussive force of the explosions, and the Germans had no way to avoid contact with us. I began to regret that I hadn't remained outside; I was becoming convinced that in the shelter we would be buried under the rubble. I didn't want to die, not when liberation was so close. Dear God, I prayed, let me live. Let me stay alive! As so often before, I was overcome with despair. I wanted to scream, "Let me out, let me out of this underground trap."

After the raid, the cellar door opened only a crack; there was scarcely enough space for us to squeeze through, even though we were very skinny. The stairs were gone, and we had to crawl on all fours up a steep incline. Seized by panic, all we wanted to do was get out into the open and breathe fresh air. As soon as all seven of us had reached street level—the five girls, the truck driver, and the soldier—we reassembled and tried to get our bearings. All around us, where there had been rows of houses, nothing was left standing. Our truck had vanished. Smoke, dust, flames, and the desperate cries of the wounded surrounded us. That day a large part of Halle was destroyed. It seemed miraculous that we had come out of this inferno without a scratch.

We stood there, not knowing what to do or where to go. Suddenly I thought, Here's our chance to escape. But the next moment common sense prevailed. After all, how far would we get in our convicts' clothing before someone reported us? In the shelter we had seen how the Germans reacted to us. At this point, as though he had read my mind, our soldier pleaded with us in a tremulous voice, "Please don't run away. I'm responsible for you, and if you escape they'll punish me. I don't know what to do now. Without the truck, how are we going to get back to Taucha?"

It gave us a certain satisfaction to hear him whine like that and to see that he was afraid. We really felt like running off so that he would be punished. Was this the time to switch roles? We outnumbered him, and we could overpower him. But again we realized that we were in enemy territory. We couldn't take such risks now that we were so close to the end. We wanted to get back to our homes alive. Therefore we promised not to run away and proposed that we start walking back to Taucha. The soldier was quite desperate, and he accepted our advice. When we passed through a small village I saw a post office, and I suggested to the soldier that he could get in touch with Taucha by telephone and explain our situation to the camp administration. Perhaps they would have a solution to our dilemma. It took quite a while to get through to the camp, but when he finally reached Taucha he was ordered to come back on foot—we would have to walk some thirty miles in our wooden clogs. At the outset things went quite well, but gradually our pace slowed and we began to hobble and drag our feet. Blisters developed, but we couldn't take off the clogs because it was too cold to walk barefoot. We were hungry and thirsty, and still there was no visible end to this journey. It was already getting dark when finally—far away—we saw the outlines of the factory. From there it was still quite a distance to the camp.

The events of the day had eclipsed all thoughts of the dress rehearsal that had been scheduled for that evening. Everybody involved would be waiting for me. It was very late when, completely exhausted, we arrived at the camp. We were given a warm welcome. They had all heard that the Leipzig detail had been caught in an air raid, and they thought something dreadful had happened to us.

Despite my exhaustion, I immediately went to the dining-room block, where the performers were waiting impatiently. Kurt told me that I should first go to the lavatory because he had hidden a little package there for me. When I opened it, I stared in disbelief. It was an apple! I hadn't eaten anything like this in nearly three and a half years. Where had Kurt gotten an apple? The explanation was simple. Instead of eating the bread I gave him, he had exchanged it for cigarettes in the factory. And then he had given the cigarettes to a German worker in exchange for the apple, which he gave me to thank me for the bread. Kurt actually needed the vitamins in the apple more than I did, because by eating the stolen carrots I was getting my share of vitamins. But I accepted his priceless gift as tears of gratitude ran down my cheeks. Later I shared the apple with Berta.

The dress rehearsal finally started, three hours late, and my exhaustion vanished. Instead of weariness, I felt dismay because the show was really bad, and we knew that the performance the following day probably would be no better. None of us felt like doing our best for the Nazis. The show did turn out to be a fiasco, but the Germans applauded nevertheless. We gloated. Did our cabaret really distract them from worrying about the approaching cataclysm? Let them worry; they knew that after the war they would have to atone for the atrocities they had committed. If that was what the camp commandant wanted to distract them from, it wouldn't do them any good. I hoped only that we would be given the chance to accuse them before a court of justice; we wanted to see them suffer. Perhaps then at last they would realize what they had done to us.

The camp commandant decided that this time the inmates, too, should be permitted to see the show. We therefore gave two additional performances, one for the male and one for the female prisoners. I was standing behind the stage peeking through a small chink in the boards, looking for acquaintances from Theresienstadt in the audience, when I felt someone touch me. It was Kurt. He had put his arm around my shoulder. I was stunned; I had forgotten what tenderness was. It wasn't just the touch but the sense it gave me that perhaps I would no longer have to rely only on myself in this crazy world. Standing next to me was someone who needed me and whom I needed, a friend with whom I could share the difficult days ahead. These were merely passing thoughts; neither of us knew whether we would see each other again after this performance.

Kurt was working in the factory as a carpenter, a trade he hadn't learned; nor had he ever worked at it before. When he arrived at Auschwitz from Theresienstadt in 1944, there was a drastic labor shortage in Germany because virtually all the able-bodied men had been inducted into the armed forces. Like everyone else, he was asked what his trade was.

"Carpenter and plumber," Kurt answered.

"That's like pastry chef and butcher," one of the SS men replied, and put the lifesaving stamp on Kurt's forehead. And that's how he came to Taucha.

The German workers in the factory treated Kurt decently; they didn't assign him arduous jobs, and now and then they handed him a potato. In camp the SS would ask him to do carpentry jobs. Sometimes he had no idea how to do the work. But usually he had to build partitions or make repairs, and this he managed well enough. He often worked in the living quarters of the SS people. The SS women, he said, would walk around half naked in front of him, probably to show that they considered him to be a creature of an inferior order.

Before the war Kurt had studied medicine in Prague. By the time the Nazis closed all the universities, he had completed four semesters. He was forced to do hard labor, working on a dam on the Moldau. Later he was assigned to remove furniture and belongings from the apartments of Jews who had been transported to Theresienstadt. These things were taken to a warehouse where Germans could help themselves to anything they wanted to furnish their homes.

In 1940, in Prague, Kurt got married. He and his wife, Lisa, had a daughter whom they named Evička. The baby was only one and a half years old when they were all taken to Theresienstadt. There Kurt worked in one of the communal kitchens as a coal carrier. He would eat in the kitchen and give his ration card to his family. In October 1944, when Evička was three and a half years old, all three were put aboard a transport to Auschwitz. There Lisa and Evička were separated from Kurt, who did not know what happened to them. I thought I knew, but I didn't have the heart to tell him.

We did not see each other after the cabaret performances. Our only connection was Alex, who was always willing to take a piece of bread from me to Kurt in the men's camp.

Early on April 14, 1945, we were awakened for a special roll call. The camp commandant announced, "This camp must be evacuated immediately. Each of you will be given some food for the journey. There are about fifty sick people in the camp, and I need twenty-five women to stay here with them. Who will volunteer?"

Without giving it much thought, I raised my hand. The other volunteers and I were sent to the medical block. I ran all the way there, hoping to find Alex. He was just leaving for the men's camp. Breathlessly, I told him about the imminent evacuation and asked him to put Kurt on the sick list so that he would not have to leave the camp.

What I was doing may seem paradoxical. For three years I had yearned for nothing so much as to get out of the camps, weighing any and all possible avenues of escape, and now that freedom was at last in sight I wanted to stay here. Was it instinct that again governed my actions? Or was it just a fear of the unknown? Perhaps it was not liberation that awaited us outside the camp. But what would happen to us if we stayed behind? What sort of plans did the Germans have for us? We could only wait and see, and be on our guard. All those years as prisoners had made us distrustful and suspicious. We knew nothing good awaited us. We were so close to freedom yet so far.

The volunteers were ordered to stay in the hospital barracks. We couldn't even say good-bye to our friends. From a distance I saw Rosa throw a loaf of bread to each of the prisoners. Then they lined up in rows of five, were counted, and led to the camp gate. SS people and soldiers carrying rifles flanked the prisoners. The gate was opened and the long column started out, first the women, then the men, all in their blue-and-gray striped uniforms. Where were they going? Dear God, protect them, save them, let them survive, now that freedom is so close.

An eerie stillness descended on the camp. All the SS men and women and the soldiers were gone. Would we ever be able to track them down, to bring them to justice? Who would condemn them? Who would convict them? After all, their crime was merely the persecution and gassing of Jews. Who would support the cause of a few Jews?

We began to get organized, and Alex and I decided to move the sick men and women into two blocks in the women's camp so that all of us would be closer together. There were about one hundred of us. In the food-storage depot we found adequate supplies of bread, horse meat, carrots, and potatoes—enough to last two to three weeks. One of the first things we did was to post guards. Scarcely two hours had passed since the column of prisoners and the Germans had left when six armed men in their fifties entered the camp. Later we found out they were with the *Volkssturm.*[1] Alex and I told them that we were in charge of the prisoners and that they had to report to us. The Volkssturm men set up guards at the camp gate, and we in turn set up our guards to watch them. Alex, Bobby, and I went to the spot where the Germans had hidden their weapons. How disappointing to find only ammunition there, no rifles. We had hoped the SS had not taken all their weapons with them. Of course we told the Volkssturm men nothing about the secret cache.

Now it was time to set up some sort of camp administration. We prepared a nourishing soup made of horse meat and lots of carrots. The soup and as much bread as people wanted was served at our first lunch. After many months, there was contentment and happiness on the faces of the prisoners. The first day went smoothly; we went to bed dead tired.

In the middle of the night we were suddenly roused by one of our guards. He told us that Leo Demner, a prisoner who had left on the march that morning, had returned with important news. "We thought that they would be taking us to another camp by train," Leo said. "But instead we were marched right past the train station, and then we went on and on. It finally became clear to us that there was no train or other means of transportation waiting for us, but that we would be forced to keep walking as long as our strength held out. By afternoon, several of the prisoners said they couldn't go on; they were exhausted. Others took turns supporting them, encouraging them to keep going. But some who had collapsed had lost their will to live and didn't want to or couldn't get up. The Germans shot each of

[1] Germany's last-ditch people's army, composed of conscripted older men, boys, and invalids.

them in the head. Evening fell, and we got ready to spend the night out in the open, surrounded by guards. I was able to slip past the guards and retraced the way we had come. I didn't know the surroundings and really had no choice other than to return here."

My God, what a tragicomedy! A prisoner who had been led out of the concentration camp comes home to the camp because he has no place else to go. It was another reminder that we were in hostile territory and that we could not count on help from any of the people who lived nearby. They considered us criminals and enemies of the Third Reich. From Leo's description we could picture the sufferings of our friends on this death march. We hoped that many of them would follow Leo's example and return to camp. Here, at least for the time being, we were still safe. But how much longer? About ten other prisoners succeeded in reaching the safety of the camp. But this safety was mixed with uncertainty and dreadful worry.

We were watching the Volkssturm, and they were watching us.

6

Liberation and Return

THE VOLUNTEERS WHO HAD STAYED BEHIND performed all the essential services, working hard to make everything function smoothly. Since they were indispensable to the camp, our three electricians, Bobby, Erich, and Polda, had also stayed. Babika, Bobby's girlfriend, moved into one of the empty barracks with him, but their happiness was short-lived. Three days after the SS and the prisoners left, Bobby went into the high-voltage house to get some things he had "organized" and stored there. Somehow he touched the high-voltage connections, collapsed, and died after dragging himself to the front of the little house. It took us a long time to come to terms with the fact that Bobby, who had a friendly word for everyone and was always ready with a joke or words of encouragement in his Viennese dialect, had died on the eve of liberation. A sad funeral cortege left the camp that day to dig a grave for him in a field beyond the barbed wire. The grave probably is gone by now, but Bobby continues to live in our memories.

When April 18, 1945 dawned, the Volkssturm men were gone. At first, our own guards didn't notice that the Germans had left, then with great excitement they came to tell us about it. Could it be that we were at last free, without any to-do, without any formal announcement?

Alex and I ran to the gate, opened it, and hesitantly stepped through. We didn't say a word to each other; both of us were extremely tense and uneasy. Could it *really* be that we were free? After more than three years of imprisonment, we were walking down a road without guards; there were no SS, no soldiers with rifles and bayonets. Since the camp was quite a distance from the nearest residential area, there was no one in sight. We decided to walk on a bit, just to savor our freedom.

We hadn't gotten far when we heard peculiar noises that sounded like groans coming from a ditch by the side of the road. Three men in prison clothes lay there, writhing in pain. It was obvious that they were suffering from burns—their clothes had been singed by fire. When we tried to help them up, they gasped in Polish, "*Utijekajte utijekajte!*" ("Run, run away! The SS are coming and they'll kill you!")

We raced back to camp, screaming at everyone to drop everything and run for their lives. Then we helped the sick to get out. Two people, holding each other's wrists, made a kind of seat to carry those who were too weak to walk. When we came to the three Poles in the ditch, we took them with us too. At that point we left the road and crossed into an open field to avoid any built-up area where we might fall into the hands of the enemy.

Then I remembered that I had forgotten my lucky horseshoe. I turned around and ran back to the camp. The others called after me to come back. I was courting disaster, they yelled, the SS men were probably waiting for me and would shoot me down. I ignored them. I found the horseshoe under my straw pallet in the barracks and quickly ran out again, thinking only, I hope I'm running toward a better future.

The Poles told us a horrible, tragic story. They had been in a labor camp located not far from ours. There the SS had also moved out on a death march with the prisoners and, as in our camp, the Volkssturm had come and gone. The prisoners who had been left behind thought they were now free, and they stayed in the camp. But a short while later the SS men returned. They herded all the prisoners into a barracks, covered the windows with blankets that had been sprinkled with gasoline, and set fire to them. Guards with machine guns surrounded the barracks, and prisoners who tried to escape were shot. And so, shortly before liberation, most of the prisoners were burned alive. The three of them were able to get out. Knowing the location of our camp, they started to crawl in that direction to warn us. It was almost inconceivable that with their injuries they had made it this far, but by their courage and selflessness they had saved our lives.

We could hear distant gunfire and headed toward it, assuming this was the way to the front. It would be easy to get there, we thought. We had no idea what the front might be like, whether we would have to pass through the German lines, or what lay ahead. Again it was pure instinct that drove us, a hunch that this was the way to freedom.

Alex and I were walking at the head of our slow and labored procession when a man on a bicycle passed us. "Follow me," he called. "I'll take you to the Americans." Some of our camp mates recognized him as a German foreman from the HASAG Works who, they said, had treated the prisoners decently. We had no choice but to believe him and to follow him because we really didn't know the area. What we did know was: The SS wouldn't be able to shoot us quite so easily in an open field as in camp.

Slowly we dragged ourselves along, trying to care for the sick, some of whom were in excruciating pain, especially the burned Poles. Some refused to keep going, begging us to leave them behind. But Alex did not relent, and we managed to continue. Whenever we didn't know which direction to take, the man on the bicycle would reappear. We followed him unquestioningly. It was already late in the afternoon and beginning to get dark when we came to a forest. The man on the bicycle said, "Go into these woods; about a hundred yards in you'll see a telegraph pole. You can rest there until I return."

We found the pole and dropped to the ground, exhausted. In the safety of the forest we would at least be able to relax a little. But suddenly I sensed danger. We were all concentrated in one little spot—wasn't this an ideal trap! They could surround us, murder us, and no one would be the wiser. I talked things over with Alex, and we decided to explore the area. We had to find a way out. To stay here and wait for the man on the bicycle was potential suicide. We walked to the edge of the trees; there was a road leading through the forest, and we decided to investigate it. I was terribly afraid. We hadn't gone far when suddenly we saw a machine gun in a nearby ditch. It was trained on us. "Don't stop," I whispered to Alex. "Keep going. It's either life or death now." Then someone yelled, "Stop!"

We stood there, petrified, as a soldier jumped out of the ditch. He was the first American soldier I had ever seen. But he spoke no German, and we didn't understand English. The only thing we could say was "concentration camp." Surely he must have recognized our prison clothes!

As the soldier turned to go back to his post, I suddenly remembered the daydreams about our liberation that I had had in camp. I always imagined that I would embrace my liberator and give him a kiss. So I ran after the American, threw my arms around him, and was about to kiss him when he pushed me away. Later I saw myself in a mirror for the first time in years: No wonder he didn't want to be kissed by someone who looked so repulsive.

The soldier activated a field telephone and a few minutes later a jeep carrying other American soldiers drove up. An officer jumped out and spoke to us in English. Again we couldn't understand him, and in my desperation I said, "*Deutsch?*"

The officer countered with, "Yiddish?"

I couldn't believe my ears, but Alex had already nodded.

"My name is Captain Winter," the officer said, extending his hand and adding, "*Sholom aleykhem, ikh bin oych a yid.*" ("Peace unto you. I, too, am a Jew.")

Tears came to my eyes, and they still do today whenever I think of this encounter. In all the excitement, I had trouble explaining to him that there were more than a hundred former concentration-camp prisoners waiting in the forest. He asked how we were able to get through the enemy lines, and we told him that we hadn't seen a single German soldier.

Accompanied by several Americans, Alex and I returned to our fellow ex-prisoners in the forest and explained to them that all of us had been liberated. There was absolute silence. They could not believe it, could not grasp it. It sounded like a fairy tale. But there was no time to celebrate; we had to get out of there as quickly as possible so that the Germans would not find us.

The Americans took us to a nearby village, and there a doctor tended to the sick. Those who were able to walk and were relatively healthy were led to a large hay barn, where we would spend our first night of freedom. Captain Winter apologized for the primitive lodgings. He couldn't have known that like caged animals, we had been sleeping in quarters that were much worse. He promised that we would be given better facilities the next day.

And then they served us food, and there was no end to our astonishment: bread, salami, cheese, and real coffee. I woke up during the night and had to make sure that I wasn't dreaming. So I opened the barn door, and found a black soldier standing guard outside. There was a full moon, and as a smile spread across his face, his white teeth gleamed. Unfortunately, because of the language barrier, we couldn't talk to each other. But now I knew that we, the former prisoners, were human beings again. Someone was actually protecting us. An immense feeling of joy came over me, and I had to wake up Kurt, who had been sleeping beside me.

Kurt had not left Taucha on the death march. (The SS commandant had also appeared at the men's quarters to tell the prisoners there that they would be leaving the camp and to ask for twenty-five volunteers to remain behind with the sick.) As I had requested, Alex had taken Kurt to the men's hospital block and reported him sick and unable to walk. Kurt then moved with the other men to the women's camp, and he and I had been together ever since. Kurt was by my side during the escape from the camp, and he, Berta, and I had stayed close together. Now in the barn, lying there on the straw, Kurt and I knew that in each other we had at last found someone with whom we could share our most intimate feelings. We were no longer alone, no longer lonely. We embraced for the first time, we kissed—and then, exhausted after the strain of the preceding days, we slept, but this time nestled closely against each other, enjoying a wonderful feeling of security and freedom.

Early the next morning, Captain Winter asked if I would accompany him. We got into a jeep—my first time ever in such a vehicle—and drove off. He told me that we were in Pönitz, a small village near Leipzig. Almost all the residents were old people, because the younger ones either had been drafted or were working in a factory that had been vital to the German war effort. We drove from house to house, and in each house the captain requisitioned the living room and at least two bedrooms for our group. A lot of things were changing for the Germans; we saw their hate-filled looks as they were ordered to clear out to make room for us. They regarded us as criminals and did not want to understand what it meant to have been a concentration-camp inmate. They protested that they hadn't known anything about the persecution of the Jews and all that followed. Hadn't they read the newspapers? Hadn't they heard Hitler's inflammatory speeches on the radio? Didn't they applaud these speeches and raise their right arms in enthusiastic "Heil Hitler" salutes? There isn't a German who can make me believe that he or she knew nothing about what happened. This was an excuse they gave after the war—very convenient, indeed! We ignored the Germans in Pönitz. It wouldn't be easy to wipe away the hatred we felt for them in our hearts.

The former prisoners were now assigned to their quarters. We drew up lists and allocated the rooms on the basis of a prisoner's origins. For example, there were twelve Czechs, and we moved into adjacent houses. Berta, Alex, Kurt, Erwin, Babina, and I lived together in one of these houses. In addition, a field kitchen and a food depot were set up.

After three years of deprivation, constant filth, and strenuous physical labor, how did it now feel to sit in a bathtub and to wash ourselves with soap? And after the bath to climb into a bed with clean white sheets, a pillow, a down quilt, and a mattress instead of a straw sack? We felt euphoric. For years I had dreamed of a soft white bed, of real coffee and fresh bread and real butter for breakfast. Now all my unattainable wishes had been fulfilled: Our very first breakfast included all these delicacies.

In the food storehouse there were other things we had dreamed about: chocolate, sausages, cheese, cigarettes, cookies, and cakes—incredible treasures. On our first day in the village we caught a few chickens, and at noon we had real chicken soup. Incredible that all this was real. Unfortunately, no one had warned us that our stomachs weren't used to such rich fare and couldn't adapt overnight. Consequently, some of us became seriously ill. But who could restrain himself after having been hungry for so long? For three years each of us had eaten "soup" out of a tin bowl with a spoon that hung from a piece of string tied around his waist so that no one could steal it. If someone lost that spoon he had to slurp his soup directly from the bowl. We even slept with these spoons attached to us.

After three days of freedom, we Czech Jews decided to prepare a festive meal in our temporary home. There was a large table in the dining room, and in two cupboards we found beautiful porcelain dishes, linen tablecloths, and silverware. Everything had been stored in perfect condition; no sign of the war was evident in this house. For that matter, a pastoral peace prevailed in the little village. If it hadn't been for the American occupation forces, you might have thought you were in a country vacation spot. We began to cook. The menu consisted of soup, chicken, vegetables, potatoes, and American canned fruit for dessert. The largest and most beautiful embroidered tablecloth we could find was put on the table. Someone turned up candles for the silver candlesticks, and flowers were brought in from the garden. Having nothing else to wear, we put on our striped prison clothes, but everything had been boiled, washed, and ironed so that we were free of lice. Nervous, excited, and self-conscious, we sat down to dinner, watching one another to make sure that we still knew how to use our knives and forks properly. You should understand that we had become accustomed to quite a different way of eating. In the end we laughed—a mixture of embarrassment, self-satisfaction, and joy.

Captain Winter and his men spoiled us, and in their care we regained our health. One day he told us, with a smile, that a delegation of villagers had come to see him requesting that he get rid of the criminals quartered in the village. Imagine their heightened indignation when they were told that we weren't criminals but Jews and Gypsies. After that the villagers made every effort to avoid contact with us. Nor were we interested in having anything to do with them; they were our enemies. We were sure that even after our liberation they gladly would have killed us because we had committed the unspeakable crime of being Jews.

Two weeks later, Captain Winter informed us that the Americans were leaving Pönitz and it would be extremely dangerous for us to stay behind. He said that the American army was responsible for us and could not permit this. He had been in touch with the occupation authorities, and they had ordered him to take us to a reception camp set up by the Americans specifically for former concentration-camp inmates. The thought of going back into a camp made us all quite unhappy—back to the wooden barracks, the mass feedings, the same sort of life we had only recently escaped and that had such ominous connotations for us. More barbed wire? How brief our halfway free and normal life had been! And now a return to regimented camp existence. We dreaded it, yet it was obvious that we could not stay in Pönitz without our American protectors. Captain Winter added that the American authorities were eager to send us back to our homelands at the earliest opportunity. This prospect made it somewhat easier to resume camp life. We realized that repatriation would take some time; there was still a war going on, and we had to wait out the end of the fighting.

It was hard to say good-bye to our liberators in Pönitz. Many tears were shed as we were loaded into American army trucks and driven off to yet another unknown destination. Would this wandering never end?

We arrived at a huge camp near Leipzig; it had been set up on the site of what previously had been a German antiaircraft base. It was run by the Americans. Former concentration-camp prisoners as well as others who recently had been forced laborers were being brought here to be registered; it was an effort to bring some order into the widespread chaos. Thousands of people were already in the camp when we arrived; most of them, like us, still were wearing their prison clothes. There was a babel of languages, because these former prisoners had come from all the countries the Germans had occupied. The Taucha group was split up and assigned to different barracks. But we twelve Czechs refused to be separated, and luckily we were allowed to stay together. Like most of those in the camp, we wanted to leave Germany as quickly as possible, to go home, and above all to see our families again. In Pönitz there had been radios, and we could keep abreast of the news. But here we had no way of staying informed.

Then came the day when the camp loudspeakers carried word of the collapse of the Third Reich. There was incredible jubilation in the camp; the end of the war was finally near. Several days later, an announcement in several languages informed us of an urgent need for nurses and medical personnel. Alex, Kurt, and I volunteered. Because he was a doctor, Alex was sent to one of the hospitals. Kurt and I were asked to find sick people in our camp and either to provide treatment on-site or to see that they were taken to one of the temporary hospitals that had been set up by the American army. This was not easy; all of us were weak and in need of help—if not medical, then psychological. In making our rounds we heard that there were concentration camps and labor camps nearby where many inmates were in critical need of assistance. We reported this to the American authorities, and they asked us to care for these people as well. We were given passes that enabled us to leave the camp; until then this had not been permitted because it would have disrupted the registration procedures. We also received a letter addressed to the American headquarters in Leipzig, instructing the administration there to provide us with a car because we were performing an important service and could not possibly walk to all the camps.

Furnished with all the necessary passes and documents, we left camp early in the morning. Practically no public transportation was functioning in Germany at this time, so we had no choice but to walk to Leipzig. When we arrived at the American headquarters, a uniformed German guard was standing in front of the building. He asked us what we wanted, but after we explained why we had come, he refused to let us in. We showed him our letters of introduction, explained the critical nature of our work with the sick—nothing helped. He wouldn't budge. All the anger and despair of those long years in the concentration camps came to a head, and I blew up. Like a crazy woman I screamed that he, a Nazi, had no right to keep me, a former prisoner, from entering. At the top of my voice, I asked him if he still felt like a superman and I told him that I had suffered enough under the Nazi terror, that I wasn't going to let any more Nazis tell me what to do. I threatened to kill him, there on the spot, just as the Nazis had killed so many innocent prisoners.

At that point, an American soldier walked by. He grabbed me and pulled me aside. It took me quite a while to calm down, to stop crying, to come to my senses and think rationally again. The American soldier understood a little German, and after we told him why we had come he took us to the appropriate office.

The Americans were extraordinarily kind and courteous, always good-humored, friendly, neat, and clean. Everything was done with a pleasant "no problem"; our admiration was boundless. They showed us that they understood and felt sympathy for the terrible suffering we had endured. The same soldier who had come to our assistance now took us to an office where there was a female German interpreter. But because of the incident at the building entrance, I refused to talk to her. The soldier therefore took us directly to a lieutenant and told him what we had come for, and within an hour we were taken to a garage to pick up a car, along with the necessary documents. No one had bothered to ask whether either of us knew how to drive or had a driver's license. With great pizzazz, an American soldier drove the car out of the garage, and Kurt and I stood in front of it without a clue of what to do. I asked how one shifted gears. I was thinking of Lada, our chauffeur back home, who, when I was a little girl, had allowed me to sit in his lap while I steered the car and later even permitted me to shift gears. He also explained to me how a car works, so theoretically I could drive. But I had no practical experience, none at all. At home our car had had a stick shift on the floor, but this car had a small manual shift at the dashboard level. After a couple of tries I figured out how the gear shift worked, and we drove off. Luckily for me as well as for the cars we met on the road, there wasn't much traffic in those days. Occasionally we met an American military vehicle or a cyclist. Kurt, who sat next to me, was terribly nervous, and whenever another car approached he poked me. I still marvel that we arrived back at camp safely. There was no need to wonder what had caused the black and blue marks on my thigh; we both knew.

The following morning we loaded a supply of medicines and bandages into the car and drove to the various camps in the area to help the sick or to take those who required additional care to a hospital. Once again we saw the consequences of the suffering the prisoners had had to endure. There would be physical and mental aftereffects from which each of us would suffer for a long time to come. It broke my heart to see these poor people just lying there, apathetically waiting for what would happen next. Kurt and I probably would have been in the same condition had it not been for the work we were doing. As it was, we worked hard, and we came back to camp late every evening, dead tired yet with the good feeling that we had made a difference.

The other Czechs stayed in the camp, taking care of bureaucratic formalities and in the process making friends with the Americans. One of these Americans, who fell in love with one of the young Czech women, felt that we had been living in camps long enough and should be provided with better housing. Before long he had requisitioned a villa for us. We were to move in the following day. "Move" is perhaps too dramatic a concept; after all, we owned nothing but the clothes we wore. Nonetheless, armed with the required passes, our Czech friends climbed into two American jeeps, and Kurt and I followed in our car. Escorted by the Americans, we drove up a beautiful winding driveway to the villa, which, it turned out, belonged to the director of the Mitteldeutsche Motorenwerke (Central German Motor Company). The driveway was flanked on both sides by huge purple and white lilac bushes in full bloom, perfuming the air. Seeing the lilacs, I remembered my grandmother's yard in Marianské Hory and her enormous lilac bush, and suddenly everything in me cried out, I want to go home!

The villa was tastefully furnished, with an enormous living room that led to a lovely conservatory. But what immediately caught my eye was the grand piano in one corner. I couldn't concentrate on anything else. Entranced, I walked over and lifted the keyboard cover. At first I didn't dare to touch the keys. What had happened to all those years of studying music? What had become of my aspirations? When I tried to play, my fingers would not obey; they had become stiff and swollen from chilblains and heavy work. I don't know whether my friends who were watching understood or were even aware of what was happening within me, but at that moment I was again reminded of the harm the Germans had done to us. How could we have survived all that? What sort of inner strength had kept us going?

A wide flight of stairs led to the first floor of the villa, where there were several bedrooms with baths and toilets. We made ourselves at home. In these elegant surroundings our striped prison clothes seemed particularly ugly and inappropriate, but we had had no opportunity to exchange them for something better. Moreover, we had found these clothes useful in our dealings with the authorities.

From our first day at the villa, the generous Americans supplied us with all the food we needed. Kurt and I continued our visits to the various camps, and the other Czechs cooked and kept house in the villa. There was an immense kitchen next to the living room. I had never seen anything like it except in movies before the war. Huge brass pans and pots hung on the walls. Every evening when we returned from work there was a wonderful dinner waiting for us, and gradually our shrunken stomachs grew used to accepting larger quantities of food.

At first we thought we had the villa all to ourselves; then we discovered that the wife of the owner was still living there. Her husband had been arrested as a war criminal shortly after the Americans occupied Leipzig, and she had vigorously protested the quartering of "convicts" in her house. After we moved in, she was restricted to an attic room. The Americans had ordered her to give us whatever we needed and not to bother us. We told her that we were not criminals, we were Jews. As far as she was concerned, that was much worse. She quickly withdrew to her garret, and we were glad that we never saw her again. The feeling, no doubt, was mutual.

Once again we had to adapt to new surroundings. There were several radios in the villa, and we set up a regular schedule for monitoring the newscasts. That's how we heard of the total collapse of the Third Reich, and a few days later about the end of the war in Europe. We accepted the news as inevitable because we had expected it ever since we fled Taucha. What did surprise us were the many references on the radio to people and places that were completely foreign to us. For six years we had lived without radios, and for almost four years we had read no newspapers. Now we realized how much had happened in the world during this time; we just couldn't keep up with all the political developments.

We decided to disregard the news reports and concentrate on the "search reports." The International Red Cross had set up a search service, and all day long, from morning until late at night, these reports were broadcast. Each of us had drawn up an alphabetical list of our relatives, and the first question Kurt and I asked when we came back from work each day was whether the names of any of our relatives had been mentioned on the radio. Invariably, the answer was "no." Desperation set in.

The Americans came to visit us regularly; we had managed to create a pleasant, cozy atmosphere in the villa, and it reminded them of home. They always brought us food and all kinds of little gifts. At this stage in the transition to a normal life it was important to get rid of our prison clothes, and the Americans supplied us with regular things to wear. Another U.S. soldier had begun to show up more and more often at the villa. He seemed particularly interested in a young Czech woman; a second love affair blossomed, and in this respect, too, normality returned to our lives. Gradually I started to play the piano again, and our evenings resounded with music, singing, and laughter.

Our conversations dealt with the future. We were restless and wanted to return to our homelands, to the people we loved. But our American friends advised us against going back to Czechoslovakia. Instead, they offered to make it possible for our group to go to the United States. We categorically declined. After all, we knew nobody in the United States, but in Czechoslovakia our families were waiting for us. Or so we thought.

One day the radio reported that Czechoslovakia was dispatching buses to the various concentration camps to pick up Czech nationals and take them home. The first buses would be leaving from Buchenwald. Two of our group went to Buchenwald to apply for

The group of Czechs revisiting Taucha, several weeks after liberation. Ruth Elias (with checkered dress), Berta Reich (beside her, in white blouse), Leo Demner (under the "7"), and Kurt Elias (beside Demner).

repatriation and to reserve twelve seats on the buses for us. In those chaotic postwar times this trip took an entire day. When they came back, they told us that we would be able to start our trip in four days. There was great rejoicing. But our happy anticipation also had an element of foreboding, of fear. What awaited us at home? What had happened to the families we had left behind? Where could we go, now that we had no homes anymore?

Each of us carried a little travel bag, which was more than enough to hold our meager belongings. My bag was the heaviest, because I was still carrying the lucky horseshoe I had found in Taucha. No longer was it necessary to hide the St. Anthony medal under my tongue; now I wore it around my neck. These two things were my most valuable possessions, and I guarded them carefully. They sustained me, so I clung to them. Why? I have no rational explanation.

The Americans drove us to Buchenwald, which was under U.S. control. Again we entered a huge concentration camp, but this time as free men and women. The place was teeming with American military personnel and people wearing prison suits. At the camp's administration building we were told to stay close by, as the Czech buses were expected any minute. We asked if they had a list of Buchenwald inmates, and when they produced it we sat down, anxiously looking for the names of people we knew. Suddenly I spotted the name Kurt Meier—Kurt who had lent me his accordion to play in Theresienstadt and with whom I had spent many enjoyable hours making music. The list indicated that he was in the hospital block. I ran over to see him, but I was not allowed inside. Kurt was seriously ill, I was told; he had typhus. I don't know if the attendant gave him my regards and good wishes, or if in his condition he even would have remembered me. Then, as I ran back to the administration building, I could see that the buses had arrived and I climbed aboard. Where to now?

On the journey out of Germany we passed through several bombed-out cities. Seeing that gave me a certain satisfaction. Those who make others suffer should be made to suffer, too. In driving through Germany we saw what war meant, the devastation, the destruction. We went through Dresden, which had been totally destroyed except for one big church that was undamaged. We saw the remnants of the walls of buildings, and they seemed to be saying, "No more war, no more destruction of people and houses!" Will future generations heed this cry? Aren't there still people in Germany who support Hitler and his ideas? Are they blind to what happened? The cities will be rebuilt, but the shameful stain called the Holocaust will remain forever.

When our bus arrived at the border of the U.S. occupation zone near Leipzig, the Americans said good-bye to us and the Soviets took over. What a difference between the easygoing attitude of the Americans and the heavy-handedness of the Russians. The Americans were neat and trim, and the Russians, wearing a jumble of different kinds of sloppy uniforms, were crude and ungainly; the Americans always had a friendly smile, and the Russians were sullen and serious; the Americans rode in jeeps, the Russians in wooden horse-drawn carts. These were our first impressions, and for a moment we were sorry that we had exchanged the Americans for the Russians. But these thoughts had to be pushed aside. After all, we were going home. That was all that mattered!

Twelve of us sat squeezed together on the bus with former political prisoners we didn't know but with whom we had much in common. Yet we were all silent, each of us deep in thought. What awaited us at home? What had happened there while we were gone? We wondered how we could go back to living normal lives after all we had experienced. How would we be able to support ourselves without a trade or a profession?

Our excitement grew as we passed the first houses in the Prague suburbs. There wasn't much to see because it was already dark, but after so much misery the feeling of being back home was overpowering. We cried, we sang.

The city of Prague had set up a repatriation office that had been doing an extraordinary job in the short time since the war had ended. We were taken to a large house where clean beds, food, and a bath awaited us. Friendly people welcomed us. There wasn't much conversation because all of us were exhausted after the long trip. The next morning we registered. They gave us five hundred koruny as pocket money and told us that we could stay as long as we liked.

Berta had lived in Prague before she was deported, so we went first to her apartment in Praha-Liben. She was told that the apartment was empty. Germans had lived there during the war, but as soon as peace was declared they had fled. At the housing office Berta asked for the keys to her apartment. They were handed to her after she obtained a letter from the police registry confirming that she had indeed once lived there. Apprehensive and nervous, Berta opened the door to the apartment. As memories of her husband and son Pavliček (both of whom had perished) came flooding over her, she began to cry bitterly. It was fortunate that I was with her; she needed an understanding friend at her side. How painful her return, how full of grief.

Berta was surprised to find all her furniture just as she had left it. Almost nothing was missing, so she was able to start her new life in her own apartment. She invited me to stay with her, and I accepted. We went back to the repatriation center and told the staff that we had found a place to live, giving them Berta's address. The apartment became the meeting place for those of our friends who had nowhere else to go. Kurt had moved in with a friend from Theresienstadt, but during the day he spent his time with us in Berta's apartment.

Next we went to the Jewish Community Center to find out whether any other Jews had returned from the camps and if a list of their names had been compiled. No members of Berta's or my family were on the list they showed us. We left our address with the center, and after registering we were given food-ration cards. The Community Center had set up a large kitchen for returning deportees, where they could eat free of charge, but because it was too far from our apartment, Berta, Kurt, and I went there only for lunch.

After a few days in Prague taking care of essential official formalities, registration, and so forth, I decided to go to Brno and Pozořice to find out if any members of my family had returned. When we parted in Theresienstadt, we had agreed that we would first meet at the home of the Žalmans in Pozořice. Our second meeting place was Aunt Alma's apartment in Brno. The third was Ostrava.

Unfortunately, travel right after the end of the war was almost impossible. There was utter chaos; no timetables existed, and if one wanted to go anywhere by train one often had to be at the station twenty-four hours before departure, spend the night there, and then hope to get a seat on a train going in the right direction. Nevertheless, I decided to take a chance. However, I had to postpone the journey for a few days. Something came up.

When we returned to Berta's apartment after making inquiries about train schedules, we found a friend of Kurt's waiting for us. He had spotted Kurt's name on a list at the Jewish Community Center. He told us that at the selection he had seen Kurt's wife, Lisa, and their little daughter, Evička, being sent to join those who had been designated for the gas chambers. At first this devastating news did not sink in, but gradually Kurt began to understand the dreadful meaning of the words. He began to cry and ran out of the apartment house. I went after him, because I was afraid that in his despair he might do something rash. He didn't notice that I was following him at a distance. He headed for the Moldau riverbank, and when he leaned over the embankment wall I stepped up and began to talk to him.

Having scarcely begun to hope that we could start to live normal lives again, we were confronted with an immense sorrow. We who had gone through hell and had only recently been liberated, now were being bludgeoned by additional calamities. Shortly after Kurt received this grim news, he heard that his mother and his younger brother Leo also had been killed in the gas chambers. He was devastated.

No one who did not go through the concentration camps him- or herself can imagine what happened to us there. Only someone who endured the hell of the camps was able to take on the task of helping friends regain the courage they needed, through understanding and support, and that task demanded great effort and spiritual strength. We would often sit across from each other without speaking, because we felt that our silent presence was more helpful than banal words. I still don't understand the reserves from which we drew the strength to do this. Bonds of friendship and comradeship developed between us. They would never be sundered.

I stayed in Prague for several more days, but when I saw that Kurt was slowly recovering from his profound shock, I set out on my mission. To be honest, I was afraid and would have liked to postpone this journey indefinitely. In those days the Prague streetcars didn't run at night, so I started out on foot at 2 A.M. to catch a train that was supposed to leave for Brno at 10 A.M. I was lucky to get a seat. The train was crowded; people even sat outside on the train steps, which was against the law. But in those chaotic times prohibitions like these were meaningless. After a long trip, with stops at every local station, the train came to a halt several miles from Brno. It was getting dark, and I had to walk the rest of the way. Passing through a village, I asked a farmer how far it was to Pozořice. It was only about six miles, he said, and because that was just about the same distance as to Brno and I had no one to look up in Brno, I decided to walk to Pozořice instead.

I arrived at the Žalmans' house in the middle of the night. Standing there in the dark, I thought about the many wonderful hours I had spent in that place. I resolved to spend the night outside, because I didn't want to disturb the sleeping family. But there was a light on in Miloš's room. I whistled our old signal, and seconds later Miloš opened the garden gate and we fell into each other's arms.

"Where's Edith, where's Edith?" he asked impatiently.

"I had hoped I'd find her here," I told him. "Haven't you heard from her?"

I had expected to get some news about my family in Pozořice, but no one had turned up. Hope began to fade. I had seen too much, experienced too much. Suddenly I heard myself say, "They've probably all been gassed."

During the past three years this sentence had become deeply ingrained in me. For those of us who had been in Auschwitz the words spelled out a dry fact, a reality. I didn't realize that others might not understand. I can still see the horror in Miloš's eyes. He must have thought me mad or unfeeling. Had the years in the camps really made me this insensitive?

Without waking his parents, Miloš took me to the guest room. The next morning, as the first member of our family to have come back to Pozořice, I was welcomed warmly by the Žalmans. Surely, they said, my relatives would show up in the coming days. When they offered me a room in their house, I gratefully accepted.

The next morning Miloš took me on a long hike through the woods and urged me to tell him what had happened. I talked and talked for hours, finding in Miloš a sympathetic listener who never interrupted me. We walked past all the places that were so closely linked in my memory to the happy times we had spent together, past the huts where Miloš and Edith had had their trysts and that later housed the group of Jewish woodcutters. Where were they now? Would they ever come back? Here was the brook where I had spent hours alone fishing for trout in order to give Edith and Miloš some privacy in their hut. There, the tree where Koni and I had buried his parents' jewels; Miloš and I looked, but we couldn't find anything. It didn't matter. Jewelry and material things had lost all value for me; there was only one thing of value: life.

The next day, my heart aching with memories of the few happy months we had been allowed to spend in Pozořice, I took a walk through the village. Here was the house where we had lived; there, the place where we had worked, Edith, Father, Lore, and the others. The villagers greeted me shyly, not sure whether they should ask about my family. They had heard about the extermination of the Jews, and they kept saying, "It's good that you have come back." And then, overcoming their hesitation, "What happened to the rest of your family?"

I would answer, "They've probably all been gassed."

Each time I said it, I saw the same look of shock and horror I had seen on Miloš's face. It was he who took me aside and asked me to change the wording of my answer. Anyone who hadn't been there, he said, would misinterpret my words and would think badly of me.

Here in Pozořice we had left all the things we could not take to Theresienstadt, including my accordion. It was the only thing that I wanted to get back. None of the other stuff interested me; I didn't even want to see the things that belonged to my family. But I was now told that it wasn't the Germans who had taken the accordion but the Russians; they had left a worthless old instrument in its place. I would never again see the accordion that had been so dear to me and was so closely bound up with my youth. Slowly I began to realize that everything that connected me to my past had been taken from me. Only the memories were left.

Miloš told me that he had been picked up immediately after we were transported to Theresienstadt. The reason given: He had had contact with Jews. He spent three years in Czech prisons, but at least he hadn't been through the hell of a concentration camp. Before the war Miloš had studied medicine, and now that the universities had reopened he immediately resumed his studies. He felt utterly disconsolate that Edith had not returned. He had waited and waited for her and could not, would not, accept the idea that Edith, the beautiful Edith he loved, would never come back. Life in prison had been bearable because the hope that she would return gave him strength.

I stayed in Pozořice for three days, three difficult but lovely days. After giving my friends my Prague address, I said a sad farewell to them in order to go on to the next stop: Ostrava. I waited at the Masaryk train station in Brno for a long time until an overcrowded train going in the direction of Ostrava pulled in. I had to stand, but compared to the cattle cars this was luxury.

Late that afternoon I arrived in my hometown. The train stopped in Přívoz, a short walk from Uncle Hugo's house. The house was still standing, but everything in it and in the factory had been stolen. The bare walls seemed to mock me. It was getting dark, and I began to look for a place to spend the night. Because the Žalmans had given me some money, I went to the first hotel I saw. The hotel owner had known my family; my father had delivered meat products to him. But when I asked for a room, he said, "We're really glad that you've come back, Miss Huppert, but all our rooms are occupied by the Russians."

Přívoz had three hotels, and I received the same answer in each. I became desperate, standing there in the market square and feeling like a complete stranger in my native town. (The Jewish Community Center was closed at this late hour.) After six years of exile and concentration camps, I didn't know where I could find a place to stay for the night. I felt utterly helpless and began to cry.

Suddenly I heard someone say, "Miss Rutinko, is it really you?"

A little woman stooped with age was standing beside me. I didn't recognize her. "Yes, it's me," I said.

"Why are you crying?" she asked.

"Because I've finally returned home from the concentration camps, and I can't find a place to spend the night."

"Don't you remember me, Miss Rutinko? I'm Mrs. Polaček, the midwife who helped your mother when you and your sister were born. Now that you're reborn I'd like to help you again. Come sleep at my house."

I think you can expect this kind of empathy and understanding only from simple, kindhearted people. Mrs. Polaček led me to her apartment, which consisted of one room and a kitchen. We spent the night sleeping in a gigantic bed under a huge feather coverlet. Mrs. Polaček told me all she knew of my family, with whom she had kept in touch while we were still living in Ostrava. (She used to go to the shop every week to get her gift of meat and sausage. After we left Ostrava she missed these weekly gifts, because she didn't have enough money to buy such things.) She said she hoped that I would find my family again, and she asked me to keep her informed. I couldn't thank her enough for her kindness and promised to come back to visit her. (A few months later when I tried to keep my promise, Mrs. Polaček was no longer there. After doing her last good deed she had died, quietly and peacefully.)

The next morning I went to the Ostrava Jewish Community Center to search through its lists and to find out whether anyone in my family had registered there. But the closer I came to the building, the more timorous my steps became. I already knew what I would find there: No one had been heard from. Could it be that out of such a large family not a single relative had returned? Could it be that all of them had been murdered? My own trauma was still too fresh for me to comprehend the extent of the tragedy. There was nothing left to do but give the center my Prague address and leave my hometown where I was now a stranger.

But one more stop had to be made. I went to see Gustav, our former employee. We had left almost all our things, including our jewelry, with him for safekeeping. He also had the two hope chests that contained the trousseaux. I was received coolly; it was obvious that Gustav and his family were disappointed that I had returned. Where were the friendly smiles that used to welcome us to this house? We went into the living room, which was outfitted with my family's furniture. And there, surrounded by our possessions, they plied me with lies, telling me that the Russians had taken most of our belongings. What a convenient excuse! Gustav went on to say that only a few of our things were left. Of course, they would be glad to return these to me if I wanted them. At that moment a great indifference came over me and I thought, I'd gladly give it all up if only a single member of my family were to come back. After all, what were these but things? They were replaceable, whereas nothing could replace my relatives.

Gustav and his family didn't understand what had happened to me, and how brokenhearted and crushed I felt when I arrived at their house. They, who had continued to live normal lives in spite of the German occupation, couldn't empathize with me. In the end it was *I* who tried to understand *them,* and before I left I asked them to put our things aside because someday I would come back to pick them up.

Not far from Gustav's house in Marianské Hory was my grandmother's house, and I decided to walk over. Strangers were living there now, and I didn't even tell them why I had entered their yard without asking permission. Across from Oma's place was Uncle Otto's house. It had been looted and stood there, deserted. It never occurred to me to ask the authorities to return these properties to me. My grief was too great. Wherever I could, I left my Prague address; then I took the train back to the people who had become my friends and to whom I now felt close.

In Prague a surprise awaited me. Koni was back! I was happy to hear that he had survived. At the same time, I remembered the pain he had caused me and that had been deeply carved in my memory. After he, too, had escaped from hell, how would I now tell him that I couldn't go back to him? Neither Kurt nor Berta was able to advise me. They could give me only moral support. I felt sorry for Koni, but I knew that I had to remain firm.

The following morning he came to Berta's apartment, and I asked Kurt and Berta to leave us alone. My first words, like the lashes of a whip, must have hurt him. I said, "Koni, I'm really happy that you managed to survive, but I can't come back to you." Even today I wonder how I could have treated him so harshly. Was it due to all I had experienced in the camps? Had that really robbed me of all compassion?

I blurted the words out, just like that, in one breath. Even now, I can still see his shocked expression. He couldn't understand my attitude, and I'm not sure he ever fully grasped the reasons for my decision, because it was hard for me to find the right words to express my motivations clearly.

We spent an entire day together. Koni told me about his experiences in the labor camp, and I briefly told him about the baby. After all, it had been his child too. I did not know how he would feel about what happened, whether he could understand what had been at stake. Would he condemn me for what I had done? We were both somewhat embarrassed, searching for words that came only haltingly. How had it come to this? Once we had loved each other very much. It was Koni who had proposed marriage in Theresienstadt. Had I left with my family on that transport east, I would have shared their fate. I owed my life to Koni. But then came Auschwitz, the estrangement, and my disappointment. I could not forget or get over what had happened there. Now, so soon after our return, and while I was still under the influence of those terrible experiences, it was difficult for me to forgive him. I felt truly sorry for Koni, who stood there looking so unhappy. He, too, was alone, lonely and in need of friends—and now I, on whom he had placed all his hopes, was leaving him. At that moment I had the urge to take him in my arms and give him the warmth and comfort he needed. But I knew that if I did that I would weaken and stay with him. Reason triumphed over emotion. Were we to get together again there always would be a shadow between us—the shadow of the Auschwitz family camp and what happened there. Even though it was hard, it was

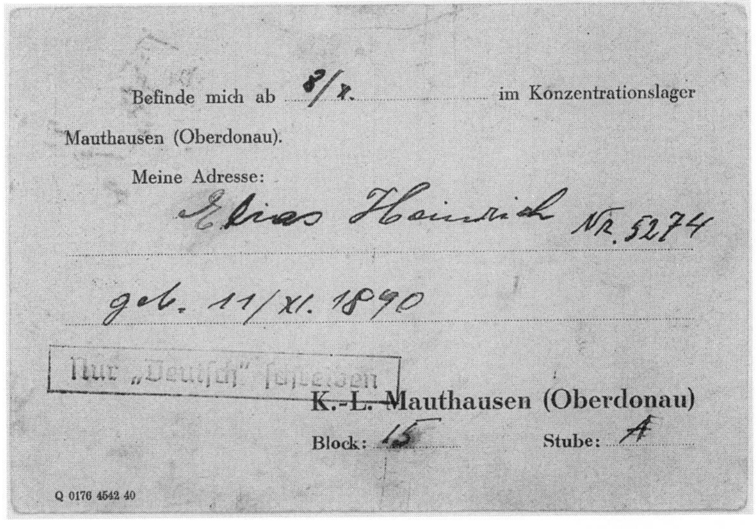

Befinde mich ab 8/I. im Konzentrationslager Mauthausen (Oberdonau).

Meine Adresse:

Elias Heinrich Nr. 5274

geb. 11/XI. 1890

Nur „Deutsch" schreiben

K.-L. Mauthausen (Oberdonau)

Block: 15 Stube: A

Q 0176 4542 40

...ntrationslager
...usen, Oberdonau

...ordnungen sind beim ...r mit Gefangenen zu

...der Schutzhaftgefangene darf im ...at zwei Briefe oder zwei Karten ... seinen Angehörigen empfangen und an sie absenden. Die Briefe an die Gefangenen müssen gut lesbar mit T i n t e geschrieben sein und dürfen nur 15 Zeilen auf einer Seite enthalten. Gestattet ist nur ein Briefbogen normaler Größe. Briefumschläge müssen ungefüttert sein. In einem Briefe dürfen nur 5 Briefmarken à 12 Rpf beigelegt werden. Alles andere ist verboten und unterliegt der Beschlagnahme. Postkarten haben zehn Zeilen. Lichtbilder dürfen als Postkarten nicht verwendet werden.

2.) Geldsendungen sind gestattet, doch ist dabei genau Name und Vorname, Geburtsdatum, Häftlingsblock und Stube anzugeben.

3.) Zeitungen sind gestattet, dürfen aber nur durch die Poststelle des K.L. Mauthausen bestellt werden.

4.) Pakete dürfen nicht geschickt werden, da die Gefangenen im Lager alles kaufen können.

5.) Entlassungsgesuche aus der Schutzhaft an die Lagerleitung sind zwecklos.

6.) Sprecherlaubnis und Besuche von Gefangenen im Konzentrations-Lager sind grundsätzlich nicht gestattet.

...le Post, die diesen Anforderungen nicht entspricht, wird vernichtet.

Der Lagerkommandant.

Postkarte

K. L. M.

Deutsches Reich

Frau

Erna Elias

Brünn XII

Auf den Bergen

Protektorat

From Mauthausen concentration camp, this January 25, 1941, postcard is the last received from my husband's father. He perished several weeks later.

better to put an end to it now, while we were still in our early twenties. Surely the pain would heal with time. The next day Koni left Prague and went back to Brno, his hometown.

After that I received several letters from him in which he begged me to come back to him, but I stuck to my decision. I even returned his last letter unopened. I wanted to close this chapter in my life; it brought back too many painful memories. Later Koni met a former girlfriend in Brno, and eventually they were married. They started a family, and I heard that he was happy.

During the first two months after our liberation we lived in a state of inner turmoil. Our lives revolved around the constant but ever more hopeless search for surviving members of our families. Right after the German troops had invaded Czechoslovakia, a few Czech Jews were able to escape to Poland and from there to Russia. After enduring deprivations, torments, and internments these men were at last taken into the Czechoslovak Army brigades formed there. Many of these served in heavily Jewish units, and after the war many of them returned home. When the first members of the brigade came back to Prague, we went to see them, hoping that someone from our family might be among them. They promised to look into it, and one day I received a report that there was a man named Huppert in their ranks. For days I searched for him—perhaps it was my father. When we finally met, I found that we were not related.

Throughout the search Kurt was at my side, accompanying me and giving me moral support in those nerve-racking days. He, too, was alone, the sole survivor of his family. Even before he and his family were taken to Theresienstadt, his father had been picked up and sent to the Mauthausen concentration camp. From there Kurt received a printed postcard filled in by a shaky hand:

"Since the *8/X* [8th of October—the date is handwritten without the year] in the concentration camp Mauthausen (Oberdonau).

My address: *Elias Heinrich, No. 5274, born 11th November, 1890.* Block: *15,* Room: *1* [again written in a shaky hand]."

A short time later the announcement of his death, dated 1941, was sent to Brno. Three months later, a longed-for affidavit from an uncle in America arrived. It would have enabled the entire family to emigrate, but it came too late.

When Brno was being made *judenrein* by the Nazis, Kurt's mother and his brother Leo were sent directly to Poland to be gassed. All of his mother's sisters met the same fate. Of Kurt's entire family only one uncle, Karel, survived. He had escaped to England, but we had heard nothing of him or his family. Kurt tried to get his uncle's address, but in the widespread disorder of the postwar period this was not easy.

Berta, Kurt, and I now began to make plans for the future. We were still being cared for by the repatriation office, which gave us some pocket money and one hot meal a day. Naturally, we knew that this support would not last the rest of our lives, and besides, we no longer wanted to be dependent on their assistance. We wanted to stand on our own feet and provide for ourselves. What's more, I couldn't continue to stay with Berta. She had met a friend who had lost his family and had moved in with her, so Kurt and I decided to look for a place of our own. The housing shortage made it hard to find an apartment, and we ended up renting a small furnished room. We would start a new life together, but it was agreed that if Kurt's wife, Lisa, turned up, he would return to her. Living together gave us the mutual support both of us needed so badly. We didn't give up looking for our relatives, and we followed up every little clue, yet we knew that it was getting more and more pointless.

My will to live slowly ebbed away. One hope had kept me alive throughout the long and difficult concentration-camp years: that one day I would see my family again, the one thread that must not break. The prospect of being reunited with those I loved kept me from giving up, kept me going. And now that I was at last free and could begin a normal life, the thread was broken. I no longer wanted to go on living.

I was sent to a sanatorium near Písek. The doctors there didn't know what to do with me. They prescribed various baths and many walks in the beautiful countryside surrounding the sanatorium. But nothing helped. I just got worse, because I was all alone.

The doctors had long talks with me, a peculiar form of treatment, I thought. Today I know that they were psychiatrists who made every effort to help me, but there was nothing in the psychiatry textbooks on how to treat patients suffering from concentration-camp trauma. Humankind had never before experienced such a tragedy. Finally the doctors decided that I needed drastic treatment. One day when I came to my doctor's office I saw a heavy rope lying on his desk. The doctor said, "You see that big tree outside in the garden? It has sturdy branches. If you don't want to go on living, then the best thing for you to do is to take this rope and hang yourself. But should you decide to go on living, you must draw a firm line under the past. You must start anew. Those are the two alternatives open to you. There is no third. Let me know within an hour what you decide to do."

Youth triumphed. I decided it was senseless to kill myself. Only a short time ago my life had been saved, and now I had a lifetime ahead of me. Reason and the will to live won out, and I decided to return to Kurt immediately. He was anxiously waiting for me. Now we knew that we belonged together, that we depended entirely on each other. All the things we had shared in the past seven months—the labor camp, our flight, and our return home—forged a firm bond that would hold us together, no matter what. We loved each other honestly and deeply, and this love had a firm foundation in our shared experiences.

The next step was to find a way to earn a living. Neither of us had a profession, because our education and training had been cut short by the Nazi invasion. Kurt did not want to continue with his medical education. He wanted to look for a job so he could support me. However, I suggested that *I* go to work so he could continue to study. No matter how little I earned, it would surely be enough for us; we were not spoiled. When Kurt came back from his first visit to the university, he was certain he would not go back to medicine. It would have taken five years. At the university it was suggested that he study pharmacology instead, and the administration promised to make it somewhat easier for him. After all, he was a former concentration-camp prisoner. Although the course of study was not reduced, he was permitted to take the examinations whenever he felt that he had mastered a subject. Kurt studied day and night. He finished the four-year course in two years.

We were delighted when Kurt's Uncle Karel came to Prague from England with his wife and child. At last we had a family. And then one of my father's cousins, Paul Wurzel (not to be confused with the Dr. Paul Wurzel to whom I had turned in Theresienstadt when I wanted to terminate my pregnancy) arrived with the Palestine Brigade. When he saw our little furnished room, he was appalled. Dressed in his uniform, he went to the housing department and refused to leave until he had obtained a small apartment for Kurt and me. It was quite an achievement.

We proudly moved into our new home. It had one room and a small bathroom. There was no kitchen, but I placed a large board over the sink in the bathroom and on that we put an electric cooker and a small toaster oven. Voilà, an ideal kitchen. The apartment had been occupied by a German officer who must have fled in haste. It was completely furnished, so we didn't have to buy a thing. That would have been impossible, anyway, because we had no money.

As soon as we moved in, I began to look for a job. But everywhere I went I was asked what experience I had. I had had a lot of experiences, but in the concentration camps I had learned no profession, no trade, nothing useful for earning a living. I now had no choice but to accept the first poorly paid office job I was offered—filing letters, which was mindless work. I decided to take an evening course in shorthand and typing, and two months later I began to answer advertisements for secretarial help. Each time, after I took a brief test, I was told that the company would let me know, but because I had no experience I was never offered a job. This did not surprise me.

Then came a lucky break. A new international freight forwarding agency, Intrasped, had just been formed in Prague, and it was hiring many clerks and secretaries. If a test had been required, probably I never would have been taken on. However, there was a shortage of qualified personnel in those days, so I got my first job as a secretary. The department chief called out, "Miss, come take a letter," and equipped with a stenographer's notebook and a sharpened pencil, I took dictation—more in longhand than in shorthand. I must have copied and recopied my first letter ten times. But with a lot of patience, especially on the part of my boss, I got some practice and self-confidence. This job paid quite well, and Kurt and I were able to live simply but free from financial worry.

Kurt studied hard, and every day after I got home from work I would go over his classwork assignment with him. We would sit there, poring over his books, sometimes until late at night, and often Kurt would have to poke me awake. He was the only student in his class who had his own apartment. His colleagues often came to our place to study; they liked the cozy atmosphere.

We never gave up the search for our families, and left our address everywhere so they could find us. One day my father's cousin, Dr. Wurzel, came to see us. I knew that he had come back to Prague—his name was on the list at the Jewish Community Center. But, still influenced by the conventions of my upbringing, I was embarrassed to look him up, because I was living with a man to whom I was not married. As he stood in our doorway, I felt uncomfortable because I had not tried to get in touch with him. But Paul immediately understood when he saw two names on the door; he didn't find the situation embarrassing and sympathized with our decision. He had been in Theresienstadt and had even been shut up in the Little Fortress, the dreadful prison of the ghetto. He constituted a link with my home and family, and I was truly happy to see him and to learn that he had been reunited with his wife and two daughters, who also had returned from Theresienstadt. He invited Kurt and me to visit him and offered to be a father to me. From that moment on we had a second home; Paul was always there, ready to help us.

Paul's home became the meeting place for our surviving relatives and those of his wife, too. Regrettably, there were few survivors on our side. In a letter from Palestine Aunt Regina, Father's sister, wrote that she would try to visit us as soon as possible. I immediately wrote back, asking her to let us know when she would arrive and inviting her to stay with us.

In the meantime, Kurt and I went to Ostrava to fetch the few things Gustav might be willing to return to us. Without telling him in advance that we were coming, we arrived outside his house. Imagine my surprise when I heard someone playing a piano inside. An embarrassed Gustav opened the door. Our arrival just then probably wasn't convenient. I asked him who was playing. He had no choice but to take me over to the piano, which turned out to be my piano from home. I would have been willing to leave all our other things with him just to get it back. Gustav said he was prepared to return some of our things: half of our beautiful trousseaux, an Oriental rug, a part of the large collection of jewelry, and small knickknacks such as the porcelain figurines that had belonged to Uncle Hugo and Father—and the piano. Without any regrets, I let him keep the pictures on the walls, the furniture, and the china. If only I could have found my family in this house rather than these things that were of such little value to me now!

Our next stop was Kurt's hometown, Přerov. He went to his grandparents' house, where he was born, and there he was confronted with poignant memories of his youth. Apart from Uncle Karel, no one had returned. Kurt remembered that somewhere in the house his parents' jewelry had been concealed in the walls. He asked an old friend, a man who had been decent to the family during the German occupation, to try to find the jewelry. When the man found it, Kurt let him keep half. Our values had changed. We had little use for material things and money. Life, human beings, and character—these were what now mattered.

But I still had two of my most precious possessions: the talisman on the little gold chain, a present from a criminal prisoner in Auschwitz; and the Taucha horseshoe, which now hung above the bathroom door in our apartment. Sad to say, when the chain broke, I put it into my change purse. That day, while I was riding on a streetcar, the purse was stolen. For a long time I was inconsolable, not because of the money in the purse but because I had lost my talisman. The theft must have occurred just as I heard someone on the streetcar call out, "Ruth! Is it really you?"

It was Houština, with whom I had shared a wooden plank, our bed in Auschwitz. We hugged each other, the world around us vanished, and only later did we become aware of the amazed and uncomprehending looks the other passengers on the streetcar were giving us. This was my first meeting with someone from the Auschwitz family camp who later was also in Hamburg with me.

Houština told me that those who had stayed in Hamburg were sure that Berta and I had been sent to the Auschwitz gas chambers. (God, how easily I just wrote down these words, and how momentous they are.) Houština couldn't believe I was alive. She didn't know what to say. She and I have remained true friends. Houština was reunited with her beloved Erischek, whom she had met in Theresienstadt. They moved into an apartment together. Kurt and I got along well with them, and we spent many happy hours together.

Houština's reaction prepared me to expect expressions of disbelief and amazement whenever I met someone from the family camp or the Hamburg transport. It happened a few times—too few times, unfortunately—that people would recognize me but at first would not believe that it was really me. I had to convince them that I wasn't just a ghostly apparition, that I really had survived.

Coming home from work one evening, I found a woman wrapped in a woolen blanket sleeping on our doorstep. When I woke her up, Ženka came out from under the blanket. Faithful Ženka had been lying there, waiting for me. Ženka, who had been at my side in Auschwitz when I had my baby, during my most difficult hours. Those moments again flashed through my mind. Neither of us could speak. We just hugged each other and cried, overjoyed to be together again.

In Auschwitz Ženka had been assigned to work at the "Union," the Weichsel Union Metallwerke, where she had to load gunpowder into various munitions. From Auschwitz she was shipped to Ravensbrück, and from there she had been forced on a death march until she was liberated by the Russians. Somehow she made it to Prague, went to the Jewish Community Center, and there she found my name on a list. For her, I was like an orienting anchor, and for me she represented home. She stayed with us for a few days and then, like the rest of us, she moved on to look for her family.

In the months after we came back from the camps we had tried to return to a normal life, but it was impossible suddenly to shake off the trauma of those terrible years. The search for relatives who might still be alive was ongoing. We had to find apartments, build new homes, establish new lives, earn money. We wanted to study, start our own families, learn how to dress and how to shop, and most difficult, we wanted to fit in again, to adjust to normal social relationships. Often we behaved in ways that were quite different from what was expected of us, and we were frequently criticized for it. But we weren't even aware of how odd our behavior was and the reactions that it elicited.

The return to normal living was difficult. Every day we encountered circumstances that reminded us of the concentration camps, and it was all we could do not to run away from these encounters. To this day, we haven't been able to avoid them. We had lost the ability to trust people, and a certain mistrust remains. Even in the most mundane situations the past comes to the fore. For instance, I can't throw away a crust of bread; it has to be used up or eaten, no matter how hard and stale it is. We always have to have stores of groceries in the house so that there'll be something to eat in case of famine. The best thing is to have a small garden where you can plant potatoes and vegetables. I am confronted with reminders of the camps almost every day. Worst of all are the nights when I dream that "they" have gassed our children, relatives, parents, and friends. Often Kurt has had to wake me up because I was screaming in my sleep. The dreams never let go of me. In those dreams I am riding in a cattle car, singing the song about the pink crinoline. How often I used to run to my children's bedroom to make sure that they were safe in their little beds, and breathing. Sometimes we would wake them, and of course they couldn't understand why. How could they know about the hell their parents had been through?

We were young. We wanted to enjoy life, to be successful, perhaps to make up for all that we had missed during that long period of deprivation. Kurt and I were passionately in love. We admired every flower, marveled at each bird we saw. We took long hikes; we swam; we walked through the beautiful streets of Prague and up to the Castle and its gardens. We went to the theater, to the movies—we couldn't get enough of it all. One day I saw an announcement that the Philharmonic was going to play "My Homeland" by Smetana. With the little money I had, I bought a ticket, and after so many years I sat in a concert hall again and listened to this wonderful music. It lifted me into a trance from which I awoke only when the audience applauded at the end of the performance.

Our attitude toward life had changed. We began to see beauty all around us, and to be aware of life in a deeper sense. We had many friends, but all of them were former concentration-camp inmates. It was hard to make contact with people who had not gone through the camps and whose way of thinking and views of life were different from ours.

Many couples we knew were living together without being married. Almost all married couples had been separated, and in many cases it could be assumed that the spouse who had not yet returned had been murdered by the Nazis. But because there was always the possibility that the missing partner might turn up, there was a mandatory two-year waiting period before a remarriage was sanctioned. We knew that Kurt's wife, Lisa, would never return, but we agreed to the waiting period nonetheless.

Any day now, Aunt Regina was expected to arrive from Palestine. We decided to remove Kurt's name from the front door so that she would not immediately be confronted with the "shameful" fact that I was sharing my apartment with a man. We planned to break it to her slowly, but she arrived a day early without warning. I was overjoyed when I opened the door and saw her there, a stately, good-looking woman. Finally, my first really close relative, my father's sister, whom I had so yearned to see again! We had barely exchanged kisses and greetings and I was introducing Kurt to her when she asked, "Ruth, why are there two names on your door?"

Matter-of-factly, I explained that Kurt and I were living together although we were not married. Aunt Regina stared at me thunderstruck. "That means," she blurted out, "that you are bringing shame to our family!"

Why this harsh reaction? How could we be bringing shame on the family? We loved each other, and our love was honest and straightforward. What crime were we guilty of? Why didn't she ask us about the ordeal we had been through? Why didn't she ask about what happened to her brothers and sisters? Why was this "family shame" so important to her?

I moved closer to Kurt, as if for protection from Aunt Regina's verbal onslaught. Kurt was speechless, and I knew how hard it was for him to restrain himself. All the while she was looking around our modest living room, in which I had put the few things Gustav had returned to me, among them a small Oriental rug that had belonged to Uncle Hugo. It was the only item among his things that I had taken—to remember him by. Staring at the rug, she asked, "Didn't this rug belong to Uncle Hugo? What right have you to take his things? The inheritance has to be legally divided among the heirs."

I had had enough. "Get out, get out of our house!" I shouted, and she had no choice but to leave without saying another word.

I felt pain, disillusionment, and shame at the behavior of my only aunt who had survived. When she called on her cousin Paul Wurzel (the doctor), he told her what had happened to us and explained that our psychic wounds had not yet healed. The least she could do, he said, was to make an attempt to understand the incomprehensible.

But she did not understand, and she was not the only one. She immediately started legal proceedings, expecting to inherit as much as possible of the assets left behind by her sisters and brothers who had been killed in the gas chambers. I was not interested in any of that; let her take the rug if she wanted to. My memory of Uncle Hugo wasn't contained in that carpet; it was preserved deep in my heart. I decided that Aunt Regina lacked the sensitivity and insight to comprehend our tragedy, perhaps because she and her family had been in Palestine throughout the war.

Bit by bit we received news about family members who were living abroad. Stella, Aunt Resi's daughter, had escaped to England and survived the war there. Another of my father's cousins, Paul's brother Sigi, had also emigrated there before the war started. He often came to visit his brother in Prague, and Kurt and I got to know him better.

Kurt's Uncle Karel, his wife, and their son Tommy returned from England. They came back with the Czech government-in-exile. Karel was an agricultural engineer and was immediately given a high position in the Czech Ministry of Agriculture, where he eventually rose to the rank of deputy minister. Kurt was his uncle's only surviving relative, and we stayed in close touch with him.

We were always happy when we heard about members of our family who had survived, even if they were distant relatives. On the other hand, these were saddening reminders of the dreadful fate our large families had met. So few had come through the catastrophe. Moreover, we did not know how the missing had died. Where had they been taken? Had they been starved to death? Had they been gassed? Did they suffer terribly? When did it happen? To this day I know of no gravestone, no grave on which to place flowers and say Kaddish, the Jewish prayer for the dead.

Obtaining personal documents was a complicated procedure. We had handed all our papers over to the German authorities when we were deported to Theresienstadt, so we had no official identities. Actually, I could have taken on the identity of someone who had died, and the authorities probably would have believed me. We went from one government office to another. My birth certificate and certificate of citizenship were on file in Ostrava, and I went there in person to pick them up and pay a fee for them. Then I had to go to Pozořice to get written confirmation of my last residence and registration, and to bring witnesses to the appropriate Prague offices to testify to my identity. A lot of time was consumed in filling out forms and waiting. But finally we had all our papers in order.

The required two-year waiting period before we could be married was over. Kurt's wife, Lisa, and their little daughter, Evička, had not come back; it was almost certain that they had been killed. We took all our papers to the registry office to set a date for the wedding. The clerk asked when we wanted to get married, and we said, "The first date you've got available."

He leafed through his book until he found a date. "April 18th, if that's all right with you," he said.

We burst out laughing. The clerk gave us a blank look, and we explained why this particular date had such a special meaning for us. It was Kurt's birthday, and it was also the day on which we were liberated. Now, on top of that, it was to be our wedding day. We were only too happy to take that date. It meant that we would always be celebrating three anniversaries on the same day.

Paul, who had become my father's surrogate, offered to have the lunch after the wedding ceremony at his home. We were a small party: Uncle Karel and his wife, Paul and his family, and the two of us. A few of our friends came to the registry office, among them Berta and her new husband, Jirka Weil, and Houština and Erich Jokl. I kept thinking of all the missing members of my family who surely would have attended the ceremony. On such occasions the wound I hoped was healing would invariably break open again, and I was hurled back in time, whether I wanted to be reminded or not. I suppose we shall never be able to tear ourselves free of the past, for there will always be occasions that evoke certain associations, and we will involuntarily recall similar situations from the past.

We had invited a few friends to come to our sixth-floor apartment that evening for a small celebration. Food and clothing were severely rationed, and it was not easy to buy something that was not covered by our ration cards. I had been given a wonderful wedding gift, something quite new in Czechoslovakia at the time, that could only be purchased abroad: two pairs of nylon stockings. Nylon had just been invented, and stockings made of this miracle yarn were very expensive. My friends admired the stockings; they may even have envied me. It was a pleasant evening, and after all the guests had left I began to clean up the apartment, asking Kurt to take the trash down to the courtyard. When he came back upstairs, he helped me finish with the cleanup. Suddenly I remembered my precious stockings. We turned the apartment upside down but couldn't find them. Then it hit me. We had probably thrown the stockings out with the garbage. Down to the courtyard we went and rummaged around in the rubbish barrels, until just before dawn we found them. What a way to spend our wedding night!

At breakfast, our first as a legally married couple, we talked about Aunt Regina. Had she been in Prague, she would have congratulated us, overjoyed because she could be proud of me, now

The wedding of Ruth and Kurt Elias, Prague, April 18, 1947.

that I was married and no longer represented a blot on the family's reputation. I also thought of the woman doctor in Taucha who had said that I would meet a widower and later marry him. I had laughed at her prediction then. But a good-looking young widower now sat across the table from me, and we loved each other very much.

Kurt studied hard, passing one examination after another. He also took a job in a pharmacy. I managed to become quite good as a secretary in the freight forwarding company. After I had been working there a year, I asked the director of the company for a more responsible position. I told him that I was capable of writing the kinds of letters that had been dictated to me by the various department heads, and that I was losing interest in secretarial work. I also indicated that I would have to look for another job elsewhere if he couldn't find a more interesting assignment for me. He thought it over for a moment and decided to entrust me with responsibility for the smallest department in the firm. That's when I became the head of Package and Sample Shipments, corresponding with major firms in Czechoslovakia and with businesspeople all over the world. It was meaningful and challenging work. Several months later I was put in charge of a bigger department, which was responsible for our company dealings with three large European ports—Amsterdam, Rotterdam, and Antwerp. I was the only woman who held such a position in the forwarding business.

It was extremely difficult to ship goods in the postwar period. Germany had been subjected to heavy bombardment, and there was widespread destruction and hunger. Trains were often sidetracked, and all the goods they carried were stolen. To prevent such losses, the Dutch came up with the idea of transporting goods to and from the ports in large closed trucks. Each truck had two drivers who took turns at the wheel so that the goods could be transported safely through Germany without stopovers. One day the Dutch owner of one of these trucks came to our firm in Prague and asked to speak with the head of the department. Our director brought him to see me, and the Dutchman seemed taken aback when he saw a woman sitting behind the desk. He turned to the director and asked, "You mean to say this girl knows something about forwarding?"

He came to our office several times after that, and about a year later he offered me the job of setting up and heading a Prague branch of his firm, handling all of Czechoslovakia. I accepted. The job paid well and would help Kurt and me improve our living standard. Meanwhile, Kurt had completed his coursework with honors, mastering a wealth of material. It was an admirable accomplishment, considering the long break in his studies and the trauma of internment. Once again, here was proof that the Nazis had not succeeded in annihilating us spiritually and intellectually.

In April 1948, I invited our relatives—Uncle Karel and Paul and their wives—and Ženka to come to Kurt's graduation at the famous old Charles University in Prague. It was the first time I had ever attended a graduation ceremony. This one was very festive and had been lent a special dignity by the grand and venerable surroundings. I was bursting with pride when Kurt accepted his diploma, a large red scroll. I thought of Kurt's parents. How proud and happy they would have been! If it hadn't been for the Nazis, Kurt might have been receiving a degree in medicine that day.

Kurt and I embraced, and at that moment we thought we were the only two people on earth. Who at the ceremony could understand our emotion? And who could have an inkling under what circumstances Kurt had managed to complete his studies so quickly? Who knew of the close ties that bound us together, the months we had spent together in the work camp and our return, the start of a normal life, the difficult readjustment, the annihilation of our families, the financial worries, and the many late hours spent studying. It had been a tremendous struggle, and the harder things got, the closer became the ties that bound us to each other. We'd go through life, unfalteringly sharing everything, the beautiful as well as the ugly. We loved and respected each other. We were immeasurably proud of what we had accomplished and resolved never to submit or to give up. I don't know how long we stayed in each other's arms. But I would have held on to this moment forever if our relatives and friends had not become impatient as they waited to express their good wishes and congratulations to Kurt.

They were all invited to a feast at our apartment after the ceremony. I had bought some wonderful meat on the flourishing black market and had lovingly prepared it, with all the trimmings. This was to be the first time our families would get a taste of my cooking. Before we left the apartment to go to the university, I had asked Ženka to put the roast and vegetables into the electric oven and set it on low to keep things warm. That way, we could eat as soon as we came back.

I walked back to the apartment as if in a dream, hearing and seeing nothing of what was going on around me. Then I tripped on a step I hadn't seen and, with a scream, I fell. A crystal box I was holding shattered, but there's an old saying: Broken glass brings good luck. Unfortunately, my precious nylons had a big hole and many runs in them, and my knee hurt. But I had learned to ignore pain, so, gritting my teeth, I walked on without even limping. I didn't want to spoil everyone's good mood. My thoughts were on the feast that was waiting for us at home. The table had been beautifully set, and the roast and vegetables were being kept warm in the oven.

Ženka and I took the elevator up to the sixth floor. We were still in the hall when we smelled smoke. Before I could unlock the apartment door, the rest of our party arrived. I ran into the kitchen, scarcely able to breathe because the entire apartment was filled with smoke. After opening all the windows, I went back into the kitchen. The electric oven had been set on high rather than low, and the expensive meat and everything else had burned to cinders. I stood there helpless, embarrassed to be making such a negative impression on Kurt's aunt and uncle. Then a practical solution suggested itself. I ran downstairs to a delicatessen, which was about to close, and bought some Vienna sausages and rolls. These became our graduation feast, and because we were all in a great mood as a result of Kurt's accomplishment the food itself was really unimportant. What mattered was the goal he had attained and the fact that we were able to celebrate his triumph together.

The political situation in Europe was changing. We had misgivings when Czechoslovakia joined the Eastern bloc and came under increasing Soviet influence. There were endless discussions about the prospects of Jews in Czechoslovakia, and we concluded that we had two alternatives: We could either assimilate or emigrate. Many hours, often late into the night, were spent grappling with this problem and trying to arrive at a decision. Those of us who had gone through the concentration camps knew that assimilation could only be one-sided. Even in the postwar years, and after all that was now known about the intended destruction of the Jews, most

Czechs were still antisemitic. Their hatred of Jews was too deeply ingrained to change in a few months. How often I had heard one of them say, "Oh, if all Jews were like you, but. . . ."

I always interrupted when they got to "but," because that little word said more than all the words that might follow. Gradually Kurt and I arrived at the decision to leave Europe, where so much suffering had been inflicted on us. By now we were eagerly following all the news about Palestine and efforts to build a free and independent Jewish state there.

Kurt and I came to realize that there was only one country for us: Israel. Both of us had been brought up with Zionist ideals, and we knew that we wanted to live in a country of our own. Had we wanted to be among non-Jews, we wouldn't have had to emigrate. We could have stayed in Czechoslovakia, where we were born and raised. Unfortunately, we had to delay our plans to leave for several months because Kurt had to perform his Czech military service. Although at the beginning I could visit him in his army camp in Prague, later he was sent farther away, and we saw each other only rarely.

I continued to work, but whenever I met Jewish friends and acquaintances the conversation inevitably turned to emigration. We were worried about the political situation of the Jews in Palestine, the coming fight for independence, and the threatening posture of the Arabs. A Haganah group had formed in Czechoslovakia. This Jewish underground army unit made up of soldiers and airmen—in a camp established for that purpose—was training not only Czech Jews but young people from Palestine who told us about Eretz Israel. We hung on their every word and could hardly wait to go there. We stepped up our efforts to complete the necessary bureaucratic paperwork for emigration. We longed for the homeland we had never had. This could only be Israel. Without exception, we were willing to risk our lives for this new homeland, even though many of us had escaped death only a short while before.

In the meantime, word came of pogroms against Jews in Poland.[1] Jews who had survived the camps and were returning to their hometowns to live were attacked; some were killed. Polish Jews streamed into Czechoslovakia. Because they had no passports or other identification papers, they could not register in hotels or other public places. Those of us who had apartments made room for them. They told us about the dreadful, tragic things that happened in Poland after the war. So few had managed to survive the concentration camps, and now they were again being attacked and murdered! Where was human compassion? Where was the International Red Cross? The Church? The Pope? Where were other nations? Few people during and after the war helped the Jews. Six million of our brothers and sisters were murdered, and when the surviving Jews wanted to return to their old homes or reclaim the belongings they had given to non-Jews to keep for them, they had to listen to sentiments such as, "Too bad they didn't gas you, too. Why did you of all people have to come back?"

The Hebrew Immigrant Aid Society (HIAS) in Prague was able to furnish the refugees with the required documents and to send them on to the Jewish homeland. The war for independence was well under way there, and young men were mobilized as soon as they got off the ships. Without much prior training, they were sent into battle against the attacking Arabs. Many concentration-camp survivors did not live to see the creation of the state for which they had fought. Having only recently escaped death in the Nazi hell, they now lost their lives in the fight to reestablish their national home.

Toward the end of September 1948, an important meeting took place in our apartment. David Taussig, a young Jew from Haifa, had arrived in Czechoslovakia to explore the possibility of building an

---

[1] Publisher's note: On July 4, 1946, Jews who had survived the camps and returned after the war to the Polish city of Kielce were the victims of a pogrom. Forty-two people were murdered that day by Polish antisemites. This pogrom induced many Polish Jews to emigrate.

Israeli branch of the well-known pencil factory Hardtmuth Koh-i-noor. The negotiations and the prospects looked promising. David was looking for young men who could be trained in the factory in České Budějovice and would then set up a branch in Israel. He told us that the company had already started building the physical plant in Israel and was also constructing residences for the specialists being trained in Czechoslovakia. It sounded like a good idea. Knowing that we would have a place to live and work in Israel gave us a sense of security.

After Kurt had returned from military duty in October, he found a job as a pharmacist and was happily at work. But he gave up this job to go into training for the new project in Israel. A group of eleven men went to Budějovice to begin their training at the factory. Kurt, who knew chemistry, was responsible for the coloring and impregnation process. The wives, who stayed in Prague, began the thorny process of dealing with Czech bureaucracy to get the group's emigration documents in order.

Each family was allowed to take one lift (a large wooden container) filled with furniture and belongings out of the country. We had to make detailed lists enumerating every plate, spoon, and handkerchief we wanted to take. These lists were then checked at the customs office. When we got them back, we found to our dismay that everything of any value had been crossed off the list: pictures, rugs, musical instruments, glassware, and china. We had all spent a lot of effort, money, and patience in making new homes for ourselves after we came out of the camps. The Germans had taken everything from us, and now the Czechs were trying to do the same. But in one respect things were different: Our possessions were not confiscated; we were allowed to sell them. But many Czechs exploited this situation and paid us very little. We couldn't take any money with us, and only the rich could afford to buy foreign currency on the black market. Officially, we were permitted to take out only five British pounds, which we picked up at the Czech National Bank. But our bitter experiences in the camps had taught us that money and material possessions count for nothing compared with one's life, so we quickly got over our material losses. We drew strength, courage, and confidence from the thought that we would be going to a new home. Still, it was very hard for me to part with my piano. It stood in our apartment, and I played only when I was alone. Once more the piano had become my good friend, and now I had to leave it behind again.

There was a new round of farewells. Berta and Jirka did not want to leave Czechoslovakia because they had just had a baby. Houština and Erich also stayed behind because Erich had become a confirmed communist and was incensed that we would want to leave a country with such a splendid regime. He saw our emigration as betrayal of our Czech fatherland. It was also hard to say good-bye to Paul Wurzel, my surrogate father. Kurt's Uncle Karel, who held a high position in the Ministry of Agriculture and was also an enthusiastic communist, would never have left his fatherland. It wasn't hard to leave my colleagues at work, for I had never formed close contacts with them.

However, I shall never forget saying farewell to the director of Intrasped. He was a Jew and had been my boss at the forwarding firm. I had asked him to write a letter of reference for me in English. When he called me into his office, he went over to the radio and turned on some loud music; evidently he thought our conversation was being bugged. He asked me about our emigration, and he seemed full of longing to join us. But when I asked him why he did not emigrate too, he did not reply. As we parted, he shook my hand warmly and said, "How very much I would like to be in your shoes. I feel that I'm not going to make it here."

What he meant by that I did not then know. He was relatively young. But his forebodings proved correct. He was sentenced to death during the Slansky show trial.[2]

---

[2] Publisher's note: Rudolf Slansky, who was born in 1901, had been general secretary of the Czechoslovak Communist Party since 1945. During a show trial in November 1951, he was accused of "Titoist and Zionist activities" as the head of an alleged conspiracy. He was sentenced to death and executed a year later.

A moving van took our things to a collection point, where customs agents examined every item, checking it against the numbered list before it could be put into the lift. It was hours before everything was packed and sealed and loaded onto a Dutch truck that would go to Rotterdam. From there our things would be shipped to Haifa. This was my final task as head of the international forwarding department of my firm.

For three days all of us in the Hardtmuth group were put up in a Prague hotel. Then, on April 1, 1949, we and a thousand other emigrants got on a train for Naples, where we would board a ship for Haifa. A last handshake with friends who had come to see us off, a few tears, and we were on our way, proudly singing our national anthem, *Hatikvah*.

This brought to mind two moments from my past: being loaded into cattle cars when we left Theresienstadt for Auschwitz, and the Birkenau family-camp inmates singing *Hatikvah* as they went to the gas chamber.

The train stopped at the Czech border, where customs guards boarded. They asked whether we had any illegal items. When no one spoke up, they selected several individuals and led them to the customs building. This was repeated several times. When these people came back, they told us they had been made to undress and then searched minutely for smuggled goods. Again those frightful associations: undressing, Mengele, selection. Would it never stop?

We were relieved when the train began to move again, leaving Czechoslovakia and crossing the border into Austria. (Some years later, we heard that an arrest order had been issued for the Hardtmuth group on charges that we were taking industrial secrets abroad. The warrant missed us by only a few hours.) There was a brief stop in Vienna, but guards on the platform made sure we did not leave the train. Then onward to Italy. For us ex-prisoners this trip was full of associations. Although we were free and heading for life in our new homeland, we were not permitted to leave the train. We had to spend the night in the passenger compartments; at least this time it was not in cattle cars. Each of us had taken a bag of food along, because the train had no dining car and we could not get off to buy anything to eat; in any case, we had no money. We were provided with drinking water.

In the port of Naples our train was switched to a siding. We waited. A second train stood on a track near ours. We heard singing and loud voices speaking a language we did not understand. There were many people on that train, most of them somewhat darker-skinned than we. We tried to find a common language and discovered that some of them spoke French or Italian. It turned out that they were Jews from Morocco and Tunisia who were also going to Israel, on the same boat.

A small steamship, the *Galilah,* was waiting for us. It had an all-Israeli crew—the sailors, officers, and the captain were all Jews. I was amazed and felt immensely proud. About two thousand of us were crowded together belowdecks, each assigned a hammock for sleeping. During the three-day voyage we spent most of our time up on deck, but one of the men had to stay below at all times to watch our baggage. It seemed that for some who had been long deprived, temptation was proving to be too strong. We took our meals in shifts, sitting at rough wooden tables, the food served on tin plates. I ate nothing but bread, because the meals consisted largely of olives and halvah, foods that were strange to me. Later, in Israel, I got used to these things.

The first evening on board I heard someone playing the accordion. The music drew me like a magnet. I asked for a chance to play, and a circle of Israelis and Czechs immediately formed around me. We sang and played till late into the night, and through the music we got to know many of the other passengers. The rest of the night was spent with members of the crew, listening entranced to their stories about our new homeland, the hard life there, the strenuous work of the pioneers, the hot climate, the sea, the hills, the desert. They told us about the cities, the villages, the kibbutzim—all of which had been built by Jews. They also talked about the recently concluded war of independence and the heroic deeds of the Israelis, who had defended their country, often with only a few weapons. We became more and more impatient to get to our new homeland. Why am I writing "new" homeland? We didn't have an "old" homeland. Until now, we had been at best a tolerated minority all over the world. In Czechoslovakia we had citizenship, but now, for the first time in two thousand years, we had our own country: Eretz Israel.

After a few wakeful hours in our hammocks—because of the heat, sleep was out of the question—we went back up on deck. There, to our astonishment and horror we saw that our North African brothers had built a little fire and were planning to cook a meal. Warned to stop, they simply couldn't understand why. Most of them were pleasant people, and I was sorry that because of the language differences we could not talk with them. It was the first time we had encountered a completely different culture, and this was a source of constant surprise to us. They had brought some musical instruments on deck, mostly large square metal cans that had once contained olive oil. With their fingers and palms they began an intricate drumming, producing fabulous rhythms. At first they hummed along softly, but gradually the drumming and the songs grew louder. One by one they got up and, carried away, began to dance with ecstatic exuberance. We stood around and marveled at so much natural joy. Having been raised to behave with European decorum, I envied their spontaneity and lack of inhibition.

The sea was calm, and the sun shone in a cloudless sky. This was the adventure of a lifetime; for many of us, it was the first trip on a ship and the first sight of the sea. The ship sailed past the Greek islands, but with our thoughts fixed on the future, we scarcely noticed. On our last night on board I again played the accordion while the Europeans sang. On the other side of the ship the North Africans drummed on their metal cans and danced. Word spread that at dawn we would be able to see Israel. There was great excitement and restlessness; no one had any desire to go belowdecks to sleep. Each of us wanted a spot at the ship's rail; we hardly felt the nighttime chill. When the sun began to rise, we could see Haifa in the distance. The beautiful city rose majestically from the sea up to Mount Carmel, the golden dome of the Bahai temple gleaming in its center. Someone started to sing *Hatikvah,* and tears came to many eyes. We had made it to the promised land.

7

My Israel

SLOWLY THE SHIP MOVED INTO THE HARBOR, and the harbor pilot came on board. On shore, there was great activity, with some people carrying burdens on their backs and others pushing heavy handcarts. Cranes were loading and unloading goods. It was a scene of enormous animation in these early-morning hours. One of the ship's officers pointed to the dock area and said, "Those people, the workers you see down there, are all Israelis."

Coming from a Europe that historically had cast most Jews in certain roles, denying them others, I saw for the first time free Jews—my brothers—doing hard physical work, just like people in other countries, and I was very proud. Finally, we were like other people, not just a minority. This was my country, and I vowed that I would do everything I could to preserve it for the Jewish people. How often had I had to knuckle under in Europe, how often was I reviled because of my Jewishness. Holding my head high, I descended the steps of the ship's ladder and swore never again to bow down before anyone. From now on, I would fight.

A reception of sorts had been prepared for us. First we were dusted with DDT in a small room, from which we emerged white and smelly. Then we were loaded onto trucks—what memories that brought back—and after riding for a few miles we arrived at St. Lux, near Haifa. There a camp had been set up surrounded by barbed wire; formerly it had been a British army camp. We were horrified. Hadn't the Israelis heard about the German concentration camps? Why were they putting us behind barbed wire again? No one seemed to have the answers to these questions. We were taken to huts made of corrugated metal, and with rounded roofs. Inside were iron bedsteads. (The mattresses for these were distributed much later.) Everyone in our Czech group was assigned to the same barracks. Some of the women began to cry. Never had we imagined a reception like this! Behind the barbed wire, all the pride and joy we had felt only hours earlier vanished.

Didn't anyone realize what connotations barbed wire had for us? Why did we have to be subjected to this again in our own country? Still intoxicated with their glorious victory on the battlefield and with the creation of the state of Israel, the Israelis in charge seemed not to be interested in our past. Apparently they considered us to be cowards, because instead of fighting, we had too easily surrendered to the enemy. They didn't know how heroically many of us had persevered during the terrible Nazi time, how we refused to be crushed, and how we resisted spiritually and physically. It was not until later, much later, that they began to listen to us, and to understand. But when we first arrived, the Israeli authorities were no different from other immigration officials the world over.

Although people in Israel sometimes asked me about the past, as soon as I began to tell them about my experiences, I sensed that they did not or would not understand, so I stopped talking about the Nazi years. Instead, we discussed the future. If we could wipe the past from our minds, perhaps we would be able to forget, and forgetting would help us to build the future, to start families. But as the years passed, we realized that we couldn't simply encapsulate and forget such a trauma. Again and again, in very different situations, the memories resurfaced. There was to be no escape.

The men in our group went to see the camp authorities and told them that we had come to Israel to set up a pencil factory in Safed, and that we were expected. They were given permission to make a day trip to Safed. The women, however, were not allowed to leave the camp, which was called Shaar Aliyah (Immigration Gate). This only heightened our desperation.

After numerous inquiries, I finally found out why we were interned. All of us, men and women alike, would have to undergo medical examinations, because the immigration authorities wanted to prevent the introduction of contagious diseases. Had they told us this at the outset we would have understood, but not knowing made us increasingly angry. However, once again my natural optimism took over, and adapting to my surroundings, I tried to make life a little more comfortable for us. There were two sheets and two pillows in our luggage. I put them on our beds and placed a board between the two beds to make a sort of night table. I covered it with a little doily and then I put our toilet articles on top of the doily. The other women watched me as though I'd lost my mind, but when I helped them do something similar their sadness and apathy began to lift. And so we occupied ourselves with minor tasks.

Unfortunately, our spirits plummeted anew when the men came back that evening with the news that there was no factory in Safed; no houses had been prepared for our arrival. The local authorities said they knew nothing of the pencil-factory project. Then why had the Israeli representative come to Prague? Why did they go to all the trouble of training us? The letters of reference from the Israeli Consulate in Prague turned out to be worthless. As a result, we had no choice but to share the fate of other immigrants to Israel, to wait and see. Not until David Taussig returned from Prague did we get a partial explanation of what had happened. David had had great difficulty getting out of Czechoslovakia. The machines, packed and ready for shipment, had been confiscated. Years later, there was testimony about the Israeli pencil-factory case during the Slansky trial, and I found out that the director of the Hardtmuth factory had been arrested by the Czechs and sentenced to prison for betraying industrial secrets. He was also charged with planning to smuggle foreign currency out of the country by exporting the machines.

Meanwhile, three or four additional transports, each carrying some one thousand immigrants, arrived at the camp. It was said that the Czechs were not permitting any additional transports to leave, and I thanked God that we had made it out in time. I had become quite prepared to deal with all the difficulties that would come our way in the process of acclimating ourselves, and I was determined to do everything in my power to help in the building of our new homeland.

The time we spent at Camp Shaar Aliyah, with no work and nothing to do except pick up our food and wash our clothes, was demoralizing. We all smoked, and out of sheer boredom we smoked too much. Soon we had spent the five British pounds we'd been allowed to bring with us on cigarettes and chocolate. We urgently needed more money.

A onetime business contact, Wolfgang Lesser, who lived on Mount Carmel, imported lumber to Israel from Czechoslovakia. I had assisted him in business transactions in Prague, and he had given me his Haifa address, urging me to get in touch with him if I needed anything in Israel. Kurt and I decided to look him up. We crept through a hole in the barbed-wire fence and climbed up the mountain, all the while debating which of us would ask Mr. Lesser for a small loan. He welcomed us warmly, serving us delicious coffee and cake. As we were leaving, he asked whether we needed anything. Could he help us in any way? In unison we said, "Thank you so much. We really don't need a thing."

We had never before asked for charity and were reluctant to start now. But there was no way out. The following day I again squeezed through the hole in the fence, and this time I went to Mr. Lesser's office in Haifa and asked him for a small loan. Without hesitating he gave me ten pounds, wondering why we had not mentioned it the previous day. I was so ashamed to find myself in this predicament that I may not even have thanked him as I took the money. Tears came to my eyes, and I quickly left his office. We paid him back with the first money we earned, and for many years we remained good friends.

Immediately after the new state was founded, Israel opened its gates to Jews from all over the world, inviting them to come and help build the new land. This was the beginning of a massive influx of newcomers. It is miraculous that this tiny country managed to absorb them all. The first challenge was to house and feed the new arrivals, which was no easy task. There was no housing available, and the newcomers had to be put up in tents. Given the acute shortage of food, it was truly remarkable how efficiently the Jewish Agency (Sochnut) organized everything in such a short time. Still, it was awful that the immigrants had to live in tents without electricity or running water, pestered by swarms of flies and mosquitoes. (We had come from civilized countries and had lived there in nice homes.) Also, the food was pretty bad, and hundreds of people had to make do with only one shower room. The spring khamsin, the winds that blew in from the desert, made it so hot that we had to wash off the sand and sweat several times a day. The lines of people waiting to take showers were long, and it was a real contest to keep one's place in line.

After two weeks in the reception camp, a doctor examined us and established that we were not carriers of infectious diseases. We left Shaar Aliyah to make room for other immigrants. Our next stop was the Brandeis tent camp on the outskirts of Hadera, which in those days was a very small town. This time there was no barbed wire around the camp, so we seemed to be making some progress. There were endless rows of tents, each with its side walls rolled up to allow the air to circulate. Our group was put into two tents that had iron bedsteads and mattresses. We stashed our suitcases under the beds, and someone stayed in the tents at all times to stand watch over our belongings.

After a brief council we decided that we simply had to do something about our situation. The men went out to look for work, Kurt to the Ministry of Health to apply for a job as a pharmacist. What we didn't know was that there was a surplus of academically trained and professional people in Israel at the time. No pharmacists were needed. The secretary with whom Kurt spoke was an old-timer. She looked at him and said, "First pick up a *turia* (a combination shovel and mattock) and go to work for a few years. After that maybe we can find something for you. And if this doesn't suit you, you can go down to the *yam*, the sea"—in other words, you can drown yourself.

Kurt couldn't believe his ears. Here was complete incomprehension and lack of interest; it was humiliating. He came back to camp unhappy and discouraged, first because of the shabby treatment he had received, and second because there seemed to be no prospects for him to make a living here.

The next day Kurt and the men in the Hardtmuth group decided to try their luck in Tel Aviv. There Kurt also visited Mrs. Alice Eisner, who had been a good friend of his mother's. She welcomed him like a son to her small two-room apartment, and he stayed with her for several days. During that time, he managed to find a job as a pharmacist in a suburb of Tel Aviv. It was arranged that he would stay at Mrs. Eisner's apartment during the week while I watched over our suitcases in Hadera. We saw each other only on weekends. We were not happy with this arrangement, but we had heard that there was no hope of finding an apartment in Tel Aviv. Apartments had to be bought, and we had no money.

One day a Czech woman who had been in Eretz Israel for a long time came to our tent to visit friends, and she told us about a small village called Nirah, near Netanya. It had been built by Czech Jews who had emigrated from the Sudetenland. She had heard that they were building wooden houses for new immigrants there. Kurt Louda, who was from the Sudetenland, and I borrowed money to take the bus to Netanya. There we asked about Nirah. The bus had gone right past it, we were told, and we'd have to walk back about three miles. It was noon on a hot day in May, but we were young and so we started to walk. (On the way to Nirah we passed through the village of Bet Yitzchak, which would be my future home.) By the time we arrived it was three o'clock, and the village looked deserted; not a soul was on the streets. Finally we met a man on a bicycle. I asked him whether this was Nirah. He looked at us in disbelief, nodded, and asked what we were doing there at this time of day. Being newcomers, we didn't know that the time between two and four o'clock is the sacred nap time—an unwritten law says that nobody should be disturbed during this siesta.

"We're new immigrants from Prague," I said, "and we're looking for other Czechs so that we can get some information about friends of ours. We also want to find work."

"You're from Prague?" he said. "I'm Freda Weiss. Come with me." He led us to a little house, where he woke his wife, Else, from her nap. At first she seemed rather grumpy, but when she found out that we had recently arrived from Prague she cheered up. Freda and Else welcomed us warmly, offering us food and drink, and then we talked and talked. Else was from Prague, and Freda had lived there for many years. Both had fond memories of the city even though they were confirmed Zionists. Kurt asked who in Nirah was from the Sudetenland. The Weisses mentioned the Konirschs, who had been good friends and neighbors of Kurt's parents. As soon as the siesta hour was over, Kurt and I went to see them, and there was an emotional reunion after so many years of separation. The Konirschs' son-in-law noticed the number tattooed on my forearm and asked about the concentration camps. He said his brother Heini Schönhof had also been deported to one of the camps.

I remembered Heini. He was in the woodcutter group in Pozořice and had often come to our house. We had been good friends, and we later met again in Theresienstadt. He had spoken of his brother in Palestine and of his hope of following him there someday. Instead, he was taken to Auschwitz and never returned. Suddenly I was hurled back into the past and was unable to hold back my tears. Afterward, I marveled at how dispassionately they had all listened to my story about Heini and the camps. It confirmed once more that some of our own people lacked interest in and understanding of our experiences.

According to Mr. Konirsch, some wooden houses were being built on a hill behind Nirah. He suggested that we apply for one of these and then took us to see the head of the community council of the village, Mr. Fleischmann, a former lawyer who was now a farmer. Mr. Fleischmann's first question was, "How much money do you have? We're a middle-class settlement, and to get in you need money."

Good Lord, are these people crazy or am I? How were we supposed to get money? Don't they know what's going on beyond their village? Are they living on a desert island? I decided to lie. I just had to get out of that tent camp, had to get a real roof over my head, so I asked how much money was needed. Mr. Fleischmann named what seemed an astronomical sum to me. In a matter-of-fact voice I said it wouldn't be hard to put that together. I had no idea what a middle-class settlement—or any other kind of village, for that matter—was supposed to be. I knew only one thing: We had to start a new life. I told Mr. Fleischmann about our group, and we agreed that all of us would soon come to Nirah to get more information. That meeting took place in the courtyard of Rudl and Gretl Hirsch's house.

But it turned out that nobody in our group, not even Kurt, wanted to stay in this rural area; they all wanted to live in a city. I, on the other hand, was ready to settle down either in a kibbutz or, if worse came to worst, in a village; I did not want to live in town. Even today, I still have the feeling that I must own a little piece of land so that in a time of hunger we will have a place to plant potatoes to keep us from starving.

Kurt finally agreed to give up his job in Tel Aviv. After all, he couldn't live with the Eisners or in the tent camp forever. We moved to Nirah, and there the villagers welcomed us. Gretl and Rudl Hirsch offered us their daughter Susi's room; she was serving in the army at the time. I helped around the house and on the farm, while Kurt worked first as a farmhand and then with horses tilling the land. With time Kurt became remarkably proficient at cultivating the tiny fields with a horse-drawn plow. Later he became an expert at cleaning out cesspools. Everyone in the village agreed to give him something to do, so he worked in a different place each day, getting to know all the settlers. The village of Nirah gave us a plot of land, where we planted vegetables for our own use and for sale.

Nirah was founded by twenty-five families, all of whom were emigrants from the Sudetenland. Some of the settlers were textile experts, and they set up a small communal textile factory to produce curtain material. Everyone had to work in the factory a certain number of hours per week. Each family owned a two-room house with a little garden in front. At the back was a chicken coop enclosed by a wire fence to keep out the jackals. Beyond that lay the farm fields, which were divided into small squares, each planted with a different vegetable. Because it doesn't rain during the summer in Israel, the fields had to be irrigated. This required a complicated installation of iron watering pipes that had to be moved every day. It was hard work.

We developed a wonderfully close relationship with the Hirsches, calling them Tato and Mamo, the Czech for father and mother. When construction of the wooden houses behind the village began, Kurt learned a new trade as a construction worker. Within two months the houses were ready, and we left Tato and Mamo, who had temporarily provided us with a real home, and moved into our own apartment.

There were now eight brand-new wooden houses, four on each side of a broad unpaved road that ran up a small hill behind Nirah. They were called *zrifim* in Hebrew. Each little house, or *zrif,* contained four little apartments—more accurately, four rooms. Every two apartments were served by an open passage at each end of which was a door. One of the doors led to a small toilet, the other to a tiny cold-water shower. From the passage you entered our apartment: a tiny anteroom with a sink that also served as a kitchen and a small room about nine feet square. The walls and ceiling were covered with artificial wallboard that could not be painted. There was no electricity. Instead, our home was romantically lit by kerosene lamps. It was small, but it was ours. We were young, gloriously happy, and convinced that we could make it here.

Twenty-four new immigrant families from ten different countries moved into the *zrifim,* producing a babel of languages. We hadn't been in Israel long enough to have learned to speak Hebrew well. It's amazing that we were able to communicate with one another, but almost everyone in the *zrifim* spoke a little German or Yiddish. Our immediate neighbors were two families from Britain; they spoke only English. I am forever grateful to Joe and Fay Isaacs, Coral Benjaminn, and Grandma Lyons. They were wonderful people, and because I wanted to talk with them, I was forced to learn English. They spoke to me very slowly, and gradually I learned the language. A lasting, sincere friendship was forged.

Evenings were our happiest hours. Because we had no radio or electricity, my accordion-playing brought people together. We would sit outside during the hot summer evenings and there would be singing and dancing.

Economically, things were not going well for the state of Israel or for us. This was the so-called *Zena* period, when everything was rationed: meat, sugar, oil, and flour. However, living in a rural village made things easier; we had enough vegetables and potatoes, so it was not as hard for us as it was for people in the cities.

I started to work, at first in the fields, then as a maid, and finally I got a job in the Nirah textile factory. One day two women came to see me: Grete Brunn, a settler from the neighboring village of Shaar Chefer, and Ivriyah Wurm, a folk-dance teacher. They asked if I might be interested in playing my accordion for folk dances.

"I'd be happy to play for you," I said, "but I don't know any Israeli music. We have no radio here, so I've never heard any. If you'll get me some scores I can play from them."

"Unfortunately we don't have any printed music, not yet," Ivriyah said. "But I think that if we sing the melodies you'll pick them up in no time." I had some doubts.

Ivriyah was a sabra, born in Israel, whose family had lived here for generations. I was drawn to her, to her openness, her warmheartedness, and her sympathetic manner, so I agreed. I've never regretted it. This was the beginning of one of the most joyful times for me in Israel. I was now Ivriyah's accordionist and went with her from village to village, from kibbutz to kibbutz. I got to know people, places, and Israeli folklore, and that brought me closer to my new country. We lived rather primitively in the *zrifim*. There wasn't much to eat and we had no money, but we were very, very happy.

Cars were unable to climb up the road that led to the *zrifim*. Only jeeps could drive through the deep sand. Every morning it would take us twenty minutes to wade down to the Moses farm to get milk and to shop at the only store in the village. Packs of jackals howled in concert every night. They made it dangerous for us to walk alone in the evenings; consequently, we always went in pairs, equipped with long sticks to ward off a possible attack by these creatures.

With the first money we saved, we bought a small chicken coop and a wire fence, happy to have our own chickens and eggs. But one night a jackal dug a hole under the fence and managed to drag several chickens out of the coop.

Jackals weren't our only nighttime visitors. Groups of fedayeen came over from Jordan, which was only five miles away. These terrorist raiders not only threatened human lives but caused enormous damage in the Israeli villages. We were never sure when or where they would turn up next. They stole whatever they could. Laundry would disappear from clotheslines, irrigation pipes and tools would vanish. We had no choice but to set up watches, and our men, who worked hard all day long, now also had to take turns doing guard duty at night.

Caught up in our new life, we began to forget the past, or rather, we thought we were forgetting it. Kurt and I made plans for the future. Both of us longed for children. At first it didn't occur to us that something might have happened to me in Auschwitz that would prevent us from fulfilling our wish. I couldn't seem to get pregnant. The doctors I consulted assured me that they would do everything they could to help us, but nothing worked. Gradually we grew accustomed to the idea that we would never have children. I continued to work in the fields and in other people's homes as a maid. I thought that perhaps I could forget my sorrow by doing hard physical work.

And then one day I realized that I was pregnant. Overjoyed, I went to see a doctor. If I wanted to carry the child to term, he cautioned me, I would have to stop doing physical work. So from then on I limited myself to taking care of our little household. I took long walks in the environs of Beth Yitzchak, Nirah, and Shaar Chefer—so happy that I would have the chance to have a baby in a normal world. I enjoyed every flower I passed, and I sang with the birds. All that mattered was the future. I didn't give a thought to what had been.

Because he still had hopes of getting work as a pharmacist, Kurt went to the Health Ministry in Tel Aviv at least once every three months. I was five months pregnant when he heard that the army was looking for pharmacists. He immediately applied and was hired; finally he'd have an opportunity to practice his profession. That day he came back to the *zrifim* carrying a huge bag. In it were uniforms, underwear, socks, shoes, towels—a wealth of gear in this *Zena* time of shortages. At the bottom of the bag was a thick book of rules and regulations—in Hebrew. Kurt bought a dictionary and deciphered every word, working day and night trying to understand it all. He had to leave the *zrifim* at five in the morning in order to arrive for work at the army camp by eight o'clock. After eight in the evening he came home dead tired but content with his work. His first paycheck would be forty Israeli pounds, only a little more than he had earned as a day laborer.

Unfortunately, the army had run out of money to pay salaries, and Kurt was told that his first paycheck would be three months late, coming at just about the end of my pregnancy. But I had to buy at least the bare essentials before the baby came: clothes, diapers, and a little crib. I didn't know how to pay for it all because our savings were gone. Once again I would be forced to borrow money, something I found quite distasteful. I was earning very little at the time. Only now and then did I still accompany Ivriyah on the accordion. But to hell with money. I was sure we'd be able to pay back any debts we incurred. It was wrong to worry when such a happy event was just around the corner.

With borrowed money I bought the baby's layette and crib in the nearby town of Netanya. But finding a place to put the crib was a problem. In our small room we already had a bed, a cupboard, a table, and two chairs—there was no space for anything else. After some ingenious rearranging, however, we finally created a spot for it. I now had only one worry: that Kurt, who sometimes could not come home because of his work at the army camp, would not be with me when the baby arrived.

At three in the morning on March 7, I felt the first labor pains. I awakened Kurt, who wanted to go to the hospital immediately. I asked him to let me sleep a little longer because I knew I had a long day ahead of me. But he was adamant, so I got dressed, took my carefully packed satchel and a walking stick, and accompanied by the howling of the jackals, we made our way through the deep sand down the hill. We were going to phone for a taxi in Nirah to take us to the hospital in Hadera about twelve and a half miles away. There was only one telephone in Nirah. It was inside the factory, and the factory was locked. We waited in the cold until the first settler came to work so that he could let us in to use the phone.

By now it was time for Kurt to go to work, so he dropped me off at the hospital. How I wished he could have stayed with me! I didn't want to be alone, not again. Kurt promised to come back as soon as possible. After a while I got caught up in the hospital routine and I forgot about him: undressing and putting on a hospital gown, labor pains, registration, bathing, and food, which I couldn't eat because of the labor pains. I was taken to a large bed with smooth white sheets. But whenever the contractions came I had to get up and walk up and down; I just couldn't stay in bed. As the pains came more and more frequently, I marched back and forth in the corridor. Whenever they were particularly bad, I clung to an old refrigerator that stood there. Under no circumstances did I want to cry out; I knew that each contraction brought me closer to the happy event for which Kurt and I had been yearning. Late in the afternoon a nurse said it was time for another examination. She took me to a large room and after one look called for help from a midwife. Turning to me, she angrily asked, "Why didn't you tell us you were in the bearing-down stage?"

In contrast to most other women in labor, I had been very calm, and if the nurse hadn't taken me to be examined I probably would have delivered the baby in the corridor. I felt an enormous pain as the baby left my body, followed by a tremendous sense of relief.

"You have a beautiful, healthy son," the midwife said. "Mazel tov."

I couldn't say a word. Tears of joy ran down my cheeks. I felt at peace, happy and content. This was the beginning of our new family. If only Kurt were with me to share this joy. All about me the nurses and midwives were busy with things I did not understand. I wasn't interested in what they were doing; I cared only for the happiness that filled my being. A nurse came over holding a bundle from which peeked a little red face. The baby was crying.

"This is your son, a lovely baby," the nurse said.

Taking a diaper from a nearby table, she wrapped it around the infant. Then she started to walk out of the room with the baby. I began to scream, "Don't take my baby away! Let my child live! My child must live! Don't take my child away!"

Terrible sobs shook me. I couldn't think clearly. Memories that I thought were forgotten pressed in on me with unexpected vehemence. Even after the nurse left the room, I continued to cry and scream, "Give me back my child! Don't take my child away! You mustn't kill my baby! Please let him live!"

A doctor approached my bed. He yelled something I didn't understand and resoundingly slapped my face twice to calm my hysteria. Gradually I calmed down. The doctor pulled up a chair, sat down, and said, "Your child is going to live. No one is going to take him from you."

He then asked one of the nurses to bring the baby back to me.

They put my son next to me in the bed, and although I was still crying, the agitation had drained away. In a concerned voice the doctor said, "I saw the number tattooed on your arm. What happened to you? You'll feel better if you can talk about it."

It was the first time since we came to Israel that someone had shown a sincere interest in what I had gone through. The words tumbled out, and the more I talked the calmer I became. My son, my child, would be allowed to live. He would never know what his parents had endured but would grow up happy and free in his native land. When I finished telling my story, I said, "Today is March 7th. When the nurse was taking my baby out the door, I again heard the five thousand people from the family camp in Birkenau singing "*Hatikvah*" as they were taken to the gas chamber on March 7th, 1944. How symbolic that my son should be born on this date."

We called him Rafi. He was allowed to stay with me during the day. Only at night was he taken to the nursery so that I could sleep. When Kurt came to the hospital after work, he brought me a small bunch of field flowers he had picked. He would have liked to buy me a present, but we had no money; this little bouquet meant more to me than the most precious piece of jewelry.

On the way back to the *zrifim,* we agreed that we would not tell our son, or any other children we might have, about our past. They were to grow up happy and free, without being burdened or influenced by our experiences. Once they were grown up, they could form their own opinions. Kurt and I were both completely absorbed in being parents. We stopped thinking of the past. The present and planning for the future occupied all our thoughts.

Rafi was one and a half years old when we were given a parcel of land by the village of Beth Yitzchak. I was three months pregnant with our second child when we finally moved into a house. It was tiny, but it was *our* house.

When Gabi, our second son, was born, no concentration-camp associations were triggered. The past lay far behind me, and I felt an indescribable joy in our growing family. Proudly, we brought Gabi home to our new house, which resounded with children's voices and laughter.

We planted the first trees in our garden—a clementine, a grapefruit, a lemon, and an orange tree. Firm roots in our new land.

Ruth Elias (right) with Dr. Margit Bleyer (Maca Steinberg), her camp "mother," 1977, in Israel.

Epilogue

IT WAS VERY HARD TO WRITE THIS BOOK. One cannot deal with memories without having to relive what happened. Often I had to stop writing because I was crying, and many pages of the manuscript are soaked with tears. But the thought of my family, to whom I wanted to leave this chronicle, made me press on.

It was pure chance that the manuscript was seen by the original publisher, Dr. Ernst Reinhard Piper, who suggested that it be published. When I agreed, I did not know what was involved, or what a complicated process the publication of a book can be. It marked the beginning of a crazy time for me: text corrections, proofing, checking, revising, countless telephone calls, retrieving old photographs, finding a title, deciding on a cover, graphics, approving the jacket copy, and the like—and all of this was negotiated long-distance between Israel and Germany. In addition, I had to go to Munich to read the final proofs. Only then did I realize that I would probably have to go to Germany frequently, and that caused me great misgivings.

When I came out of the concentration camps, I swore that I would never set foot on German soil again. However, when I was invited to accompany an Israeli youth-exchange group to Germany, I broke my vow. It was pointed out to me that this was not to be a vacation trip. It was a duty, and it would contribute to German-Israeli understanding. I agreed to go as a representative of my country.

I made a second trip in 1985, after I was invited to give a series of lectures in Germany. President Reagan was visiting Bitburg, and this time I had absolutely no misgivings about going. If Reagan was going to pay his respects at the graves of SS members, then I would speak out about the atrocities they had committed. I was on the road for a week, visiting five schools and taking part in three evening events.

For the first time, I met the younger generation of Germans, heard their reactions to my lectures, saw how moved they were. But I, too, was moved when a seventeen-year-old youth took me aside, and said, "Mrs. Elias, my father still has an SS uniform hanging in his closet. Please tell me what to do. After hearing what you just said, how can I face my father, how can I even talk with him?" What could I say to this young man? I felt sorry for him.

In May 1988, I returned to Germany for a few days, this time to Munich, the former Nazi stronghold. All my time was spent in the offices of my publisher, and I was occupied every minute of the day with work, so I had no time to see the city itself. But in the editorial offices I met several young people, and there were many opportunities to talk with them quite candidly. That made my stay easier to bear. I avoided going into the streets because whenever I met older Germans I wondered what they were doing during the Nazi time. Was he or she a guard in one of the camps where I was a prisoner?

Before I left Munich, the publisher asked me to go on a reading tour once the book was in the stores. I agreed without giving it a second thought. But back home, after looking at the schedule—readings in some twenty cities, radio and TV interviews, appearances at the Frankfurt Book Fair—I suddenly had doubts. How could I, who had experienced so much horror, face the Germans? How old would the people in my audience be? What would be their reaction to the excerpts I planned to read from my book? What questions would they ask? Would I be subjected to abusive comments?

I began the trip with mixed feelings. As I traveled through Germany I saw hundreds of faces, rode in innumerable trains and cars, was greeted by people who had been sent to assist me, and stayed in a variety of hotels. I didn't get to see anything of the cities I visited. Usually I arrived in the afternoon, unpacked, got dressed, did the reading, and the following morning I went on to the next place.

But at last some of my doubts were resolved. Ninety percent of those who came to hear me were born either during the war or afterward. Occasionally, there were older people in the audience who wanted to know what my attitude toward them was. I always wondered why they had come to hear me talk. Even before I started the reading tour I decided to answer all questions frankly and honestly. I had remained silent long enough. I told these older people that I had doubts about their past and what they had done during the Nazi period.

After the readings I was usually inundated with questions, but in a few rare cases not a single question was asked, not a hand was raised. Instead, a heavy silence hung over the auditorium.

At almost every reading one question was asked again and again by the younger people. The question was, "Why did our parents (or our grandparents) never tell us anything about their past and what they did during the Nazi period?" Did these young people really expect me, a former concentration-camp prisoner, to answer that, to actually deal with this reproach? Was I the one who should explain their parents' and grandparents' enthusiasm for Hitler, and their participation in the mass murder and the attempted extermination of a people? Often members of the audience looked at me in stunned bewilderment and dismay. Perhaps they were asking for a word of understanding, comprehension, even reconciliation. I couldn't provide them with consolation.

I was also exposed to a few excesses. One incident in particular created a deep impression. Although considerable time has passed,

I remember it clearly. About fifty or sixty people had come to hear me in a small town. After the reading, there was an oppressive silence. I asked whether there were any questions. A man in his early twenties raised his hand. "I don't have a question, merely an observation," he said. "You probably know that Marx and Trotsky were Jews. You Jews are to blame for your own fate. . . ." This was followed by a wild tirade against Jews. I sat there thunderstruck, unable to think rationally. There was tumult in the room; people angrily reproached the young man, and finally he was forcibly removed from the hall. It turned out that he was the grandson of the former Nazi mayor of the town. I was deeply hurt and speechless while the people in the hall apologized to me. I wondered whether I could even go on with my tour. Nevertheless, I decided to continue with the readings. Running away was useless; only an open, frank, and honest dialogue could lead to positive results.

In general, I was warmly received wherever I went, and over and over I was told how important my readings were because, people said, we must not allow this evil period in history to pass into oblivion. And later this belief was confirmed for me by several hundred letters from readers (and about 150 book reviews). I would like to quote some excerpts from these letters, not out of vanity but to show that my message was received in the right spirit by most of the Germans who read this book:

> H.H., Cuxhaven: "I can't tell you how deeply moved I am by what you and all the other people endured in the concentration camps. I am ashamed to be a German."

> M.B., Giessen: ". . . I feel that this is a very important book, especially for a German. I think your book can help see to it that human beings commit themselves to making sure that people will never do such things to one another again."

> L.G., Rosenheim: ". . . what a response your reading had. . . . I am sure that your willingness to speak out represents an impor-

tant contribution to understanding. . . . Also, attending the events that followed your evening presentation encouraged us not to let up in our efforts to find enlightenment about this darkest epoch of our history. Surprisingly many young people attended these evening lectures."

Dr. E.U., Hofheim: "We find that in Germany young people feel an increasing need to confront this darkest period [in the history] of our country. . . . I have noticed that a large portion of the students are alert, interested, and attentive. . . . If I may, I should like to cite passages from your book the next time I deliver a lecture. I have by now turned this into a sort of obligatory reading for my colleagues and students."

K.S., Munich: "Your book is so important for us! And I can only hope that many Germans, especially the younger ones and those of my generation (I was born in 1943), will find the courage to read the book. . . . What happened to all those SS men and women? How many continued after the war to live unmolested among us? Hardly anyone was called to account; they are silent. . . . But I find it unbearable that many Germans who did it or who allowed it [to be done] were silent or looked away. . . . Only rarely have I seen real regret and sorrow about what the Germans did to the Jewish people. . . . I heard that you are talking with many young people in Germany and that they want to know a lot [about the Nazi era]. That is a really hopeful sign."

W.T., Biberach: "Even today, after fifty years, we still cannot conclusively answer the question 'How could this have happened?' . . . Is it possible that the same beast that controlled the SS executioners lives on within us. . . . We know from many reports that some of the SS members were described as loving husbands and devoted fathers, etc.: 'Normal people!' I'm a normal person too: Was it only luck that my hands stayed clean? . . . My children ask me what the crimes of their grandparents have to do with them. . . . For that very reason, books like yours are important. They help to keep these questions alive and force us again and again to search for answers."

Dr. H.S., Ingelheim: "After reading your book, anyone who has to the present day suppressed his awareness of the crimes the Nazis committed in the concentration camps cannot in the future live without shame as a German. . . . Therefore it is most important, especially for us Germans, to keep the memory of these atrocities alive in the interest of today's and future generations so that such crimes will never happen again."

H.K., Schorndorff: "I speak from personal experience: I know why the young people of today don't want to let these 'old stories' bother them in their determined attempts to build their own lives. But I very much hope that they will soon be confronted by your book or a similar one so that no new 'perpetrators' will grow up [in our midst]."

M.S., Ebenhausen: "It is terrible what uncontrolled, fanatical hatred can do. We bow down [in respect] to a people [the Jews] who never gave up their culture, their faith, and their identity."

L.H., Obernburg: "When I listen to my parents talk, I hear a huge, inconceivable thoughtlessness rather than an unconscious anti-Semitism. . . . I always think that the pain of the Jews has become a message that all people all over the world should hear."

E.K., Schwelm: "We who lived through the period of 1933–1945 as children (I was born in 1934) wish we could build a bridge between Israel and Germany, between Jews and Christians. Will we be able to do that?"

M.S., Frankenthal: "When I asked my parents, 'Why didn't you do something against the racial hatred, the persecution of the

Jews, and all the misery?' they would answer: 'We couldn't do anything. Anyone who resisted was arrested.' I cannot understand how neighbors could look on as Jews simply disappeared, were picked up and never returned. . . . Your book is gripping, tremendously captivating, very moving. It is a chunk of contemporary history that everyone in Germany should read, young or old, so that something like this will never happen again."

M.S., Biblis: "I will soon be 40 years old. We didn't learn anything in school about the Third Reich and the persecution of the Jews. Only in vocational school were we made aware of this period in history and its consequences by an old teacher, who introduced us to the book by Eva von Meyer Levin. . . . And today, too, our children hear very little in school about this period."

M.P., Endorf: "Dear Mrs. Elias, the famous Nobel Prize winner (Elie Wiesel), who is also Jewish, said on television last year: If at least only one German were to publicly apologize to the Jewish people. . . . Since I cannot get in touch with this famous man, who lives in the U.S., I would like to apologize to you with all my heart for all the atrocities [committed] by our people."

I feel these letters from readers were proof that my message was being heard, and they gave me the strength and the courage to make another trip to Germany in January/February 1989. I wrote this book for future generations so that the terrible Nazi time will not be forgotten, and also as a warning that what happened must never be repeated. God grant that my plea be heard.

Acknowledgments

My deepest gratitude goes to the historian Gideon Greif, Ph.D., at Yad Vashem: The Holocaust Martyrs' and Heroes' Remembrance Authority in Jerusalem. Some years ago, on Israel Defense Forces Radio, he was the first to interview me on radio; subsequently he handed me a pen and paper and ordered me to start writing. His unabated interest and continuing encouragement enabled me to complete this book.

I owe thanks to the historian Livia Rothkirchen, Ph.D., Jerusalem, for her kindness in reading my manuscript, for her encouragement, and for her helpful suggestions.

I will never forget the late Dr. Margit Bleyer (Maca Steinberg), my camp mother. She helped me during the hardest period of my life. Without her this book never would have been written, because without her I would not have survived.

Alysa Dortort Rosansky merits particular thanks for facilitating this English-language edition by bringing my story to the attention of those who could see it into print. She has my gratitude for her skill, persistence, and devotion.

To Benton Arnovitz, Director of Academic Publications at the United States Holocaust Memorial Museum in Washington, D.C., I owe many thanks and deepest appreciation for his interest in my book and for making the arrangements for it to be published in America.

The publisher's historical notes were prepared for the German edition by Dr. Peter Longerich of the Institut für Zeitgeschichte, Munich and edited for the English-language edition by staff of the Historian's Office at the United States Holocaust Memorial Museum.

Readers who would like to fit my experiences into the chronological time frame of the camp may wish to consult Danuta Czech's *Auschwitz Chronicle, 1939–1945* (New York: Henry Holt, 1990).

Photos of the Theresienstadt barracks and the arrival of the transport at Auschwitz are from the Yad Vashem Photo Archives, courtesy of the United States Holocaust Memorial Museum Photo Archives.